PRAISE FOR MOONLIGHT SERENADE

Dr. Gordon Wallace has put together a combination of profound ideas and advice about aging, disarmingly simply described. *Moonlight Serenade* is an engaging application of the practice of mindfulness to the processes of aging. Dr. Wallace intelligently combines this potent brew with Jungian psychology, providing the reader with a practical guide to working with the challenges and promises of aging. He reveals an extraordinary level of insight into existential crises such as illness and grief. I benefited from reading this book, and I heartily recommend it to everyone approaching their later years.

—**Lionel Corbett, M.D.,** Jungian Analyst and Co-Editor,
*Jung and Aging: Possibilities and Potentials
for the Second Half of Life*

How might we use the challenges of aging to wake up and live the moments left of our life more fully? In this clear, step-by-step, comprehensive guide, Dr. Wallace blends insights from contemplative practice, depth psychology, and years of clinical experience to show us how. He provides a carefully structured path any of us can follow to become more honest, connected, flexible, and present in our later years—when we need wisdom and sanity more than ever.

—**Dr. Ronald D. Siegel,** Assistant Professor of Psychology, part time, Harvard Medical School and author, *The Extraordinary Gift of Being Ordinary: Finding Happiness Right Where You Are*

More than another book on mindfulness, *Moonlight Serenade* takes head on some of the key issues of aging. It teaches us the basics of mindfulness and then how mindfulness may play a role in healthy and wise aging. Adeptly weaving in Jungian Depth Psychology, this much-needed book serves as a practical support for those in their later years. Highly recommended!

—**Diana Winston,** Director of Mindfulness Education, UCLA Mindful Awareness Research Center and author, *The Little Book of Being*

Moonlight Serenade is a wonderous survey of the compensatory move of "mindfulness" for the compulsive thought/worry/ behavior nexus driving most of us. Regret binds us to the past, and anxiety to the future—but only mindfulness allows access to "the eternal now." This book . . . provides exercises, attitudes, and behaviors that access a fuller sense of fulfilment in this fleeting mystery we call our lives.

—**James Hollis, Ph.D.,** Jungian Analyst and author, *The Broken Mirror: Refracted Visions of Ourselves* and many other books

This book comes at an opportune (*Kairos*) moment, as the Covid19 pandemic and the looming climate crisis are eliciting essential questions about life and death, about the notion of time and, especially for older individuals, the related issue of aging. . . Here, the author has staked out a path to bring our errant minds back home to our embodied selves. Wallace offers a unique guide-book, culled from decades of experience as a dedicated psychologist in private practice and group facilitator of mindfulness skills. Insights gained from Jungian psychology add richness and depth throughout. I wish this book a widespread and grateful following.

—**Marianne Tauber, Ph.D.,** author, *The Soul's Ministrations: An Imaginal Journey Through Crisis*

'Moonlight Serenade: Embracing Aging Mindfully' is **the** book for those who are ready to start a mindfulness practice to enhance their life experience . . . Dr. Wallace draws from a well of experience that combines personal anecdotes, spiritual perspectives, and professional knowledge to present a program that is trustworthy in its research and refreshing in its honesty.

—**Trevor Josephson, M.C.,** Manager of Clinical Services, Peace Arch Hospice Society

With *Moonlight Serenade* Dr. Gordon Wallace has offered a gift to the Universe – a gift to us, its readers, which will keep on giving until our last breath, an unknown moment in time . . . The messages of *Moonlight Serenade* ring true, for though steeped in the truths of the ages, we glimpse that it is also the personal journey of its author . . . Dr. Wallace was inviting me to make a journey - whatever my age . . . While deep in contemplation – reflecting how I was ever a lifetime seeker, was now 83, and considering whether to embark on an adventure that could enrich my continuing, albeit unknown, years ... my heart responded: 'OH, YES, WE WILL'!

—**Rev. Dorothy Barklie Blandford, Ph.D.,** author,
By the Fireside with Dorothy ... Into the Mystic

Gordon Wallace and I are old friends. Its not that we have been friends for a long time its just that we are friends, and we are old (not terribly old but old). Friendship with Gordon causes me to trust him and what he has to say. He knows what he is talking about when he invites us to embrace aging mindfully. His experience of aging (and mine) comes naturally, but his insights into aging healthfully have been achieved through years of study, teaching, psychotherapy (given and received) and dedicated meditative practice. And he has poured all this personal and professional experience and learning into a thoughtfully crafted and skillfully layered manual.

—**David W Morrison, DMin, MDiv,** Retired Chaplain

I gravitate to books written by professionals who walk their talk. Dr. Gordon Wallace is one of those people who has been able to distill years of personal and professional experience into this wise and practical book. . . I envision that Moonlight Serenade will sit on many a bedside table, and continue to sing songs of reassurance, courage, and compassion to all of us who long for a conscious and grace-filled life, all the way to its end.

—**Janie Brown,** Founder and Executive Director of the Callanish Society and author, *Radical Acts of Love: Twenty Conversations to Inspire Hope at the End of Life*

Moonlight Serenade

Embracing Aging Mindfully

GORDON WALLACE, Ph.D.

 FriesenPress

One Printers Way
Altona, MB R0G 0B0
Canada

www.friesenpress.com

The author is not engaged in rendering psychological advice or services to the individual reader. The meditations and exercises are educational and not meant to replace formal medical or psychological treatment. Individuals with medical or psychological concerns should consult with their care professionals about participating in this program and discuss any appropriate modifications relevant to their unique circumstances and conditions. No expressed or implied guarantee of the effects of the use of the recommendations can be given nor liability taken.

"Talking to Grief" from POEMS 1972-1982 by Denise Levertov. Copywrite © 1978 by Denise Levertov. Reprinted by permission of New Directions Publishing Corp.

"Sweet Darkness" from THE HOUSE OF BELONGING by David Whyte. Copyright © 1997 by David Whyte. Reprinted by permission of Many Rivers Press, www.davidwhyte.com, Langley, WA, USA.

"Everything is Waiting for You (After Derek Mahon)" from EVERYTHING IS WAITING FOR YOU by David Whyte. Copyright © 2003 by David Whyte. Reprinted by permission of Many Rivers Press, www.davidwhyte.com, Langley, WA, USA.

Author photograph by Rebecca Lewis, 2021

ISBN
978-1-03-913303-7 (Hardcover)
978-1-03-913302-0 (Paperback)
978-1-03-913304-4 (eBook)

1. SELF-HELP, AGING
2. SELF-HELP, MEDITATIONS

Distributed to the trade by The Ingram Book Company

To my grandchildren, Dan, Parker, and Quinn,
whose spirits illuminate the wonders and delights of this life . . .

To my stillborn grandson, Bowen,
whose spirit illuminates the mysteries of this life . . .

Table of Contents

ACKNOWLEDGEMENTS

My indebtedness to the many who supported this project runs deep, and with heartfelt appreciation, I thank you!

The staff at Peace Arch Hospice Society have been extremely supportive of the Mindfulness course that I developed, and this book would not have emerged without their continual patronage. I especially want to thank Trevor Josephson, M.C., Manager of Clinical Services, for his unwavering program support. I appreciate the co-facilitators I have been fortunate to work with over the years to make the course the best it can be – thank you, Wendy Hazell, Smita Shah, Shelagh Boutell and Joyce Poley. I also appreciate and thank the students of the Hospice Mindfulness course and all the clients I have had the opportunity to work with over my professional career who have been my co-creators in learning how to recognize, develop and implement resilient and healthy responses to meet whatever life demands.

The professionalism, expertise and patient support of my team at Friesen Press, Jahleen Turnbull-Sousa, Jodi Sowinski, Kate Richards and my Publishing Specialist, made this later life undertaking not only possible but enjoyable – thank you!

Friends have been encouraging of this later life publishing gambit, and I have been fortunate to have received valuable feedback from early readers - thank you, Janis Kirk, Dr. David Morrison and Rev. Dr. Dorothy Blandford. I am incredibly grateful for the thorough review from David Kirk, *Word-Smith Extraordinaire*, whose line-by-line edit greatly enhanced and polished my initial offering.

My family has been a welcoming and vocal cheering section for this long-haul project, and I thank each of you – Shaena,. Rebecca, Trevor and Dan.

It is often said that book projects would not come to fruition without support from one's life partner, and I can now attest to the veracity of that claim! My wife Lynn has been co-facilitator of many mindfulness and Jungian-oriented workshops over the years, has read every word of the multiple manuscript editions, has provided critical clarity to my writing style and has been the voice (literally) of the audio-guided meditations found at the book's website. Over the years, not only her active involvement but especially her steadfast support of my next latest venture has been invaluable, without which this book would not have come to life. Lynn, you've heard this many times, but again I bow in appreciation and thanks for your supportive love on this shared journey of our lives.

INTRODUCTION:
THREE INVITATIONS

This thing, all things devours;
Birds, beasts, trees, flowers;
Gnaws iron, bites steel;
Grinds hard stones to meal;
Slays king, ruins town,
And beats mountain down.

Gollum's Riddle to Bilbo in *The Hobbit*

Parker's three-year-old gaze was transfixed on the exposed workings of my mechanical watch. Even with the scratches on the glass face evidencing years of wear, the watch's design invites a curious observer to behold the inner components that in a seemingly secret manner allow seconds, minutes, and hours to be precisely measured. Immediately evident is the large spiral ribbon of steel known as the mainspring, but what draws the eye is the gold-coloured balance wheel that hypnotically oscillates back and forth at precision speed. Pulling your gaze slightly to the right introduces the delicate escapement mechanism that allows the watch's gears to advance by a set amount with each swing of the balance wheel. Seemingly by magic, this permits the variable-sized wheel trains to sum the number of swings, which informs the rotating hands click by click by click, patiently moving the second, minute, and hour hands to calculate the spent moments of time.

I had no illusion that my granddaughter's young mind deciphered any of the mechanical intricacies of my watch. Instead, Parker's intent was more appropriately immediate as her short little fingers caressed the glass face in a frustrated attempt to touch the dance of mesmerizing intricate metal parts playing out before her. My simplistic explanation that these were the workings of a watch that allowed for the telling of time led to a long silence. With her gaze held spellbound by the sight of perpetual motion, Parker's mind suddenly seized upon a seminal topic of inquiry held for millennia in religion, philosophy, and science, as she innocently questioned, "What *is* time, Papa?"

Without knowing the question, Parker had also serendipitously stumbled upon time as the answer to Gollum's muddled riddle. Time, that elusive concept children measure by anticipated sleeps, teenagers by frustrated waits, young adults by endless horizons, and mid-lifers by subtle acknowledgement of passing years. Time, the persistent intruder during our advancing aging years asking not only in wonderment of where did it go, but more pressingly, reminding us of Napoleon's dictum that "You can ask for anything you like, except time."

TIME IS COMPLICATED

Time is a slippery concept notwithstanding its ubiquitous nature, as the iconic song of the late 1960s from the Chambers Brothers made clear when they sing that time has arrived today and there is no place to hide. Yet, I know from discussions with family, friends, and psychotherapy clients that I have not been alone in having a complicated relationship with time.

I must confess that, though that I have had seventy years to figure it out, I have never got this notion of time quite right. There have been periods when I have wanted time to slow down, especially when I am settling into a lazy vacation on the warm beaches of Maui or when I am enjoying a sumptuous meal with a rich, full-bodied merlot. But there have also been intervals when I have wished for time to speed up. Those seemingly endless days, weeks, and months while initially grieving my stillborn grandson, whom I never will be able to hold and hear his squeals of laughter: time is simply too fast or too slow.

Notwithstanding my frustrated control of time, my perceptions of it are too often skewed. Immersing myself into the flow of a Photoshop enhancement of an aged Bhutan monk's craggy face can make hours feel like ten minutes, while sitting in the dentist chair, feeling the numbness from the anesthetizing injection ever so slowly mask my toothache, can drive five minutes to feel like an eternity. Over my more than thirty-five-year professional career, I became acutely adept at sensing when my client's fifty-minute psychotherapy hour comes to an end. However, I continue to struggle to synchronize the time demanded of a roasted chicken, baked potato, and mustard carrot dinner with similar years of family culinary practice: time is simply too much or too little.

My attitude toward time reveals an underlying tension that erupts when an unspoken accord is challenged. I have ignored time structure for lengthy periods when I blithely procrastinated preparing for retirement, as I believed that there would always be a tomorrow. Still, I was flooded with anger and resentment when my mother passed at the age of forty-seven because of the limited time afforded her: time is simply just or unfair.

To Parker's innocent question, "What *is* time, Papa?" I must acknowledge that my power struggle with this mysterious concept influences any response. My life story reflects an ambivalent relationship with time over the years as consciously and unconsciously, it has been worshipped or despised, hoarded or squandered, obeyed or ignored, celebrated or denounced, remembered or forgotten, loved or reviled. Unmistakably, I am a seventy year old poster child of not only a complicated but a conflicted relationship with time!

TIME THROUGH AGING YEARS

Aging years brings your relationship with time into stronger focus because of an acute and undeniable awareness of the ever-decreasing moments available in your life. By the time you hit your mid-fifties, you have most likely lived more years than remain. How many years remain is, of course, unknown, which only adds further urgency to your quest. Time is the limited resource for which you have no control, and like it or not, it will determine not only the length but also, to a significant degree, the quality of your life to come. Aging is inextricably linked with time as aging is the embodiment of time.

While I acknowledge little Parker's childlike curiosity to understand time, what is more pressing to me and others during these later aging years is the vexing matter of determining your relationship with time: how to be with aging through time (for as the Chambers Brothers remind us, there is no place to hide) becomes the seminal exploration.

TIME AS SEASONS

My need to establish a healthier relationship with aging is certainly not novel. Time has been an object of interest to humans ever since the regular movement of the sun and stars was recognized, as evidenced by prehistoric people first recording the moon's phase some 30,000 years ago. Initially, for millennia, time had primarily been understood and measured through the seasons of the year. These divisions mark changes in daylight, weather variations, and ecological patterns from the earth's orbit around the sun and associated axial tilt. Each season denotes particular activities and attitudes, moods and visceral experiences congruent with our relationship to them.

Measurement of time through seasons was vital for agrarian societies, whose lives revolved around planting, tending, and harvesting crops—the understanding of time and its accurate measurement meant life or death. Outside of such weather task differentiation, typically, the four seasons of spring, summer, autumn, and winter also provide accessible markers of remembrance for past events and plans for future ones.

TIME AS HOURS

A deeper understanding of time's unique attributes beyond a calendar measurement manifests in the Benedictine monastic life. The monastics apprehended the hours as individual stages that follow a natural rhythm and therefore envisioned time as not seasons of the year but rather seasons of the day. The hours were initially understood through a mythical lens whereby a messenger, an angel, informed humans that each hour had its particular character, presence, and significance, making it richer and more meaningful than merely clock time. Not to be swept along by the demands of a clock, by external needs and agendas, or by impulsive reactions, but rather to live by the natural rhythms of the hours of the day offered a more conscious and purposeful response to whatever would emerge.

The distinct qualities of each of the eight monastic hours prescribe its challenges and unique response:

Vigils: Beginning before dawn, this is a time to wake up to the mystery of the darkness that unfolds into the light and to carry this wonder through the day.

Lauds: This hour takes us out of darkness and into light to receive the day as a gift.

Prime: Work duties are assigned, and it is a time to deliberate on the intentional attitude to bring to this new day through seeing task challenges, even those that have been repetitively experienced, through fresh eyes.

Terce: A prayer break in the middle of the morning, remembering and appreciating not only the gift of this moment but all the gifts of life.

Sext: A transition in the middle of the day appreciating the stillness and peacefulness of the noon hour but also acknowledging that it can be a time when good intentions and enthusiasm for the task at hand can begin to diminish. It is a time to trust and recommit to your resolve.

None: Mid-to-late afternoon brings an acknowledgement of impermanence, of the inevitable approaching end of the day with an attitude of acceptance and commitment to hold an intention to live a full and meaningful life.

Vespers: The end of the workday with evening descending accompanies this hour of peace and serenity by letting go of the day's concerns and appreciating the beauty of the coming night.

Compline: The monastic hour completes the day asking for an attitude of trust to meet the night's coming darkness as well as meet the unknown unfolding of life.

GREEKS AND TIME

The ancient Greeks were especially interested in the passage of time, valuing distinct ways of imagining the concept. The god Chronos was the personification of time regarding time's quantitative, linear, sequential measurement, so Chronos births the term chronology. You can review a lifetime through time passed in the minutes and hours recorded by clocks with days, weeks, months, and years chronicled by calendars. Any quantitative measurement of time spent or anticipated pays homage to Chronos.

However, the Greeks also recognized that there could be another way to record time, a more qualitative perspective, by identifying critical moments that measure one's life journey. Greek mythology knows Kairos as the youngest child of the god Zeus. Instead of being associated with quantitative measure, he represented qualitative aspects of moments often characterized as the opportune time, right time, or decisive time. Kairos time involves liminal moments when a question inquired, an opening appeared, options presented, a decision demanded, or an action taken. Kairos moments not only arrive through conscious deliberation and choice but can also descend upon a life unbidden beyond an individual's agency.

"RAGS OF TIME"

Kairos moments represent both the highlights and the lowlights of an individual's life story through voluntary and involuntary paths taken. Therefore, it is these moments that not only punctuate but also define a life lived. I imagine Kairos moments to be what the poet John Donne called "rags of time": moments taken and moments refused; moments of achievement and moments of defeat; moments celebrated and moments mourned; moments of pride and moments of regret. These individual rags of time stitch together to become the fabric of a particular life story. While each life shares the similarity of birth and death, Kairos's intervening experience is uniquely woven by each.

UNINVITED MARKERS OF LOSS

Kairos rags of time that delineate the aging years often underscore an individual's life story through uninvited markers of loss. You know the ones I am talking about—unwanted losses that have arrived but are not met with open arms, or ones that have visited someone else you know, or ones that actuarial predictions indicate may yet be coming. Kairos losses include the diminishment of physical functions like vision and hearing; chronic pain; life-limiting illness; dwindling vitality; decreased physical endurance or capacity; the cognitive decline of memory gaps or slowed problem-solving; loss of a partner; friends passing away; restricted independence; diminished social community; financial insecurity; loss of purpose in life; and the list goes on. No getting around it—aging is often associated with loss and decay to body, mind, and spirit.

While our incomplete list and Gollum's riddle graphically acknowledge that much of advancing years portends loss, aging can, however, also provoke a positive imperative to wake up and fully live the reality of limited time available. That is, advancing years brings not only *memento mori* as a reminder of our mortality, but it also offers *memento vivere* as a remembrance that we must fully live the time that is still available.

THE GIFT OF KAIROS

Aging is fundamentally the embodiment of time, expressed through both Chronos and Kairos. While one aspect of aging is the measurement of your advancing years, it is more than simply counting days, weeks, years, and decades gone by, for it also includes the critical quality of time spent. While the extent of time remaining in your life is usually out of your control, you do have more agency over the quality of the moments that are presented to you.

Aging, therefore, can be a gift—a gift received through conscious engagement with time empowered through your Kairos sensibility! The acknowledgement of time passing has the paradoxical potential to also give birth to new life-enhancing awareness of the possibility held in each moment. While you can try to ignore the reality of waning time, your conscious engagement and relationship to the moments that continue to materialize offer a tempting alternative proposition. Your aging years, beginning through attention to this present moment, presents a Kairos worldview—an acknowledgement that this is the right time to live this life that is yours with more intention, animation, vitality, and curiosity.

THREE INVITATIONS

This book addresses all readers, but especially those approximately fifty years and older, as an invitation to consciously live this life, YOUR precious life, in the most healthy, satisfying, and meaningful way possible. It offers a compassionate way of being during your aging years, no matter how many there may still be, by inviting the development of a vital personal connection to three aspects of time's inevitable presence.

AWARENESS

The first invitation is to maintain your *awareness* that there is no stopping time, and therefore, this book lays no claim magically to create or extend time since that is not possible. It is also not an offering about avoiding, escaping, or denying the reality that you face with the truth of ever limiting time available to live as you age. Many books on the market ring with an underlying message that growing old is not right and is not acceptable and needs to be fought. However, in a seemingly paradoxical manner, awareness and acceptance of your human limits can strengthen your lived experience of each moment. Therefore, throughout this book, a central theme to remember the reality of passing time will be frequently posed by a critical rhetorical question of "If not now, when?"

EXPERIENCE

The second invitation concerns your *experience* of time. Specifically, this book is more than just a friendly nudge not to forget the inevitable passing of time but also calls for a recognition of how you experience each moment that you are alive—to figuratively and literally wake up to the unfolding nature of each moment that defines the limited horizon under which each of us lives. Therefore, in addition to your respectful attentiveness toward time's departure, this book also petitions your attending to the visceral experiences of whatever aging presents—the good, the bad, and the ugly, as the eminent cultural observer Clint Eastwood would say. Besides, Buddhism tells us that life comprises 10,000 joys and 10,000 sorrows, so a dynamic experience of time will inevitably need to include the challenging episodes of pain and loss to which no one is immune.

RELATIONSHIP

While you can run from aging, the reality is that you cannot hide from it, so the burning question is, how are you going to meet it? During your aging years, the likelihood of pain, loss, and sorrow that you will experience heightens, so your attitude to such challenges become critically important. Therefore, the third invitation involves exploring and developing a healthy *relationship* with the previous two offers. In addition to being aware of time passing and the experience of what transpires during each spent moment, how you meet these events will, in no small measure, determine the quality of your life. To *meet* time, not harness or control or manipulate or worship or dread time, is the appropriate, respectful attitude needed to initiate a new relationship with it during the aging years. Meeting time also does not mean attempting blissfully to celebrate every painful experience with a false bravado but rather to learn honestly and courageously to be *with* whatever arises, including more difficult and provocative experiences.

SUPPORTIVE GUIDE

However, I want to emphasize that this book is not a nihilistic treatise demanding a mournful march through your remaining years. It is quite the opposite; this book is offered as a supportive guide to enjoying an engaged and life-affirming way of being that approaches your aging years by embracing a different perspective encapsulating your awareness, experience, and relationship to time. This perspective predicates holding the value offered by both Chronos and Kairos. That is, it acknowledges the need to continue being attentive to the unfolding measurement of time, as bills still need to be paid when due, while also becoming more acutely attuned to the uniqueness and accompanying possibilities of each moment. This awareness and experience of time offers a marriage with your conscious relationship to each moment. While it is no doubt easier to experience pleasant moments, meeting the challenging ones is often not simple. This book embodies the paradoxical thesis that to live a satisfying, contented, and meaningful life demands that you recognize, experience, and meet the good times as well as the pain, loss, and sorrow that you cannot avoid.

Learning how to live the adventure of an authentic life is not easy, and in truth, I have found it to be a formidable process. However, based upon my professional experience as a psychologist (now retired) and the culmination of my personal life explorations as I enter my eighth decade of life, this book proposes that there is a way of being that facilitates meeting advancing years in a healthy, meaningful, resilient, and more satisfying manner.

WOUNDED AND SCARRED

I have come to this conclusion wounded and scarred by my misplaced and long-suffering attempts to avoid the unavoidable of my life. Like you, I have never wanted to suffer pain and loss and sorrow and so have valiantly attempted to deny, avoid, or numb myself to them. However, my good-faith efforts to live without suffering have failed dramatically. While it would be easy to conclude that I am just spectacularly poor at living life, my role as a psychologist endowed me with a more realistic close-up view of our human condition. Over the years, I have come to understand, notwithstanding at times kicking and screaming in protest, that the bottom line is *no one* gets through life unscathed!

For over thirty-five-plus years, every single client who arrived at my consulting room shared a similar path of determined pursuit for the magic beans that would inoculate them from the pains and sorrows of life, only to experience continual disappointment. I will not bore you with a recitation of my and my clients' failed attempts of searching for paradise, as they would simply mirror your creative efforts, and you know what your failed endeavours have been! In a not-so-funny sense, therefore, our shared humanity discloses not only the universal experience of life's struggles and challenges but also the doomed collective pursuit of escape—we are all in this together with no easy and painless way out.

One of my favourite characters is a fellow by the name of Wavy Gravy. He was one of the MCs at the Woodstock music festival in 1969, and if you have listened to the soundtrack or watched the movie, he is the one who suggests "Breakfast in bed for 400,000!" He is a very funny guy, but one of his quotes that I think holds much truth is his portrayal of our common humanity: "We are all bozos on the bus, so you might as well sit back and enjoy the ride."

To acknowledge your group membership as one of the "bozos on the bus" does not, however, mean girding your loins and gritting your teeth only to stagger toward the finish line of death. I have found a middle way between avoidance of and resigned capitulation to life's challenges that allows you to "enjoy the ride"—to live in a healthier, meaningful, resilient, and more satisfying manner. Even in the midst of suffering, it is possible to meet what life asks of you in an engaged, energized, and resilient way. In the spirit of shared cooperation (and to save you the expense of wasted time), allow me to reveal the crucibles that I have found to be practical containers to hold and manifest the three invitations of time: welcome to mindfulness meditation and Jungian psychology.

MY JOURNEY

My appreciation for the benefits of mindfulness meditation and Jungian psychology with aging is not new or simply theoretical. Over my lengthy professional career, I have introduced these strategies and interventions to hundreds of clients and students while continually assessing their value with my own struggles and challenges with time and aging.

I began a mindfulness meditation practice in 1990 when I attended a ten-day silent retreat high in the Sangre de Cristo mountains outside Taos, New Mexico. In hindsight, beginning with ten long days of meditation for a neophyte wasn't the most thoughtful plan! It was a stretch physically and mentally but proved extremely worthwhile as hard-won benefits became manifestly evident. I continued practising mindfulness at home, through numerous multi-day formal retreats in North America and during travels in Japan, India, Thailand, and Bhutan. With no formal mindfulness teacher available in my community, I soaked up knowledge and stratagems from attendance at workshops/retreats and writings offered by many skilled practitioners, including Jack Kornfield, Jon Kabat-Zinn, Tara Brach, Susan Bauer-Wu, Sharon Salzberg, Joseph Goldstein, Frank Ostaseski, Judson Brewer, and Kristin Neff.

After establishing my mindfulness practice, over the ensuing decades I began, initially tentatively but over time more confidently and wholeheartedly, to introduce mindfulness concepts and strategies to psychotherapy clients. In 2007, I completed a practicum in Mindfulness Based Stress Reduction (MBSR) with the Center for Mindfulness in Medicine, Health Care and Society at the University of Massachusetts Medical School.

By the time I completed the MBSR program, I had considerable experience incorporating mindfulness strategies into my psychotherapeutic intervention repertoire. To further assess the applicability and effectiveness of mindfulness treatment practices, I then began developing and facilitating workshops applied to various client groups. Workshops that I designed and cofacilitated included ones directed to hospice volunteers and the general public ("Meeting Suffering Mindfully"), school counsellors ("Introduction to Mindfulness with Adolescents"), and mental health professionals ("Deepening the Inner Eye: Mindfulness and Countertransference in Clinical Practice").

Since retiring from my clinical practice in 2017, I designed and continue to teach a mindfulness course to address complex issues presented by hospice bereavement and palliative care clients. With most hospice clients being between fifty and eighty-five years of age, I have been fortunate to incorporate their evaluative feedback to hone a course of mindfulness skills capable of effectively addressing their specific presenting issues and complicated aging concerns. My journey into the complexities of time, driven by awareness of my advancing years, continues to expand as I engage in bedside vigils with individuals close to death. To offer companionship at the end of life allows me to get closer to the final mystery of time and aging in this human existence.

My clinical journey with Jungian psychology is also not new, as it began in the mid-1980s when I started undergoing a lengthy Jungian analysis. Having been trained during my first graduate degree in cognitive-behavioural therapeutic interventions, it is no exaggeration to say that I unearthed an entirely new world through my analysis—the realm of the unconscious that I was unknowingly living within and acting out of! Through continuing psychotherapeutic analysis, self-study, and attendance at training courses, I slowly incorporated a depth psychology perspective into my clinical work. Later completing a short training course at the Jung Institute in Zurich, Switzerland, cemented my interest and desire to complete further education, leading me to complete a Ph.D. in clinical psychology with a specialization in depth (Jungian) psychology at Pacifica Graduate Institute in Santa Barbara, California.

Over the years, I presented many talks and workshops on Jungian topics (especially dream interpretation) and provided clinical consultation and supervision with mental health professionals. I also was an invited speaker at a conference on psychotherapy and Buddhism in Kyoto, Japan, which led to my contributing a chapter (Wallace 2009) to a book titled *Self and No-Self: Continuing the Dialogue between Buddhism and Psychotherapy.*

Recognizing and appreciating that to live life is to face the mysteries of everyday existence, I continue to practise what I advise—to open-heartedly meet life through the lens offered by mindfulness and Jungian psychological practices. Therefore, this book is not a theoretical discourse arising solely from academic study. With my education and training as a psychologist (now retired), I do value research scholarship and continue to review clinical studies, but I equally appreciate the importance of lived experience.

Everyday awareness of, experience with, and relationship to time, and therefore aging, based on my own and clients' lived authority, is, in fact, the essence of this book. Understood through the lens offered by mindfulness meditation and Jungian psychological practices, aging does not have to be an enemy to be resisted and fought. Rather, a different awareness, experience, and relationship to aging allows it to become a friend, one whom you have likely up to now kept at bay outside your everyday consciousness. However, when invited to share this life with you, paradoxically, aging can become your new best friend.

I know this sounds like a stretch, but this book offers you the opportunity to test out this possibility in a slow, step-by-step manner. Let's start by meeting the new lens that we will work with to see and meet aging with greater acceptance, ease, satisfaction, resilience, and well-being. Let's take a quick introductory trip through mindfulness meditation and Jungian psychological practices.

MINDFULNESS MEDITATION

Mindfulness arose from the Buddhist wisdom tradition over 2,600 years ago. While acknowledging the novel attributes and characteristics inherent in time through seasons, days, and even hours, it proposes that each singular moment is unique. Mindfulness recognizes that each moment's particularity arises because of the ever-changing nature of not only time but of everything in this world. Since change is a constant, each moment is original.

Mindfulness is the mind's quality and power that is deeply aware of what is happening in this unprecedented moment without commentary and interference. I see it as a mirror that reflects whatever is before it, knowing that each moment is distinctive in and of itself. Experiencing time through a mindful sensibility generates not only an appreciation but also an awareness of moment-to-moment existence.

While mindfulness has been practised for millennia, fast forward to the twentieth century when Dr. Jon Kabat-Zinn and his colleagues at the University of Massachusetts Medical School began to hone and refine this ancient practice for a modern medical setting.

In 1979, Dr. Kabat-Zinn founded the Mindfulness Based Stress Reduction treatment program (MBSR), anchored in mindfulness meditation practices. It has applications to stress and various physical and emotional concerns, including pain, chronic illness, depression, anxiety, etc. It is based on the premise that you miss much of your life through mindless reactivity and that your relationship with each moment is coloured (often negatively) through your judging attitude. I have found that mindfulness sensitivity allows you to experience each moment more consciously and develop a more accepting and compassionate response to whatever arises. It presents a proven methodology to enhance your awareness, experience, and relationship with time through explicitly focusing on each moment.

Dr. Kabat-Zinn presented mindfulness meditation as a practice involving four components:
1. Paying attention
2. On purpose

3. In the present moment

4. Non-judgmentally

SELF-REGULATION OF ATTENTION

This deceptively simple-sounding practice involves two discrete but interconnected tasks, with the first being self-regulation of attention. Neuroscience has found that attentional focus influences all conscious brain functioning. That is, wherever attention goes, the rest of the brain follows, which includes many mental operations, including memory, comprehension, learning, sensing how we feel, identifying emotions in others, communication, and appropriate social interactions. Therefore, where we deploy our attention determines to a large extent what we see and do, or as the wise teacher Yoda summarized, "Your focus determines your reality."

However, research has found that there is approximately a fifty-fifty chance that your mind has wandered at any particular moment, and therefore, you are not present with what you are doing. Since attention is essentially the brain's boss—it determines the moment-to-moment experience in terms of what you perceive, think, emotionally feel, remember, and do—it makes the self-regulation of attention an essential skill to consciously participate in the moments that comprise your life.

To exemplify the importance of self-regulated attention, I recommend an entertaining and informative exposé of how we miss much of life through distracted attention presented in a TED talk by a pick-pocketer. In a short video, Apollo Robbins demonstrates not only how easily we can lose our attention but also its dramatic negative consequences. The video's powerful presentation transcends what words alone can describe, so it is well worth watching!

I view the first three aspects of the mindfulness definition—paying attention, on purpose, in the present moment—as the technical skills needed to self-regulate attention. They provide a strong building structure, much like the foundation and framework of a house, that assists in placing and holding your attention where you want it to be. Thus, learning to self-regulate your attention satisfies the first two invitations involving awareness and experience of time.

ATTITUDE TO EACH MOMENT

However, the last aspect of the mindfulness definition—self-regulating your attention *non-judgmentally*—is a more challenging but equally necessary task. Surprisingly, after initially starting a meditation practice, students of mindfulness report that the mind continuously generates judgments about what you are thinking, feeling, and experiencing. Almost everything that passes through your awareness is labelled and categorized by the mind. Some experiences will be judged as "positive" or "good," others will be deemed as "negative" or "bad" while still others will be regarded as merely "neutral," all based on your emotional reactions or evaluative conclusions as to their worth.

While you may not readily recognize your reactions as judgments per se, you are likely to know what you want more of and what you want less of, which is simply you making judgments by another metric. This habit of categorizing and judging your experience locks you into mechanical reactions of which you are often not even consciously aware. These judgments tend to dominate your mind, making it difficult ever to find any ease or well-being. Dr. Jon Kabat-Zinn concludes that it is as if your mind were a yo-yo, going up and down all day long on the string of your judging thoughts.

The practice of mindfulness recognizes this destructive pattern humans have developed, and it identifies the critical component of attitude that you bring to each moment as central to your well-being. Mindfulness provides the opportunity to do away with the yo-yo by cultivating an attitude of non-judgment, impartially witnessing whatever arises in your awareness and anchoring the mind in a new, more stable foundation. It is a way you can "meet" whatever occurs with a sense of equanimity rather than reflexively grasping, pushing away, embellishing with stories, or reacting emotionally.

While not an exhaustive list, Dr. Kabat-Zinn presents seven attitudinal foundations critical to be consciously cultivated in developing a healthier, resilient, and more satisfying relationship with whatever arises in your moment-to-moment awareness. The attitudes of acceptance, non-judging, non-striving, beginner's mind, trust, patience, and letting go are not independent but rather reciprocally interact to create and strengthen a lens through which you can understand and respond to whatever arises. Of course, the attitudinal foundations will not take away the pain and sorrow that you will inevitably experience, as these are simply universal human events. Instead, they provide a framework that fosters a way of allowing you to meet and hold all your thoughts, emotions, and physical sensations more healthily and satisfyingly. This framework is like a roadmap that guides you to a new mindset of what it takes to be a better friend to yourself.

While the first three aspects of the mindfulness definition address the technical or structural components needed to build this new house, developing a non-judgmental and accepting attitude toward whatever arises makes this house feel more inviting and supportive, which I imagine as becoming more like a home you would want to inhabit. While creating this more inviting sense of home is easy with positive thoughts, emotions, or experiences, it becomes increasingly complex and therefore critically important when you bump up against or are slammed by the more challenging and difficult moments that each will encounter. You know those moments that I am speaking of, those of pain, loss, and sorrow that no one can escape. I have found that nurturing this beneficial relationship to the present moment through the attitudinal foundations represents a significant practical and useful mindfulness component, especially during the aging years.

PARADOXICAL RESULTS OF MINDFULNESS

Mindfulness presents a powerful and effective process that fosters awareness, experience, and relationship to each moment as it arrives, expanding your consciousness of inner thoughts and emotions and sensory awareness of sights, sounds, smells, and tactile perceptions. However, like much in life, there is a paradoxical reality to your newfound mindfulness sensibility. In addition to the gift of expanded moment-to-moment experience, increased consciousness also brings to light awareness of persistent and repetitive thoughts, feelings, and behaviours that negatively impact your sense of well-being. You know the ones I mean—nagging patterns or habits or personality characteristics that inevitably interfere with not only your sense of well-being but also relationships with partners, family, workmates, or friends. These pesky thoughts, emotions, or behaviours may have haunted you for many years or perhaps have only recently arrived with your aging years. No matter when current, they act as troublesome issues that encroach into your happiness, ease, and well-being.

These persistent irritants show up under many guises, with examples of thorny intrusions aging clients brought to my psychotherapy practice, including loss of control, unknown future, rigidity, criticalness, vulnerability, shame, resentment, regret, and so forth. These intrusions often give birth to distressful conditioned reactions. Notwithstanding the provocation, responses can be experienced as being angry, on edge, anxious, ungrounded, depressed, uneasy, listless, or simply out of sorts. Any one of these can be so persistent and powerful that even with the best intentions not to get pulled into their orbit, they continue to arise like an undesirable relative who shows up at your door repeatedly and will not leave. What makes them so obstructive to your awareness is that they act as a filter, a veil or haze that obscures your experience of each moment. You simply cannot see or feel or think straight when such intrusions arrive. As a result, these unwelcome intrusions can seem impervious even to mindfulness interventions.

Much of your life is influenced, if not ruled, by unconscious processes. We are all subject to such troublesome issues, and I have worked with people long enough to conclude that it is not a matter of if these disruptive issues will arise but rather when. Since they are strong enough to colour your experience and play havoc with your attempt to meet each moment non-judgmentally, additional strategies are helpful to address these conditioned reactions.

Fortunately, a psychological school of thought addresses these intrusive burdens through the aging years and, therefore, can be of assistance.

JUNGIAN PSYCHOLOGY

Analytical psychology was developed in the late 1800s and early 1900s by Dr. Carl Jung, a Swiss psychiatrist interested in human development during our later years. He noted that the elder years were the "afternoon" of life using the analogy of the sun's passage through the sky such that youth was "morning," mid-life corresponded to "noon," and "night" embraced more senior years. Thus, Jung regarded aging as a later developmental stage that, while it has its challenges, simultaneously holds a wealth of opportunities for personal growth and discovery, exploration of life's meaning, and psychological enrichment and maturity.

However, as a clinician, Jung was particularly interested in what interfered with one's ability to experience aging's positive aspects. Obstructionist struggles are not to be ignored as they can be powerful enough to derail your individuation, a process Jung identified as an inner imperative to embrace and fulfill your potential to become the unique individual you are.

Jung often found unconscious processes brought about through earlier life experiences that stifled or disrupted your personal development. Therefore, investigating and analyzing the most troublesome aspects that individuals experience were doors to unlocking your potential. Unlike many other psychological models, Jung did not vilify the challenges and struggles individuals found interfering with their quest for wholeness. Rather than attempting to quickly eradicate such difficulties, Jung's approach was to treat them as welcomed clues or signposts to understand better what interfered with a fulfilling and satisfying life.

While the praxis of Jungian psychology is considerable (evident by the vast available literature, as well as academic and professional clinical training programs), core concepts that are useful in our quest to be more mindful include curiosity, investigation, analysis, and relationship.

Entrance to the Jungian view of personal development during your "afternoon to evening" of life begins with curiosity—to observe, identify, and become acutely aware of those thorny challenges that interfere and repeatedly topple your sense of well-being. These persistent intrusions become glaringly evident within the mindfulness practice, although their origins can be challenging to identify.

Since much of your life functions through unconscious processes, an open and receptive attitude to uncover and meet these previously unidentified constituents of yourself becomes a critical process. Investigating and analyzing patterns of thoughts, emotions, and behaviour can require an excursion into exploring early developmental experiences and relationships. However, this investigation is not undertaken as a witch hunt to assign blame for current difficulties. Instead, it offers compassionate understanding and insight into what underlies and contributes to present-day struggles, including defences, projections, personal shadows, overcompensation, and the limiting persona you show to the world.

An attitude of curiosity and discovery through openly meeting, investigating, and analyzing both the conscious and unconscious aspects of psychological blockages create the opportunity to have a different relationship with yourself, and by extension, to each moment. It allows the skewed perception of yourself to be unmasked, facilitating an expanded sense of self. This new and expanded relationship incorporates previously unwanted characteristics and newly discovered positive aspects of yourself, which together create the unfolding potential of fully becoming the individual you are in each moment.

TWO DOORS OPENING TO SHARED REALITIES

While Jungian psychology is predicated upon different theories and practices from mindfulness meditation, they share similar beliefs concerning present-moment experience. As a foundation, both approaches share an attitude of acceptance of whatever is arising at the moment, which Dr. Jung (1973) characterized as an affirmation of things as they are: ". . . an unconditional 'yes' to that which is, without subjective protests."

Both platforms emphasize the critical importance of awareness through direct experience of whatever arises with thoughts, emotions, and behaviours. Investigation of present-moment incidents is undertaken through different methods in each practice, but the goal remains similar—that is, to meet and develop a more accepting relationship with whatever you experience as challenging or disruptive to your ability to experience the present moment fully.

Both platforms rest on the belief that a healthy and satisfying life journey does not depend upon excluding harmful or unwanted thoughts, emotions, or behaviours, as this would essentially be attempting to sculpt the "perfect" individual. Instead, both facilitate meeting your humanness with an attitude of acceptance and curiosity that spills over into a new, encompassing, healthier, resilient, and more satisfying relationship with yourself.

Just as Dr. Kabat-Zinn presents seven attitudinal foundations critical to be consciously cultivated in developing a mindful relationship with whatever arises in your moment-to-moment awareness, Dr. Jung (1969) notes that his therapeutic intervention could be accurately described as a "readjustment of psychological attitude." He added that "There is no change that is unconditionally valid over a long period of time. Life always has to be tackled anew."

Mindfulness acknowledges that a full, vibrant, meaningful, and enjoyable life includes not only relishing the 10,000 joys but critically through also finding a resilient approach to "be with" the inevitable 10,000 sorrows that make up each life. Dr. Jung (1954) would agree as he concludes "Therefore the principal aim of psychotherapy is not to transport the patient to an impossible state of happiness, but to help him acquire steadfastness and philosophic patience in face of suffering. Life demands for its completion and fulfilment a balance between joy and sorrow." Thus, they are two systems that share similar goals—they just come at it from different perspectives. Combining mindfulness meditation and elements of Jungian psychology practices is a gift offered to our aging years and is the premise of this book.

EMBRACING AGING MINDFULLY

Think of your aging years, as Jung did, as the nighttime of your life. This book's title—*MOONLIGHT SERENADE: Embracing Aging Mindfully*—extends Jung's metaphor by encompassing my vision of moonlight as an archetypal motif representing and illuminating the aging process. Mindfulness and Jungian psychology practices are self-sung serenades, encouraging you to lovingly court and support yourself throughout this natural, inevitable, trying, and potentially rewarding process.

Embracing the mindfulness invitation of present-moment awareness, experience, and relationship to the unstoppable nature of time married with the Jungian imperative to develop increased consciousness and associated benefits that advancing age offers to each moment are available to you right now. Acknowledging the limited and unknown span of lifetime left is the catalyst to not wait to begin, for "If not now, when?" becomes the inescapable aging question!

HOW TO USE THIS BOOK

This book presents a step-by-step course to develop a unique mindfulness practice of value to your aging life. While it draws from my professional and personal experiences, it is centred upon a training program that I have been teaching for several years to participants primarily aged fifty to eighty-five years old, addressing the inevitable challenges accompanying our advancing years. Mindfulness and Jungian psychology cannot cure such difficulties, of course. Still, they can and do provide unique perspectives on a way of being that results in greater acceptance, ease, satisfaction, well-being, and happiness in this adventure of a lifetime—*your* adventure!

The program will teach a systematic mindfulness practice useful to all ages but is unique by explicitly applying these new skills to the often-multiple complex issues arising in later years, including grief, chronic pain, and life-limiting illness. Accompanying mindfulness practice will be the application of Jungian psychological strategies to bring insight into conscious and unconscious patterns or personality characteristics that negatively colour your ability to be present in each moment. Finally, knowing that life's vicissitudes can be taxing, even with the acquisition of mindfulness skills and Jungian psychological insights, a separate chapter will present additional resources found through self-compassion and loving-kindness meditation. Combining mindfulness, Jungian psychology, and self-compassion practices, this book offers the goal of developing a new mindset of becoming a better friend to yourself through your aging years.

This program is structured into a nine-week course of mindfulness instruction, allowing time for the development and cultivation of a personal practice, as well as the opportunity to begin experiencing an attitudinal transformation of your relationship to life, to your very way of being. It is a step-by-step process best undertaken in the order presented since new skill acquisition ladders on previously learned ones.

Individual chapters will mirror the nine weekly sessions of the mindfulness course that I teach to aging clients. To vicariously experience the flavour of the course, the sessions will follow a group of participants (based on composites of individuals I have taught) in a format that I designed and have found helpful to the hundreds I have trained over the years. I recommend that you stick to the schedule of working with each session for a full week, starting with reading the session notes followed by seven days of practice. Midway through the week of practice, a section exploring more deeply how to develop a healthier relationship to your experiences is offered. Specifically, each session will contain the following:

- Detailed instructions of the structural aspects of mindfulness practice—essentially how to do it. Assuming you have no experience, we will start right at the beginning with foundational skills. Then, each session undertaken on a weekly schedule adds additional techniques to learn how to hold your attention in the present moment needed to practice mindfulness. These skills are the "house" that you will build to meet the first three aspects of the mindfulness definition of *paying attention; on purpose; in the present moment.* It also addresses the first two invitations concerning the backdrop of time in that it allows you to both be *aware* of the passing moments and fully *experience* each one of them.

- Presentation and discussion of attitudinal foundations that address the last aspect of the mindfulness definition, which is to act in a *non-judgmental* manner, will begin in Week Two. Attitudinal foundations are a critically important aspect of mindfulness training in that it fosters a healthier *relationship* with whatever arises, especially in terms of challenging thoughts, emotions, and body sensations that you will inevitably experience. Your newly unfolding relationship to each moment through the attitudinal foundations creates more of a "home" that you will want to hang out in even during challenging experiences. Critically, it addresses the third invitation of developing an open and embracing *relationship* regarding your understanding and experience of time.

- Each session will include a section that encourages you to practise what is being presented during each of the following seven days. Mindfulness is a practice that cannot be learned just through reading about it; instead, it is an embodied experience that requires the active rehearsal of new skills and ongoing practice to enjoy its benefits. Written instructions are included at the end of each chapter and audible guided presentations of each session's meditation practices are available at the book's website, www.embracingagingmindfully. com. I recommend that you engage in mindfulness meditation daily during the full week before moving on to the next session. The recommended time for each practise session starts at approximately twenty minutes a day and gradually increases over eight weeks up to forty-five minutes per day. At the beginning of each new session, a review of last week's practice with suggestions for relief of potential concerns will be offered.

- A Tracking Your Practice form is available at the end of Week 1 and on the book's website, which can be printed for ongoing use. It is recommended that you record your daily practice during the week to document your continued involvement and as a motivator to reinforce your participation. Learning any new skill can be challenging, so use the tracker as a reward to pat yourself on the back for the investment of your commitment, time, and effort!

- Beginning in Week 2, I have included a Midweek Cuppa section during the middle of each practice week that allows you to further build your relationship with each moment. Developing an open and healthy relationship depends on understanding and applying the attitudinal foundations, so I invite you to find a time later during each week (after you have read the lesson and begun your daily practice sessions) to get a cup of your favourite beverage and spend a few minutes reviewing and exploring them further. These sections provide reflection and insight on the attitudinal foundations, as well as specific insights and exercises from a Jungian psychological perspective, to address knotty issues that can act as filters or veils to negatively interfere with your relationship to each moment. To illustrate how to work with such exercises, each section will introduce you to a composite of some of my psychotherapy clients' struggles and applied interventions to change their relationship to often unconscious barriers intruding in their ability to live each moment fully. Even if the topics do not seem like pressing issues to you at present, I recommend that you review the material and engage with the exercises. Becoming conscious of these issues and exploring them will positively impact your relationship to mindfulness and present a further roadmap of developing psychological maturity that contributes to a healthier relationship to your aging years. Record your completion of the Midweek Cuppa on your Tracking Your Practice form to document and reinforce your active participation.

THE FINE PRINT

Your awareness, experience, and relationship with time are the themes and the framework upon which this book is predicated. In this vein, I honour and respect your time and therefore want to explicitly address a few issues you need to know before embarking upon this course. Specifically, I do not want to waste your precious time if these concerns call into question your intention, as well as motivation, to commit to the course.

PRACTICE

One of the gifts of aging is that you have undoubtedly been "around the block" a time or two and so realize that any offering of significant personal development and growth guaranteed through the promise of alluring and tempting effortlessness is not only *likely* too good to be true but *is* too good to be true! Therefore, the first consideration that you need to be aware of is that this course is not a magic pill—rather, it is an experiential process requiring active participation. To read the book without investing your intention, energy, and time in the practices of both mindfulness and Jungian psychology will provide you with little else but a cognitive understanding of these processes. Quite simply, you should not expect to experience any benefits in terms of your thoughts, emotions, and behaviours unless you commit to doing the work. This conclusion has been borne out through research and my experience teaching mindfulness as well as clinically practising Jungian psychology over many years. While I honour that each of you is exceptional in your own way, know that others have tried but found that there is no quick fix or bypassing the investment needed to learn and practise these new skills.

However, this need not scare you from embarking on this new adventure. Quite the opposite! I know from my own experience as both a practitioner and a teacher of both mindfulness and Jungian psychology that the required practices are anything but arduous. On the contrary, the practices are inspiring, as they unwrap the gift of agency over your life, the sense that you can impact your day-to-day, moment-to-moment experiences. While learning any new skill can initially feel somewhat artificial and awkward, students report that they enjoy the time they are investing to do so. Many students in their seventies and eighties commonly conclude that they wish they had learned these skills thirty years earlier!

EXPECTATIONS

A further issue that is important to address to be fully informed before starting this learning process concerns your expectation of what your lived experience will become. Thousands of books promise a pathway to idyllic existence in only seven or twelve or twenty-eight days. While some people may enjoy a rapid opening to paradise, my rather long professional and personal exposure to such offerings have only unearthed empty claims.

Be very clear that this course does not promise to transcend your human experience; that is, it lays no claim to create a blissful life existence after nine weeks or nine years or ever. Instead, it offers a proven theory and process of learning to transform your awareness, experience, and relationship of moment-to-moment events and encounters, especially those of a more challenging and painful nature.

Therefore, the course's tone will be compassionately supportive in its unflinching identification and understanding of the challenges that arise as you age in your human body, mind, and soul to foster an acceptance of these provocations as part of your human incarnation. Yes, you will continue to experience the inevitable pain and loss and sorrow of life's journey because no one is immune to such occurrences. However, life, including the unavoidable less-than-blissful aspects, will be shared through a different perspective, creating an open-hearted and inspirational relationship that makes for more ease, calm, well-being, resiliency, and equanimity. Language limits the complete understanding of what you can expect, but images of being more grounded, balanced, capable, and confident to live each moment consciously and wholeheartedly is the reward offered. You truly can learn to become a better friend to yourself, especially during difficult and complex moments!

PERSONAL AGENCY

It is difficult to fully advise what you can expect from this course because of not only language limitations but also the unknown influence of how each individual's differences, as well as present-day level of personal development, affect the outcome. Therefore, I would recommend that the most appropriate intention and mindset to bring to the course is to know that you are in charge of not only what you will invest in terms of time, energy and effort, but most importantly, that you are the judge as to its value. There is a large and growing body of research concluding that these practices are beneficial to participants. From my experience as both a practitioner and a teacher, I know that they can transform individuals' lived experiences. But this course is not about what I or the research believes; instead, it is *your* life, and you need to be the one to discern if it has any benefit to living your aging years. Therefore, to commit to the course with a sense of openness and curiosity, a healthy dose of questioning, and trust that YOU will be the ultimate arbiter of knowing through experience any benefits to be accrued, is, I believe, the most appropriate and valuable attitude with which to begin.

Any true adventure begins with not knowing the ending. Therefore, I offer this invitation to step into the unknown and join me in learning a new awareness, experience, and relationship with aging through its embodiment of time. Know that while the framework of this course is predicated on learning new skills through meeting and being with time, its genuine deeper thrust is learning a new awareness, experience, and relationship with your aging life. Time is aging and aging is time, so you learn and benefit through meeting each!

Not knowing is a significant issue we each have had and will continue to encounter as we age and, therefore, will be one of the major themes to be explored. However, while there is much that we do not know in this life that we live, it is abundantly clear that the best intentions or pleadings will not slow the passage of time or, by extension, your aging life. Therefore, while acknowledging the reality of limited time available in your aging life, the pressing question becomes not should you learn a new way of being, but if not now, when?

MINDFULNESS BEGINS

WEEK ONE

It is indeed challenging to transform an institutional milieu into a warm, inviting, and friendly meeting space. Still, I was impressed by a local hospice's noble attempt to host our new mindfulness course in a welcoming environment. Large paper globes hung at contrasting heights in two opposing corners to soften the sightlines of stark white walls and ceiling. Silently acting as a backdrop, the walls embraced enlarged nature scene photographs coupled with the round, white-faced industrial clock mounted at a level for ubiquitous monitoring ease. An overhead audio-visual projection system with an enormous wall screen signalled a modern building capable of entertaining attendees. One long wall of windows framed a narrow grassy belt with a waterfall feature valiantly competing for your audible attention over surrounding traffic commotion.

However, what betrayed a potentially transformational makeover was the circle arrangement of the never-comfortable blue plastic bucket chairs with legs of chrome. Even with blankets draped over the chairs offering the promise of a reprieve from the obligatory "numb bum" that occurs with extended periods of sitting, the reality that this room was a functional institutional space could not be overlooked.

However, what was lacking in the setting's ambience was more than counterbalanced by the palpable group vitality. The room was alive with greetings, tentative introductions, and small talk generated by a complement of strangers brought together for a common purpose. Each of the twenty-five individuals, ranging in age from fifty-four to eighty-three years, exuded a blend of excitement and nervousness to be starting the mindfulness course.

Beyond the commonality of interest in the subject of mindfulness, their individuality unmistakably defined this emergent community of new students. Differentiation by daily activity (retirees, homemakers, employees, professionals, business owners), education (limited schooling to professional university graduates), socio-economic (struggling with fixed incomes to affluent), relationship (married, divorced, single, widowed), spirituality (Western and Eastern established religions, nature-based faith, independently defined spirituality, atheism), physical health (pain, chronic illness, life-limiting disease, strong vitality, mobility restrictions), and emotional well-being (bereavement, low mood, anxiety, questioning life's meaning, contentment) highlighted the lived background mosaic of this cohort of new students.

Having interviewed each person independently before their enrolment, I knew that differences took a back seat to their shared objective of gathering this late February morning. From my vantage point as the course instructor, I knew they collectively would soon come to understand that even with their marked differences, all arrived in a universal search for more ease, well-being, resilience, and happiness during their aging years.

From my interview with each participant, I also knew they already had assumptions of what mindfulness entailed. This degree of awareness is certainly not unexpected, as, over the last forty-plus years, the practice of mindfulness has blossomed exponentially in Western culture. Mindfulness has even proclaimed its formidable position by gracing *Time* magazine's cover in 2014!

At the same time, and perhaps due to this publicity, superficial awareness of the concept of mindfulness has led to the inevitable co-opting of its purpose and value via misplaced association with practically all of life's activities. While there certainly is value in paying attention to engagement in any activity, attaching the label of mindfulness can sometimes be more of a marketing ploy than an accurate attribution of mindfulness's purpose and worth.

WHAT MINDFULNESS IS NOT

Labels such as "Mindful Baking," "Mindful Golf," or "Mindful Financial Planning" subvert the potential authentic mindfulness offers. However, even more deceptive than marketing gambits are the underlying misperceptions of what mindfulness practice is about. While appreciating Western culture's welcoming embrace of mindfulness, unfortunately, it is often predicated upon false or misleading understandings of mindfulness's goals. Therefore, it is critical to begin a mindfulness course with a debunking of false expectations that participants may hold. These retractions include:

1. **Mindfulness is not trying to relax.** While there certainly are forms of meditation whose primary immediate goal is to induce a relaxed state, this is not mindfulness. Instead, mindfulness has, what I believe to be, a bolder objective. Mindfulness proposes to be aware and accept what is occurring in the present moment, no matter what that may be. As you know from your history, experiencing life's moment can be anything but relaxing, especially if you are in the midst of a challenging or painful thought, feeling, or event. However, studies have shown that as participants learn to become more aware and accept what is occurring, they become less surprised, fearful, and combative to thoughts, feelings, or actions that may arise. Therefore, mindfulness allows participants to develop a less reactive, more resilient, and capable relationship to their inner and outer world experiences.

   However, I want to emphasize that while mindfulness does not directly focus on becoming relaxed, decreased stress is one of the most often reported practice outcomes. To develop a healthier awareness, experience, and relationship to whatever arises in your life generates a confident and assured attitude that naturally embodies a more relaxed and grounded way of being. The bottom line is you get relaxation—not directly but as a natural by-product of paying attention, on purpose, in the present moment, non-judgmentally.

2. **Mindfulness is not a religion.** Although mindfulness has been observed historically for over 2,600 years within Buddhism, present-day practice does not require adherence to religious or spiritual beliefs. Starting with the MBSR program at the University of Massachusetts Medical School in 1979, it is explicitly asserted that there is no prerequisite or expectation to become involved in any religious undertakings. Instead, the goal is to learn new secular skills. Indeed, modern scientific psychology and medicine consider mindfulness a core healing factor, which is why it is employed in many inpatient and outpatient treatment programs.

3. **Mindfulness is not about transcending ordinary life.** One of the goals of mindfulness is to become aware of each moment of your life, no matter how common or magnificent, no matter how pleasant or painful. Mindfulness is about experiencing yourself entirely and wholeheartedly and therefore is not attempting to bypass the mundane or the ragged edges of your life. It is explicitly not an attempt to escape from pain, sorrow, disappointment, and losses that each of you will experience. As one example, the goal is not to surgically relieve the human experience of grief but rather to allow individuals to have a different relationship to this profound and painful experience by developing more resilience and subsequent coping strategies.

   A cartoon illustrating this point depicts two characters with the first proffering, "I have been thinking . . . you know all that stuff . . . once you get it out of the way, then you can live your life?" The second quizzically responds, "Yeah, what about it?" To which the first plaintively laments, "Well, that IS your life!" Mindfulness is an acknowledgement that your short human existence encompasses

10,000 joys *and* 10,000 sorrows, so the only question becomes how you are going to be with each of them.

4. **Mindfulness is not emptying the mind of thoughts.** The mind will always produce thoughts because that is what it does. It has created thoughts ever since humans began inhabiting the earth and will continue no matter what meditation program you bring to it. Therefore, mindfulness is not attempting to empty the mind of thoughts, no matter what their content. It is explicitly not trying to rid the mind of negative thoughts and generate only positive ones. Instead, mindfulness allows you to become more aware of your thoughts and learn to be in a relationship with them in a more accepting but discriminating manner. Mindfulness enables you to develop a more harmonious and even-keeled connection with your thoughts through a deeper understanding of how the mind works. Quite simply, you learn that you do not need to get dragged around by every thought that arises. As a bumper sticker that I came upon many years ago fittingly concludes, "Don't believe everything you think."

5. **Mindfulness is not about becoming emotionless.** The goal of mindfulness is not to become a robot devoid of all feelings so that you will never be subjected to life's pains. Quite the opposite, it allows you to experience the entire range of emotions that are available to each of us—the whole enchilada of life—but with the added benefits of more tolerance, confidence, and resilience. Of course, life can still hurt, but strengthening and enhancing your capacity to be with hurt is what mindfulness offers.

   There is a charming story that I heard at a retreat many years ago from Dr. Jack Kornfield, a psychologist who was one of the first to bring mindfulness to Western culture. In but a few lines, the story succinctly characterizes our misguided expectations as to how we should experience life's emotional trials and challenges:

   "If you can sit quietly after a difficult conflict with your partner . . .

If in a financial downturn, you remain perfectly calm . . .

If you can see your neighbour travel to far off fantastic and exotic places without a twinge of jealousy . . .

If you can happily meet whatever is placed in front of you . . .

If you can always find contentment, no matter what struggles befall you . . .

You are probably . . . a dog!"

WHAT'S IN IT FOR ME?

Now knowing what you will *not* learn from mindfulness, the obvious question becomes, what can you expect? While most new group participants likely hold this query, usually only the boldest individuals will pose the challenge directly, probing what benefits there are to investing time and energy to pay attention, in the present moment, on purpose, non-judgmentally. A fair question for all to ask, so let me address it directly!

Mindfulness-based treatments are applied to many medical and psychological conditions that could potentially affect us all. A fulsome but incomplete list of these conditions includes pain, hypertension, heart disease, irritable bowel disease, fibromyalgia, skin disorders, cancer, HIV/AIDS, eating disorders, insomnia, stress, general anxiety, recurring depression, grief, addiction relapse, panic disorder, social anxiety, anger, etc. Research and anecdotal evidence have shown that participants can, through the practice of mindfulness, anticipate demonstrable support in their quest for more ease, well-being, resilience, satisfaction, and happiness during their aging years. Potential outcomes include:

1. **Reduced symptoms:** While clearly, mindfulness does not "cure" all the clinical issues it has addressed, it has proven effective in reducing symptoms associated with many medical and psychological

conditions. An intriguing, more recent finding is that mindfulness can positively affect the degree of inflammation in the body, which has consequences for reducing disease severity.

2. **Increased subjective well-being and enhanced quality of life:** Improved mood, happiness, vitality, satisfaction, and life engagement are benefits often described. Learning to be an active participant in your physical and emotional well-being generates a sense of self-efficacy, a feeling that you can control your destiny to an extent not otherwise experienced.

3. **Reduced emotional reactivity:** Relief from negative reactive symptoms such as angry or fearful thoughts/emotions by an enhanced ability to relate differently to the symptoms is a by-product of mindfulness practice. Neuroscience has shown a thinning in brain structures (such as the amygdala) that regulate fear-based reactions and increased connectivity in areas (such as the prefrontal cortex) that manage emotions. As a result, people can better respond to inner and outer events rather than unconsciously react to them.

4. **Increased emotional tolerance:** Becoming mindful of one's emotions, including those created through thoughts and physical sensations by recognizing their impermanence (left to their own, they arise and fall away), provides not only reduced reactivity but also increased emotional tolerance. Improved emotional regulation allows you to recover more quickly from upsets and enjoy more freedom from rash reactions.

5. **Improved behavioural regulation:** The capacity to "decenter," that is, to step outside your thoughts and emotions by seeing them as just coming and going rather than a mandate to act, allows more freedom from impulsive, repetitive, and often harmful behaviours such as rage or addictions. Addiction relapse usually occurs when emotional or behavioural triggers prove difficult to bear, while

mindfulness offers an enhanced understanding and resilience to cope better.

6. **Improved cognitive efficiency:** Being more fully present and attentive leads to enhanced cognitive control evidenced through increased memory, concentration, ability to manage tasks, problem-solving, and prioritizing goals. In addition, neuroscience has demonstrated thickening in brain regions that play essential roles in learning and memory through mindfulness practice.

7. **Positive brain changes:** Research on mindfulness meditation has also found that it potentially slows the normal shrinkage of the brain. At age fifty, long-time meditators' brains have been found to be "younger" by seven and a half years compared to brains of nonmeditators of the same age. While there has been no research indicating that mindfulness can reverse brain atrophy, there is the possibility to believe that it can be slowed.

DOUBTING QUESTIONS

Simply running through this impressive range of potential benefits usually fires up interest in an entire group of course attendees. However, Richard was the sole vocal skeptic on this occasion. A retired engineer in his seventies, who sat slumped in his chair with arms crossed while hearing of such benefits, had a more pressing question. "If the premise is that these benefits are available through the simple task of paying attention, on purpose, in the present moment, non-judgmentally," he slowly unravelled, "why do we need a nine-week program?" His distrust was evident, as he added, "It seems so easy that even a monkey could do it!"

I was thankful for Richard's cynicism, as it led to the group's first opportunity to be their own experiment—to test this potential time-saving shortcut and therefore be their own judge of whether my offer of a protracted weeks-long investment was necessary.

I invited each participant to sit with eyes closed and silently count backwards from 100. The catch was that every time your awareness drifted from attending to the actual numbers, you were to start over from 100. No matter how momentary an intrusion—whether it be a fleeting thought of how silly this exercise is, a physical sensation that your nose is itchy, a feeling that you are happy, a noise that caught your attention, or whatever interloper meddled into your task of simply counting backward—your obligation is to acknowledge the breach of your focused awareness and begin again. The intrusion need not be strong enough to interfere with or derail your counting—only enough that it arose in your awareness to be noticed. To provide more data for your experiment, tally the intrusive occurrences by counting them on your fingers each time you notice a loss of attention. This would be a short experiment, as I would keep time for three minutes.

As the seconds and minutes ticked by, I could see fingers extending as the count of intrusions multiplied in the silent room. At the end of the three minutes, when asked what number they could count down to, there was a perceptible hesitation until Richard sheepishly reported ninety-one. Others followed, tentatively declaring their results of eighty-seven, ninety-three, eighty-eight, eighty-four, ninety-five, and so on. The lowest number in the group was seventy-nine. When then asked how many intrusions they noticed in their quest to focus on counting backwards, in a hesitant but good-natured manner, they reported meddling occurrences ranging from nine to nineteen! While there was no prize for the lowest winning number, each benefited from experiencing the takeaway message that while mindfulness is a simple concept, it is not easy to implement. Richard sat up straighter in his chair, now convinced to participate in his nine-week investment actively.

In the spirit of self-discovery, I invite you, the reader, to try this experiment. Set a timer (smart phone, watch, kitchen timer, etc.) for three minutes and follow the above-noted instructions. This experiment is only for your information, so be vigilant and honestly note when your attention is pulled, even momentarily, from your task. See what number you can count backwards to, as well as tally the intrusions that will inevitably occur. You be the judge—can you unwaveringly hold your attention on the counting task for just three minutes? If so, you are pretty unique, as with all the students I have had over the years, no one has met that high bar—and I certainly include myself among those attempts!

WHERE IS YOUR FOCUS?

Your mind has a mind of its own. With our Western culture's emphasis on personal responsibility, it is a sobering experience becoming aware of how little control you have over where your attention is focused. The only reliable conclusion from this three-minute experiment is that your mind will do what it wants to do—like a defiant two-year-old child, it often won't willingly comply with your directives. Even when asking the mind to focus on the straightforward task of counting backward, it could not, or would not, postpone or avoid attending to intruding thoughts, feelings, physical sensations, or noise.

You have probably seen the ubiquitous YouTube videos of household cats chasing lasers. While it is entertaining, I also feel sorry for them, as they do not seem to have a choice as they frantically pursue the elusive laser. Even when they momentarily succeed, the outcome is insubstantial (nothing there!) until they are again drawn into the hunt, hoping that this time, there will be a reckoning. After your short experiment, can you relate to their impulsiveness? Do you have any more empathy for the impetuous cats? Do you not also chase after the next shiny object that appears in your awareness?

WANDERING MIND

Researchers at Harvard University set out to explore this question by studying how much our minds wander. In 2010, Matt Killingsworth and Daniel Gilbert designed a smart phone app that pinged people throughout the day, asking what they were experiencing at that moment. The app specifically asked what activity they were engaged in (such as working, shopping, exercising, grooming activities, having sex, etc.) and whether they were thinking about something other than what they were doing. Thousands of individuals participated in the study, with the results indicating that people's minds tended to wander from what they were doing forty-seven percent of the time! The degree of mind-wandering varied considerably, with the least occurring during sex while the most was during grooming activities, such as taking a shower.

The results were incredible as almost half of the time, people were not consciously focusing on what they were doing, choosing instead to follow some other thought, feeling, physical sensation, or environmental stimuli that arose in their awareness. So, any way you cut it, almost half a waking life disengaged from what you are doing means missing much of what you are experiencing.

WHAT WERE YOU THINKING?

Coming back to your experiment, take a moment to review the content of intrusions that popped up while attempting to concentrate on counting backwards. What was it that pulled your attention from your task of counting? Specifically, what was so crucial at that moment that demanded you drop your commitment?

Allow me to offer my best guess. I believe, notwithstanding any startling noise or physical sensation that grabbed you, upon reflection, you will undoubtedly find a significant theme that most of your intruding thoughts are either about the past or the future.

THE COST OF TIME TRAVEL

Our human focus on mental time travel—to focus on the past and the future—in and of itself is not to be demonized, although unchecked, it does come at a price. The Harvard study looking at mind-wandering also asked individuals how they felt in the moment when their smart phone pinged on a scale ranging from very bad to very good. Quite surprisingly, overall, people reported being less happy when their minds wandered. Neutral or negative thoughts made them less happy than focusing on the moment, but pleasant thoughts made them no happier. Even when people were involved in an activity that they did not like—commuting, for example—they were happier when focused on the undertaking than when their minds strayed. The researchers noted that people's negative moods appear to be the result of the mind-wandering rather than the cause. These findings led to the published article's title, emphasizing that "A Wandering Mind Is an Unhappy Mind," with the takeaway conclusion that people miss experiencing almost half of what they are engaged in and are unhappy during these times. Being unhappier for nearly half of your life because not attending to what you are doing is a pretty hefty cost to the mind's time wandering lust!

STRESS AND MIND-WANDERING

In addition to diminished mood arising from not attending to what you are engaged in, humans incur another cost because of mental time travel. A classic book from 1994 by Dr. Robert Sapolsky titled *Why Zebras Don't Get Ulcers* helps us understand this human dilemma that appears to be unique among the animal kingdoms.

Dr. Sapolsky notes that animals, such as zebras, are subjected to episodic stress, like being pursued by a predator. However, once that threat is over—if they have not been eaten—they can shake off the traumatic experience and carry on unencumbered by the event. Their response means that animals are not immune from stress, but they do not hold onto it by berating themselves for what they did or did not do, what could have happened, what might happen next week, what other animals will think of them, and so forth. The animals can deal with potentially life-threatening events, but critically, they can then let them go. Wendell Berry aptly summarizes this reality in his poem "The Peace of Wild Things" with the image "I come into the peace of wild things/who do not tax their lives with forethought of grief."

Humans also experience stress, but it is more chronic than episodic because of our inclination to focus on the past and future. Unlike animals who live more in the moment, we humans are adept at living as time travellers, bouncing our attention from the past to the future, which unfortunately prolongs our stressful experiences. Our continuing ruminations about what happened, what could have happened, what should have happened, what if it happens again, what others will think of you and so on, only serve to extend an already stressful episode long after the actual event.

WHAT'S SO SPECIAL ABOUT THE PAST AND THE FUTURE?

Spending any amount of time with your mind wandering aimlessly in the past brings the realization that you often seem to marinate in regrets and resentments. If you have ever woken in the middle of the night, you know what I mean! A cartoon from many years ago titled "The 3AM Brain" aptly characterizes our imprisonment to the past: "I can see you're trying to sleep, so I would like to offer you a selection of every memory, unresolved issue, or things you should have said or done yesterday as well as in the past 40 years! Just trying to be helpful!!!" Don't mistake the mind's claim on the past as only a consequence of modern life, for even the first-century Roman poet Perseus accurately observed that "we consume our tomorrow fretting about our yesterday."

Spending your moments thinking randomly about the future may seem like an attractive alternative to living with the past's regrets and resentments, but it too comes at a cost. While we may not wallow in guilt and grievances from the past, we all want to hide from the dirty little secret that we do not know what the future will bring. This state of unknowing is, to say the least, disturbing and more often ladened with a sense of fear. The resulting condition of ongoing apprehension and angst is no small matter, as anxiety is the most prevalent mental health disorder in the United States.

This is an appropriate point to discuss the differing concepts of fear and anxiety, as we will be working with both throughout the course. Fear is immediate—there is an actual danger to your physical or psychological well-being that requires a swift response. When realistic fear arrives, you want your mind, emotions, and body to respond in a life-sustaining manner immediately. On the other hand, anxiety is more of a free-floating worry about what *could* happen without there being an immediate danger.

Anxiety can be described as "fear without a face." In other words, there is no immediate actual danger that requires a quick response.

While anxiety does not require an immediate response to a life-threatening situation, it is a compelling emotion that can override your reasoning and decision-making capacities. The fact that anxiety grips the body in the same way as fear gives anxiety more credibility than it deserves. When your body reacts this way, the mind believes anxieties alert you to a genuine threat when this is not the case.

From my early career working in a psychiatric hospital, I know that taken to the extreme, anxiety of the future can leave you paralyzed, unable to function day to day. In a less intense form, worry about the future can negatively impact your decisions, your plans, and your moment-to-moment experience. Anxiety and its associated stress about the future can rob you of happiness, satisfaction, and contentment. It is powerful and truly is no fun!

WHAT IS TRUE?

Mark Twain reportedly concluded, "I am a very old man and have suffered a great many misfortunes—most of which never happened." So, honouring the spirit of Mark Twain, in addition to the emotional toll brought by aimlessly focusing your attention on mental time travel, you also must question the accuracy of your memories of the past and predictions of the future. Concerning the past, I continue to be amazed at the different versions of early family life that my two brothers and I have even though we experienced the same events. While some of these versions only represent differing vantage points, others are so different that it feels like we came from separate families. This "illusion of memory," thinking we perceive and remember more of the world than in reality we do, is well documented by researchers Daniel Simons and Daniel Levin, so if you're interested, check out their entertaining YouTube examples (https://youtu.be/6JONMYxaZ_s), including the classic phantom gorilla study (https://youtu.be/vJG698U2Mvo).

Mentally travelling to the past comes as a double whammy—not only do you experience emotional costs of more unhappiness and stress, but what you are basing your unhappy and stressful memories on is suspect and may not be accurate. Does that sound like a winning combination for you?

FUTURE PREDICTION ACCURACY

As you have likely discovered from reflecting on your thought intrusions during the counting backward exercise, the unknown future is ripe to grab and hold your attention. While you are not likely to be clairvoyant, humans have developed a remarkably sophisticated technique that allows you to fantasize effortlessly by making predictions about future events that you have never experienced.

In studying how we make predictions of the future, Dr. Daniel Gilbert (2006) has been a leading investigator. One of the classic experiments focused on how test subjects would feel learning that they had a deadly disease, such as pancreatic cancer. Most participants reliably reported that it would not be pleasant. However, they did not produce this conclusion by remembering how it felt to receive this bad news in the past, as they would with a memory, but by closing their eyes, simulating the event, and noting their emotional reactions to the simulation. Now, most of us assume that if you feel bad when you imagine dreadful news, you will feel even worse when you receive it. In essence, you generate mental previews of future events, which cause you to have emotional reactions, which you then use as a basis for your predictions about the actual event's likely emotional consequences. Quite simply, you know which future events will feel good and which will feel bad because you feel good or bad at the moment when you simulate them.

This method of mental simulation to forecast the future is ingenious but unfortunately imperfect. Along with studies that have explored this remarkable cognitive process, others document the flaws that call into question the precision of what you predict. Variables such as when in the future you imagine an event occurring, how readily you would adapt to it, the changeability of emotions over time, the tendency to omit critical factors, and the context in which you generate your forecast can affect the accuracy of your predictions. To add further injury, you are experiencing real—possibly disturbing—emotions at the moment based on nothing more than fantasy of the future!

This means that centring your life primarily on the future can be a fool's errand with the cards stacked against you. John Lennon's song "Beautiful Boy" aptly concludes that this life of yours is what unfolds while you are busy making other plans. So, it ends up that you not only are lousy at predicting what will happen, but you also are not very good at knowing how you will emotionally feel when whatever happens, happens. Add to this the research about generally how unhappy you are when mind-wandering coupled with the additional stress that comes with the unknown future, and you have to wonder why you ever go there in the first place!

EVOLUTIONARY PSYCHOLOGY'S GOOD NEWS AND BAD NEWS

To add additional weight to this discussion is that outside of your conscious time-travelling adventures, evolutionary psychology tells us that your emphasis on the past and the future is, in fact, a hard-wired inherited blessing and curse. On the one hand, it is a gift because it has kept humans alive for thousands of years. Life on the savannah was a dangerous adventure where early humans needed to be acutely aware of past events and anticipate future threats to stay alive. If your cousins Benny and Lenny were happy-go-lucky fellows with no memory for what they experienced in the past or awareness of whether a sabre tooth tiger could be waiting around the next boulder to have them as lunch, then they probably did not survive for very long. Only those who were acutely aware of the past and future survived with their genes passed to the next generation, which is a blessing.

However, what came attached with those blessed genes was negativity bias, being always primed to be on the lookout for the worst-case scenario. Since you are alive today, this ancient negativity bias lives on even though the potential of impending doom through being eaten by a sabre tooth tiger has dramatically lessened. Modern life has left us in a constant state of fight, flight, or freeze mode, even when there is no identifiable threat. The neuropsychologist Dr. Rick Hanson concludes that our brains are like Velcro for negative experiences and Teflon for positive events, which will undoubtedly colour your perceptions about past and future events. Therefore, it is helpful to know that your time travel woes represent an honest, albeit hard-wired, response passed down through the generations. That can feel like a curse!

WHY TIME TRAVEL?

I could sense the deflated atmosphere in the room as I ended my sobering discussion about the negative impacts of mental time travel to the past or the future. While many students nodded their acceptance of mind-wandering's detrimental effects throughout my presentation, an awkward but predictable question gradually appeared to be percolating through the room. Finally, Jessica spoke for many in the group, hesitantly asking, "Does mindfulness prohibit thinking about the past or the future?" The short answer is definitely not, but the question presents an excellent opportunity to revisit and reinforce mindfulness's process and goal.

As a tool, mindfulness is considered more like a scalpel than a sledge-hammer when befriending all parts of who you are, including your mind-wandering and time-travel capacity. Mindfulness does not live in the dichotomous black or white illusory realms of life but is comfortably at home in the messy middle grey zones. For example, while I do not want to spend my days floundering in the past, I, like most people, unapologetically love basking in pleasant memories. Remembering the night that my wife and I danced to an orchestral ensemble under the full moon at St. Mark's Basilica square in Venice, Italy, is still thrilling even though it was many years ago! Also, while I do not want to spend my days living in daydreams, planning for the future organizing a portrait shoot of my grandchildren, as I recently did, was terrific!

It is vital to emphasize that mind-wandering is not all negative; instead, in the spirit of mindfulness acceptance, it is crucial to recognize that it can be good or bad, enjoyable or destructive. Therefore, it need not be despised or worshipped because in and of itself, it is neither positive nor negative.

While I have focused my review on its negative implications, remember that on the positive side, your capacity to remember and learn from previous experiences is critical to developing consciousness, personal development, and harmonious relationships. Furthermore, applying learning from the past and imagining previously inconceivable possibilities have also unleashed human ingenuity to create future fantastic technology, medical advancements, and creative endeavours beyond imagination. Thus, mental time travel is essential to our individual and societal well-being.

I hoped the group was now clear that time travel in and of itself is not the issue. Instead, the mindfulness goal is to be aware of your mental time travel, fully explore the experience of it, and develop a more discriminating and healthier relationship with it. Specifically, you want to be in control when you engage in mind-wanderings.

WHO IS IN CONTROL?

Imagine you are sitting for a critical examination. If, after reviewing the questions, you begin to daydream about how you will ace the test, go on to great professional renown, and earn the Nobel prize, you are in trouble. On the other hand, if after reviewing the test questions and realizing how difficult they are, you fantasize that you will flunk the test, fail in life, and end up homeless, you are in just as much trouble. In both scenarios, you cannot harness your cognitive resources to address the task at hand in the moment, which is to apply your knowledge to the test demands. Time travel has got you in its grip; can you see how the laser beam is dragging your attention around the room?

Many years ago, I was fortunate to realize my dream of owning a horse. Fionn was a beautiful tri-coloured filly who, although very gentle, was not yet trained. I hired a younger (and more courageous) cowgirl to do the first rides, but when the initial rodeo of bucking and rearing ended, I was excited to continue her training. As I swung my leg over the saddle during my first ride, I'm not sure whose heart was beating faster—Fionn's or mine!

But as my hands tightly took hold of the reins and my legs pressed to her girth, a disturbing question abruptly popped into my awareness: Who was in charge here? Well, it didn't take long to realize that Fionn was in control, as she was the one who decided to go forward or back, to the right or the left, burst into a run or stand still, and occasionally kick front or back legs, so instead of me expecting to lead this 1,500-pound animal around the paddock, my only job became breathlessly hanging on tight. I, who was supposed to be in charge, had no say in the matter with the unplanned but sobering conclusion that I was just along for the ride.

In my daily life, I do not want to just be along for the ride, slavishly pulled from one thought to another, one feeling to another, one physical sensation to another, one sight to another, or one sound to another, like the laser-addled cats! That is not a life that would be worth living—missing your life moment by moment. But it would be a mistake to create barriers that safeguard from this out-of-control predicament because rigid decisions made from fear often evoke unintended consequences. Unfortunately, attempts to ban mind-wandering excludes you from participating in the positive allure and benefits offered through mental time travel.

The middle or grey zone of life recognizes that you are not committed to a forced-choice dilemma deciding if time travel is good or bad, wanted or unwanted, because your attitude, experience, and relationship to it determines value and appropriateness. Engaging in mental time travel then becomes a choice, selected by you when and where it is appropriate. And mindfulness, through paying attention, on purpose, in the present moment, non-judgmentally helps you make those decisions, which allows you to take more charge of your life.

MINDFULNESS BEGINS

The first goal of mindfulness is to learn to direct your attention when you want to, where you want it, and how long you want to retain it. Like holding a flashlight in a dark room, you want to control its revealing power, such as where you point the illuminating light and how long you keep it there focused.

Neuroscientists such as Dr. Amishi Jha at the University of Miami consider attention to be the brain's leader. It allows you to notice, select, and direct the immense computational resources that your brain possesses. Attention is all-encompassing as it oversees what you perceive, feel, remember, think, and do. Wherever attention goes, the brain's considerable powers follow, so in essence, it is the brain's boss.

BODY SCAN MEDITATION

Mindfulness is fully conscious of the mighty power and resultant benefits of awareness, which is why it constitutes the first aspect of its definition: paying attention, on purpose, in the present moment. To begin learning how to direct your attention, you will start with the Body Scan exercise. It is a simple process of focusing your attention on your body, an effective technique for developing consciousness and flexibility of awareness simultaneously. That is, you start to learn that you can be aware of your attention, direct where you want it to be, and hold it in that area.

The body scan instructions are straightforward: Focus your awareness on a specific area of your body and become curious as to what you experience. Attend to that body part for only about ten to twenty seconds and then move to the next part, methodically reviewing the entire body. There is no expectation as to what you should experience. Simply be interested if there is anything of note—perhaps a sensation such as tightness or pressure or throbbing or temperature or texture of clothing or aching or pain or whatever. Maybe you sense the body area, such as the size or shape of your foot or leg or arm or back. Simple awareness of each body area that you attend to is the goal of your focus.

In the beginning, you may find it difficult to experience any sensations in a particular part of your body. If so, you can wiggle or tighten or slightly move that area to derive a more visceral sense. However, it is essential to note that it is perfectly fine that sometimes you will not have any specific awareness of that body part at that particular time. If so, this is neither good nor bad; it is merely your experience at the moment. In fact, sometimes, it is interesting to notice the lack of sensation, the "nothingness" in the body area at the moment. Call me a slow learner, but after having done the body scan many times over the years, I still have difficulty feeling any sensations in my left toes unless I consciously wiggle them!

FINE-TUNING POINTS

There are a couple of additional points to remember when completing the body scan. First, the purpose is to begin working with your attention on what is truly happening in the present moment. Should you experience tension in a body part, your task is to notice it but not alleviate the sensation. Remember, the goal is not to create a different experience but rather to be aware of whatever is occurring at the moment. It may be tension, or it may not. It doesn't matter as your task is just to focus your awareness at will and on purpose.

The body scan is a way of practising your attention skills through establishing or re-establishing contact with all parts of your body, no matter what it may be experiencing at the moment. Bare attention is an essential aspect of mindfulness, and you will be building skills to accomplish more focused awareness through the course.

A second point to be conscious of is that completing the body scan allows you to dwell in silence and stillness. Should your mind wander to thoughts, feelings, sounds, or competing body sensations, bring your attention back to the targeted body part. Please do so compassionately and gently, recognizing that even though the body scan instructions are straightforward, it is not always easy to focus your attention without intrusions. This pulling of attention to something other than the intended task is guaranteed to occur, so don't be surprised or upset by it.

The complete body scan guided instructions are transcribed below for your review, and an audible guided version is available through the book's website at www.embracingagingmindfully.com.

Enjoy . . . and welcome to the first step to become more mindful!

PRACTICE OF THE WEEK

Guidelines:

- Plan to invest approximately **twenty minutes each day** with this Body Scan exercise. While the recommendation is to do a body scan each day of the week, you may want to set your intention slightly lower by committing to do them on only six out of seven days. An understanding schedule will allow you some flexibility, recognizing that life can get busy and you may need to skip one day. It is better to set a realistic target, which will more likely set you up for success rather than failure.

- Choose a time that works for you, a time you know you will not be interrupted. You may have to try different times of the day to find what works best for you.

- However, before bed usually is not a good time, as you can fall asleep quickly. Your intention is to "fall awake," not fall asleep.

- You can sit in a chair or lie down—experiment, see what feels right for you!

- If you find yourself falling asleep, try opening your eyes but keep your focus lowered on one object just in front of you—do not visually sweep the room.

- You have the option of reading the instructions or listening to the audible presentation on the book's website, www.embracingaging-mindfully.com.

- Record your practice on the daily **Tracking Your Practice** record at the end of this chapter or you can print it from the book's website. Recording your involvement will allow you to keep track of your sessions and experiment with what time works best for you and reinforce your efforts. Learning any new skill can be tricky, so use the tracking record as a motivator to pat yourself on the back for your investment of dedication, time, and effort.

- Congratulate yourself for committing to your well-being!

BODY SCAN INSTRUCTIONS:

(Note: "..." indicates pausing for a few moments)

Before we get started with the meditation, take the time to get comfortable. . . .

If sitting, position your feet flat on the floor . . . hands resting on your thighs or on your lap . . . upper body balanced over your hips . . . shoulders in a comfortable but alert position . . . bottom sitting comfortably on the seat. . . . Let the chair and floor support you completely. . . .

If you are lying down . . . feel where your body touches the floor or bed . . . feel the bed or floor supporting you. . . .

Imagine yourself on a journey . . . maybe to a place you have never been before . . . discovering . . . noticing . . . watching . . . no judgment as to what will be found . . . just being curious . . . and open to the new experience. . . .

You are not trying to change who you are . . . not trying to do anything . . . except be aware and open to what is at this very moment. . . . This inner journey will be an exploration of your body in this present moment. . . .

As we move through the body scan, you may want to gently wiggle or move that area of the body to feel if there is any sensation . . . or to stay still and just notice the lack of sensation. . . .

There is no right or wrong way to do this meditation. . . . It is only an exploration of attending to what you notice in this moment . . . to use your body as the target of your attention. . . .

When you are ready . . . allow your eyes to gently close. . . . Become aware of your body in this room . . . noticing how the chair or bed supports you, the floor supports the chair or bed . . . and the earth supports the floor. . . . Become aware of the space in this room . . . perhaps sounds . . . smells . . . just observe and notice . . . sensing the movement and rhythm of your breath coming in . . . and going out . . . coming in . . . and going out . . . no need to change the rhythm . . . just allow it to be what it is. . . .

Throughout this body scan meditation, you will notice how quickly your attention can move to other things . . . your to-do list . . . perhaps what you are making for dinner . . . appointments you need to make . . . so many thoughts. . . . Thoughts are normal and natural. . . . You are not trying to empty the mind of these thoughts. . . . You just want to become aware that they are present . . . but not follow them . . . not follow any storyline . . . to only allow thoughts to arise and, like puffy clouds in the sky, to dissipate on their own. . . .

If you notice the mind is wandering . . . that thoughts are vying for your attention . . . just gently bring your attention back to the sound of my voice . . . back to the sensation of your breath. . . . Allow your breath to become an anchor to this present moment, to the right here, right now. . . .

Become aware of how your whole body is feeling in this moment . . . calm . . . anxious . . . feeling anticipation . . . noticing curiosity . . . just be aware without judgment. . . .

On the next in-breath, let your attention be on your left foot. . . . Now the left big toe . . . the second toe . . . the third toe . . . the fourth toe . . . and the baby toe. . . . Now the space between the toes . . . the top of the foot . . . bottom of the foot . . . the heel. . . .

Do you notice any tingling in your toes or your foot? . . . Is there pain or discomfort? . . . Warmth or coolness? . . . Can you feel the texture of your sock or shoe? . . . Maybe the size or shape of your foot? . . . Perhaps you feel nothing, and that is okay. . . .

Now move your attention to the left ankle . . . shin . . . calf . . . noticing without judgment, just noticing what there is to notice . . . any sensations . . . the knee . . . the back of the knee . . . the front of the knee . . . the sides of the knee . . . the thigh. . . .

Can you feel the thigh resting against the chair or bed? . . . Perhaps you can feel the pulsing of circulation here. . . .

Notice whatever can be detected or felt. . . . Maybe you feel the weight of your clothing against your thigh . . . perhaps becoming aware of your hand sitting gently on your thigh. . . . Perhaps you are feeling nothing . . . and that is okay. . . . Whatever you are feeling is fine. . . .

Now with the next in-breath, sense your left leg as a whole . . . becoming aware of the inside and outside of the whole leg. . . .

Now on the next in-breath, let your attention shift to your right foot. . . . Notice that you can move your attention to where you want it. . . . Focus on your right big toe . . . the second toe . . . the third toe . . . the fourth toe . . . the baby toe . . . the area between the toes . . . the top of the foot . . . the bottom of the foot . . . the heel. . . .

Notice any sensations in the toes . . . any sensations in the foot . . . temperature changes . . . pressure from shoes or socks . . . just noticing curiously, as if you are exploring your foot for the very first time. . . .

Now bring your attention to your right ankle . . . the right shin . . . the calf . . . the knee . . . the front of the knee . . . back of the knee . . . sides of the knee . . . just bringing awareness to these areas. . . .

With the next breath, move your attention to the right thigh. . . . Can you feel a heaviness? . . . Feel the shape and strength of the thigh as it rests on the chair or bed beneath you. . . .

Now with the next in-breath . . . sense the right leg as a whole . . . becoming aware of the inside and outside of your whole right leg. . . . Bring your attention to the left and the right leg together. . . .

Do you notice any difference between the right and the left leg? . . . Perhaps one feels heavier than the other . . . maybe one feels more prominent than the other . . . or not. . . . Just notice . . . be curious . . . and be aware. . . .

With the next out-breath, release the left and the right leg . . . just letting it all go. . . . There is no one right way to feel as you do this. . . . Whatever you are feeling is fine. . . . It's just the way you are feeling. . . . You are not here to change anything. . . . You are here to just notice . . . with curiosity . . . with compassion . . . and with openness. . . .

With gentle curiosity, just observe whatever arises at this moment . . . in your body . . . where you are focusing your attention. . . .

With this next in-breath, allow your attention to move to the left hip . . . pelvis . . . groin . . . right hip . . . left buttock . . . right buttock . . . noticing whatever there is to notice . . . maybe discomfort . . . tensing or holding on . . . pressure. . . . Do you notice the support of the chair or bed under your bottom? . . . The placement of your hips? . . . Pressure under your thigh? . . . Where does the sensation of the chair end? . . . Behind your knee perhaps? . . . With your next out-breath releasing this part of the body, just let it all go. . . .

With your next in-breath, shift your attention to your lower belly . . . belly button . . . upper abdomen, just below the rib cage. . . . Do you notice any tightness? . . . Softness? . . . Perhaps some sounds . . . gurgling . . . growling . . . rumbling . . . or not. . . .

Can you become aware of the shape of your belly? . . . With a full deep breath . . . notice if the shape of your belly changes. . . . Does the belly rise and fall with each breath? . . . Just notice. . . .

With the next in-breath, allow your attention to move to the heart area . . . the heart centre. . . . Can you notice the rhythm of your heart beating? . . . Can you feel the movement of your heart with each beat? . . . You may feel tightness . . . pounding . . . gentle pressure . . . or nothing at all. . . . Maybe some emotions or feelings have arisen . . . such as a sense of peace . . . anxiety . . . comfort . . . fear . . . joy . . . boredom . . .

No matter what you are feeling . . . it is okay. . . . There is no right or wrong, no good or bad . . . no expectations as to what you should feel. . . . It is just the way it is . . . in this place . . . at this moment. . . .

Now allow your attention to rest upon the left and the right lungs. . . . Take a deep breath in . . . and out . . . feeling the sensations of the breath filling the lungs . . . and then releasing . . . maybe noticing coolness with inhalation . . . warmth with exhalation . . . just notice. . . . You may notice how the ribs move in a gentle rhythm with each breath. . . .

Notice how the chest expands as you take a deep breath. . . . Notice how the torso changes shape. . . . With the next out-breath, let the upper chest go. . . .

With the next in-breath, shift your awareness to your left hand . . . the left thumb . . . the first finger . . . the second finger . . . the third finger . . . the pinky finger . . . the area between the fingers . . . the top of the hand . . . the palm of the hand. . . . You may notice tingling in the fingers . . . maybe moisture on the palm . . . coolness . . . or warmth. . . . Can you feel the sensation of the left hand on your thigh or on the bed? . . .

Notice your hand at rest . . . no texting . . . no driving . . . no doing anything . . . just resting. . . . Notice the left wrist . . . the left lower arm . . . the elbow . . . upper arm . . . Just feel what there is to feel . . . if anything. . . .

Now shift your awareness to your right hand . . . the right thumb . . . the first finger . . . the second finger . . . the third finger . . . the pinky finger . . . the area between the fingers . . . the top of the hand . . . the palm of the hand. . . . Notice the right wrist . . . the lower arm . . . the elbow . . . upper arm. . . . Again, just notice your right hand at rest . . . nothing to do . . . just stillness . . . just resting. . . .

Can you notice any difference between the left arm and the right arm? . . . Any difference between the left hand and the right hand? . . . Just notice with curiosity, kindness, and non-judgment. . . .

If you have noticed that your thoughts are pulling you away from this present moment . . . gently and without judgment, come back to your body . . . your breath . . . my voice. . . . Now with the out-breath, let go of the hands and arms. . . .

With your next in-breath, move your attention to your lower spine . . . mid-back . . . upper back . . . shoulders . . . to the very top of your spine, where it connects to the skull. . . .

What do you notice in your spine and back area? . . . Does one area feel different than the other? . . . Does one area feel better than the other? . . . Perhaps you notice strain . . . stress . . . tiredness . . . pain. . . . Perhaps you feel neutral . . . nothing to notice. . . . On the next out-breath . . . let it all go. . . .

With the next in-breath, allow your awareness to shift to the neck and throat area. . . . Can you sense how you are holding your head? . . . Any tension . . . or tightness? . . . Maybe you feel a coolness on the back of your neck . . . or warmth. . . .

Now move your awareness to your jaw . . . mouth . . . lips . . . tongue . . . teeth. . . nose . . . nostrils. . . . Focus your attention on your eyes . . . left and right . . . your eyelashes . . . your eyebrows . . . the space between your eyebrows . . . your ears . . . your skull . . . hair. . . . Just notice whatever there is to notice . . . no right or wrong sensations . . . only whatever is occurring at this moment. . . . Does your face feel soft and relaxed? . . . Maybe tight? . . . Just feel what you feel. . . . Now with the next out-breath, let your awareness of your head dissipate. . . .

With the following in-breath, notice your whole body. . . . Briefly scan the body from your feet up to your head . . . quickly but purposefully moving your attention through this bag of bones that is your body. . . .

Can you recall how you felt at the beginning of this meditation? . . . How does it compare with how you are feeling now? . . . Perhaps you feel relaxed . . . more open . . . more curious . . . more grounded. . . . Or maybe you feel impatient . . . tired. . . . Maybe you are bored . . . irritated. . . . Again, without judging yourself . . . or your feelings . . . just be aware and be open to whatever is. . . . Nothing is right or wrong. . . . It just is what it is in this place . . . at this moment. . . . Be held in the stillness and the silence. . . .

As we come to the end of the body scan meditation, I will ring my bowl three times . . . just remain in stillness and awareness with your eyes closed. . . .

1 . . . 2 . . . 3 . . .

Now gently allow yourself to come back to the awareness of your body in this space. . . . Sense the room . . . the air around you . . . any sounds . . . any smells. . . .

Very gently and with awareness, begin to wiggle your fingers and toes. . . . Slowly, very slowly, open your eyes. . . . You may feel you need to stand up and stretch . . . or just sit or lie quietly. . . . Enjoy the sensation of just being present in THIS MOMENT. . . .

TRACKING YOUR PRACTICE RECORD

Week 1	Sunday	Monday	Tuesday	Wednesday	Thursday	Friday	Saturday
Time							
Duration							

Week 2	Sunday	Monday	Tuesday	Wednesday	Thursday	Friday	Saturday
Time							
Duration							
Midweek Cuppa …							

Week 3	Sunday	Monday	Tuesday	Wednesday	Thursday	Friday	Saturday
Time							
Duration							
Midweek Cuppa . . .							

Week 4	Sunday	Monday	Tuesday	Wednesday	Thursday	Friday	Saturday
Formal: Time							
Duration							
Informal: Time							
Duration							
Midweek Cuppa . . .							

Week One

Week 5	Sunday	Monday	Tuesday	Wednesday	Thursday	Friday	Saturday
Formal: Time							
Duration							
Informal: Time							
Duration							
Midweek Cuppa …							

Week 6	Sunday	Monday	Tuesday	Wednesday	Thursday	Friday	Saturday
Formal: Time							
Duration							
Informal: Time							
Duration							
Midweek Cuppa ...							

Week One

Week 7	Sunday	Monday	Tuesday	Wednesday	Thursday	Friday	Saturday
Formal: Time							
Duration							
Informal: Time							
Duration							
Midweek Cuppa …							

Week 8	Sunday	Monday	Tuesday	Wednesday	Thursday	Friday	Saturday
Sitting #1: Time							
Duration							
Sitting #2: Time							
Duration							
Midweek Cuppa …							

HELLO, PRESENT MOMENT: WHERE HAVE YOU BEEN ALL MY LIFE?

WEEK TWO

Waiting to start the second mindfulness class, I could sense my curiosity wondering if anyone has dropped out. Mindfulness is not for everyone, and the overview of what it is and isn't, what you can expect, and the need for active investment of time and energy isn't what some people are looking for. Others quickly conclude after only a few attempts at the body scan meditation that it "doesn't work!" Therefore, as participants began arriving, I was delighted that the student count did not drop and that everyone returned.

However, even with those returning, many mindfulness students report that while the instructions seem simple and straightforward, they are often surprised and frequently disappointed with their experiences. I could feel this apprehension at the beginning of the second session as the mood seemed subdued with a noticeable trepidation in the room when asked what their body scan practice experience in the past week had been.

Sybil was the first to speak, hesitatingly offering that she found it challenging to observe and not try to change the sensations that she was feeling. Betty found it hard to concentrate as her mind wandered while focusing on the different parts of her body. Sanjay reported that he sensed increased anxiety when feeling the pain in his arthritic fingers. Rachel loved the meditation, finding it very calming. Sam was surprised at how little awareness and feeling he had in his lower body. Karl reported that he found the body scan to be relaxing and fell asleep a few times. Cindy was surprised and slightly alarmed when she did not have any visceral experience of her artificial left knee. Carlos found that while he could focus his attention on different body areas, he had difficulty with his right hip that he had injured several years ago. Specifically, he found that he kept replaying stories of the incident that intruded in the focusing of his awareness. Jasmine was surprised at how tight and tense her body felt. Bethany reported increased anxiety when noticing her rapid heart rate. Cassie found the Body Scan exercise very disappointing, as she discovered that she had little awareness of much of her body. Devon simply reported that he was bored with this exercise and didn't see any point in it.

Do not be concerned if you found this Body Scan exercise challenging, frustrating, or even boring. The following sessions are designed to work with whatever you experience. It is important to remember that even though the body scan appeared to be a straightforward and effortless practice, it is not what you are probably used to regularly doing unless your daily focus involves active monitoring of your body, such as with athletes or dancers. Be easy with yourself. While noticing any negative judgments that may have arisen about your experiences, know that the Body Scan exercise is a deceptively simple practice that is not always easy.

The body scan meditation is an important beginning as it presents an opening to focus your attention consciously and deliberately on a specified target (in this case, different parts of the body) and simply notice what (if anything) is happening in terms of sensations at this moment. It is also a valuable technique for developing flexibility of attention—to shift your attention at will, consciously, which is a major goal of mindfulness. Specifically, this exercise allows you to begin accessing the mindfulness process, which, as you recall, involves paying attention, on purpose, in the present moment, non-judgmentally.

OPENING TO MINDFULNESS

Notwithstanding your specific experiences during this last week completing the body scan practice, this simple exercise presents a vital introduction to the mindfulness process. First, it asked you to set aside the time to begin establishing a different relationship with the present moment intentionally. It did not ask you to read your emails, turn on the TV, do the dishes, walk the dog, or any of the thousand and one other activities that demand the moments of your day. It merely asked you to be in the present moment and, in a curious and non-judgmental manner, check in with this bag of bones that comprise your earthly body. It is a way to become aware of what is happening in this body at this present moment.

For many of us, our mental life is primarily an "out of body" experience. Therefore, the second concept introduces a practice using your body to intentionally re-establish, or perhaps even initially establish, a relationship with your body. Your body is always present in your moment-to-moment existence, yet it is often ignored or taken for granted. However, until you have drawn your last breath at death, your relationship with your body is critically important. It directly impacts your experience of each moment, as anyone with chronic pain or physical limitations will attest. The mindfulness practice will continually use your relationship to your body not only through the ability to use it as an object of awareness but also that attending to its ever-changing experiences will become a dominant theme with which we will work.

Many new mindfulness students report that while they initially found it interesting to explore the body, repetitively completing the exercise lessened the experience. For example, Malik found that his initial couple of body scan sessions were informative and noteworthy, but the exercise's novelty diminished as the week progressed. For instance, he noticed few sensations while focusing his attention on his right foot during the initial sessions. Therefore, Malik concluded that there would not be any new information obtained in future practice sessions, so he simply fast-forwarded his scan through that part of his body. That is, he found himself more quickly going through the body scan in a rote-like fashion, relying on his previous experiences as the basis for his mistaken belief that there was limited new information available to observe.

Malik's conclusion brings us to a third important concept. While his experience of "been there, done that" is typical for new mindfulness students, it illustrates not a mastery of the practice but rather a fundamental misconception. One of the basic understandings of mindfulness practice is that everything is in a constant change process and that without noticing such changes, we miss a significant part of everyday life.

As you look out your home or work window, you can witness that not only do the seasons change but daily and even hourly shifts occur with the weather. This sense of constant change is also evident within yourself. Whether it is the body's cells regenerating, the air you breathe continually being in motion, the diversified emotional expressions, or just the inevitable aging of your body, nothing stays the same. However, a basic premise of mindfulness practice is that if you are unconscious of the inevitable constant flux of change and inattentive to it, you are blind to the individual moments that populate your days, weeks, months, and years. The mistaken belief that you know what will come acts as a veil that clouds your perception and experience of each moment. You simply miss this life that is yours—you miss it moment by moment!

BEGINNER'S MIND

Countering this tendency to falsely believe that we already know what the next moment will bring is supported by developing an attitude of "beginner's mind." Quite simply, beginner's mind is an acknowledgement that we do not know what the next moment will bring, and therefore, we need to cultivate and hold an attitude of attentive curiosity and receptivity to the arrival of each moment. To let go of our misplaced belief that we know what the next moment and the next moment and the next moment will bring is to let go of preconceived notions and cultivate an experiencing of the unfolding world through new perceptions.

Beginner's mind is a central aspect of your awareness, experience, and relationship to time. It is also a core characteristic of mindfulness because not only is it an acknowledgement of our limited foresight into the future, but more importantly, it is a declaration of our intention to be open and receptive to experience each moment as though it is the first one we have ever felt. And in a not-so-surprising way, this is a declaration of reality. We are opening to the next moment as if it were a brand new one never before experienced—because that's precisely what it is. And to the next moment and the next moment and the next moment. Each one is a moment that no one in the world has ever experienced. The moment is uniquely experienced through your senses, against your particular history, in this specific environment, with these conditions and all the interacting variables that come into play at just this time—this particular moment is truly a brand new one never before experienced!

The negative consequence of not holding a beginner's mind is illustrated in the old Christian story about a man who lived in a house at the bottom of a valley. One day, the rains began and continued for days after days after days. The water continued to rise, resulting in a flooding of the first floor of his two-storey home. The man moved to the second storey, and as the waters continued to rise, a boat came by to rescue him. However, he said, "I have full trust in God, and therefore, I do not need to be saved. Go away." The boat left, but unfortunately, the waters continued to surge, and the man had to move into the attic of his house. A second rescue boat came by floating at a level equal to the attic where the man had retreated. But the man went to the attic window and again declared, "I have full trust in God, and therefore, I do not need to be saved. Go away." And so, the second rescue boat left. Unfortunately, the rains continued, and the man found himself standing on the house's roof, which was now completely underwater. A helicopter arrived from overhead to rescue him, but again he said, "I have full trust in God, and therefore, I do not need to be saved. Go away." The waters continued to rise, and the man eventually drowned. When he got to heaven, he had an opportunity to meet God. As he sat down before God, he said, "I don't understand! I had such faith in you!"

and God replied in a very empathic tone: "I don't understand either—I sent you two rescue boats and a helicopter."

The drowned man missed God's offerings because he lacked the appropriate awareness, experience, and relationship to each lived moment. Beginner's mind aptly describes the opportunity to cultivate and bring to each unfolding moment a new lens to meet all that arises. It is an attitude of attentiveness, openness, curiosity, and receptivity that declares your intention to experience each individual moment that comprises a life lived. Beginner's mind is, in fact, one of the attitudes that Dr. Jon Kabat-Zinn (1990) identified as being a foundational aspect of mindfulness, with him concluding that "The richness of present moment experience is the richness of life itself." As discussed earlier, mindfulness not only encompasses self-regulation of our attention to this moment, it is also the attitudinal foundations we bring to the moment that critically determine our relationship to this life we are living.

FOCUS ON ONE OBJECT

While mindfulness meditation's overall goal is to practice ongoing attention in a non-judgmental manner to whatever arrives in each moment of our lives, you need to start by first practising a more structured process—learning to consciously hold your attention on a defined object. This task builds on the body scan by steadying and stabilizing the mind in its present awareness through continually focusing on one—and only one—thing. The following images will help to understand better how to learn this skill.

Picture a stormy day at a lake: Dark, ominous thunderclouds overhead, the wind whistling through the shoreline trees, white caps building offshore, and the waves driven with increasing speed and force to crash onto the beach. A sailboat anchored just offshore bobs and tacks in the direction of the wind, feeling the energy and pressure of the waves that vociferously command the boat to move beyond the tether line holding it to the anchor. But it stays put, held in place by the anchor.

Paying attention to a specific object is like anchoring the boat of your mind and thereby keeping it from drifting aimlessly or blindly following the ever-changing water currents. Just as the sailboat remains in place due to its anchor, your focus of attention can help cultivate a reliable and known place or marker that holds your awareness. Should your attention begin to drift from your anchor (like laser addled cats), you can quickly return to it time and time again, a safe haven in the frequent storms of daily life.

YOUR FRIEND: THE BREATH

There is an infinite number of objects that you could choose as your anchor of attention, but you require a neutral object of focus, one that does not evoke strong emotions or physical reactions. You want an impartial object to which you continually return your attention.

The breath is the most common neutral point of focus within mindfulness meditation and has established itself as the primary anchor because of several attributes. The first is that the breath is always present. As long as you are alive, you are breathing. There is no need to do anything specific to bring about the breath, and therefore, there is no need to be concerned or vigilant as to whether you are still breathing. You can trust that breathing simply happens and will continue until your death.

A second attribute is that the breath is portable—it comes attached to your body and is always with you. As a result, the breath is something that you can focus on no matter where you are or in what situation you are involved. Associated with this ownership of the breath is that it also does not cost anything financially—a genuine bargain in this day and age!

A third important attribute is that the breath helps you cognitively understand and viscerally experience each moment's continually changing nature. You will find that each breath can vary significantly in its depth, duration, and smoothness depending upon many ever-changing factors both within your mind and body as well as the environment around you. You already know this from experience when the breath has changed significantly depending upon whether you are relaxed, stressed, scared, excited, or with any of the multitude of other emotions arising from experiences or even from just thoughts.

Breathing is a mighty friend and teacher in the mindfulness experience. Over time, it will become your best friend as the anchor to which you can always return your attention no matter what is occurring in your thoughts, emotions, or bodily sensations.

FIND YOUR BREATH

Having decided to use the breath as the anchor of attention, it becomes necessary to choose where to locate your focus within the body. There are many different places in the body to observe your breath, which offer choices for your anchor's location. One of the obvious ones is the nostrils. If you decide to focus on your breathing here, you will be focusing on the breath's feeling as it passes in and out of the nostrils. There may be a cool sensation as the breath comes in and a warmer sense as it is exhaled. Being aware of the breath coming in and out of the nostrils can provide a steady anchor of your awareness.

You may find it easier to focus on the breath coming in and out of the body through your mouth. The sensation of the breath coming through your mouth and passing the back of the throat can also present a strong anchor of awareness. Another body area on which to focus your attention is the chest and how it expands and contracts as it rises and falls. The fourth area as an option for your attention's anchor is the lower belly as it too expands and contracts, moving in and out with each breath.

No matter which location you choose, mindfulness asks you to be aware of the sensations accompanying your breathing at that particular place and use those sensations as the anchor for your awareness from moment to moment. Thus, it is not thinking about the breath coming in and out that is required. Instead, it is the acute awareness of your *experience* of the breath entering and leaving the body that makes it your anchor of attention.

MEETING YOUR BREATH

So, there you are, afloat in your boat on the shifting seas of your restless mind, anchored by your resolute focus on your rising and falling breath. Let's take a moment to get to know it better, this breath, this life-giving force that has been with you since the moment of birth and which will accompany you through all your days. In the spirit of mindfulness, this means "meeting" your breath in a curious, open, and receptive manner as if it were the first breath you had ever taken.

Find a seated position with eyes closed that allows you to feel relaxed but alert. Place one hand gently on your abdomen just above your belly button. Place the other hand on your upper chest just above your breastbone. Now close your eyes and pay attention to your breath. Simply observe the breath as it comes in, stays for a short period, and then leaves. Don't try to control the breath in any way; just breathe normally. Do not try to make the breath faster or slower, deeper or shallower—simply pay attention to it. Get to know where you most easily notice your breath coming in and going out. Is it through the physical sensation of the air coming through your nostrils? Or your mouth? Is it more easily felt as your chest rises and falls? Or is it your belly expanding and contracting with each breath? Spend a few minutes shifting your awareness to each of these potential anchor points of attention to identify your new best friend—that place in your body in which you will be developing an intimate and long-term relationship.

Now that you have an anchor of awareness to initiate your sitting mindfulness practice, spend a couple of moments with the breath—again, not consciously trying to change it in any way but simply to get to know it at this moment. Become curious about the breath itself. It obviously will change from moment to moment, but at *this* moment, what are you experiencing? How long is the in-breath compared to the out-breath? Are they similar or different in length? Which one is longer? Are there pauses or gaps after either the in-breath or the out-breath? Does the breath flow smoothly, or is it ragged, jerky, or broken in places?

NEED FOR AN ANCHOR OF AWARENESS

An obvious question that may have arisen while exploring your choice of placement for the anchor was asked by Betty, who quizzed, "Why do I need it? What is so special about having an anchor of attention?"

During this brief exploration of the breath entering and exiting the body, you no doubt found moments when your attention was drawn away from the task. Perhaps thoughts crossed your mind and you began thinking about them. Or emotions arose that caught your attention. Or physical sensations in the body pulled your awareness. Or perhaps a sound in the room became interesting and took attention away from noticing the breath as it came in and out of your body. Any or all of these experiences are certainly not unusual. As you will soon experience yourself as you enter the sitting practice meditation, they are exceedingly common.

The activity of thought, emotions, and physical sensations in your mind and body can quickly become the primary focus of your attention, pulling it away from your breath. Even though the task assigned was simply to watch your breath coming in and out of the body, your attention was easily hijacked! It's not that the thoughts are especially critical or that the feelings demand a review or that the physical sensations make an absolute claim for a response. They were merely cognitive, emotional, or physical stimuli that overrode your intention to watch the breath coming in and going out of the body. Very demanding, aren't they? They won't easily take no for an answer!

While it can feel frustrating to experience what limited control we have over our attention, it is also instructive as to why the mindfulness process becomes critical. To simply bounce from one thought or feeling or physical sensation to another and another results in frantic pursuit of whatever arises in your awareness field. Like the cats mentioned in the previous section, uncontrollably and excitedly chasing a laser beam of light, your attention can be just as overzealous and mesmerized with following the latest thoughts, emotions, and physical sensations that arise.

You found from the counting backward exercise that, just like the cats, if you pursue whatever stimuli come into your awareness, if you cannot maintain your attention on what is most important at this moment, you will miss much of what life offers. Mindfulness presents you with an alternative way of being—more present and attuned on purpose in this present moment to what arises both within and around you.

ALTERNATE ANCHOR

However, sometimes the breath is not enthusiastically embraced as the potential anchor of awareness. For example, individuals with a history of high anxiety or panic can often find it challenging to use the breath as the anchor of attention. Their often-frightening experiences with the breath can initially make the thought of using the breath as their focus of attention overwhelming. However, experience has shown that even with high anxiety levels, gradually and gently focusing on the breath as your anchor of attention for even initial short periods can result in a different relationship to the breath, allowing it to become your neutral anchor of awareness. To learn that the focus is simply on the breath itself and not trying to change it in any way can be helpful. Therefore, I encourage you to experiment gradually and gently with this life-sustaining process called breathing.

However, even with such a gentle and gradual desensitization process, it still may prove challenging to use the breath as your attention anchor. Perhaps breathing is more difficult for you because of physical illness or disability. In these situations, the breath would not be a neutral anchor, and it could even create more discomfort, pain, or emotional distress. Therefore, in these cases, it is necessary to identify another neutral point that will be your anchor of attention.

It is best to select an alternative anchor of awareness as a part of your body since you will want to have it readily available no matter where you are or in what situation you find yourself. Therefore, this could include any other body part that does not generate discomfort or emotional reaction, a neutral focus point. For example, in our meeting room during the second session, Beth found that her left hand, placed on her thigh, could become her anchor of attention. Moving one of her fingers or the whole hand created a focus for her awareness. Merely being aware of her finger or hand's sensations slowly moving over her clothing fabric allowed Beth to hold her attention and therefore became her personal anchor of awareness.

Using the hand or any other body function is simply a place or marker on which you can consciously focus your attention. When you notice that your awareness has strayed, the identified body area is the place where you can return to refocus your awareness. Be creative and experiment with what alternative body part will become your anchor of awareness and which, over time, will become your friend and partner in the mindfulness way of being.

While your anchor of awareness can be your breath or any other body function, I will only address the breath as the anchor in the following instructions for ease of reading. However, know that the instructions are referring to whatever anchor of awareness you have chosen.

SITTING MEDITATION PRACTICE

So now, let's put this all together and begin a formal sitting meditation practice. The instructions for the sitting meditation practice are surprisingly straightforward. First, using your anchor of attention, notice your breath coming into the body and leaving the body. Second . . . Guess what? That's it—that is the essence of the practice! Nothing fancy, just being aware of this moment through your anchor of attention on the breath as it comes into the body, is held for a while (however long or short it may be), and then leaves the body. There is no attempt to try to change the breath in any way. The breath may be rapid or slow, shallow or deep, smooth or ragged—just pay attention and be present with the experience of the breath coming in and going out. Believe it or not, that's the fundamentals, the scaffolding of the mindfulness practice you will be constructing.

It sounds easy. But as you experienced with the experiment of counting backward from 100 and will again experience within a brief period of beginning this practice, attention is a slippery concept that can seem to have a mind of its own. Thoughts will arise that will pull your attention away from your primary task of merely noticing and concentrating on the breath's movement. Thoughts occur that may be important to you or, more often than not, ideas about "things" that do not require your attention at this time. Thoughts may be about the past or the future: a seemingly bottomless catalogue of ideas, plans, memories, random ideas, loose associations, and so on.

When any thoughts arise that pull your attention away from the anchor of awareness, your breath, simply notice them and return to your breath. There is no need to argue with, judge, or feed them with more thoughts or engage in any manner with them. As my mother told me when I was in elementary school, don't make eye contact with the bully! The same applies to intrusive thoughts—they are simply thoughts that have arisen into consciousness and, like a bully, are demanding your attention and pulling you away from your goal, which is simply to concentrate on your breath. They need to be recognized as the intruder they are and let go. Gently bring your attention back to the breath, again focusing on the breath's intake and outtake to hold your awareness.

At times, your thoughts may be positively charged with emotions so that it's not even the thought that pulls you away from the breath as your anchor of attention, but rather the emerging feelings that accompany it. Sometimes it's merely emotions that erupt on their own into consciousness, such as worry, excitement, dread, sadness, boredom, or the thousand and one other feelings that accompany our human existence. The feelings may again be in connection with past or future events. They may be positive emotions that you enjoy having or negative ones you would not volunteer to entertain. But no matter what the feelings may be, when they take your attention away from the breath, simply notice and gently bring attention back to your anchor of awareness, your breath.

At other times, physical sensations in the body can hijack your attention. These phenomena may involve discomfort or even pain within the body, while conversely, you may become aware of very positive and pleasant physical sensations. Physical feelings of discomfort are not uncommon during sitting meditation, as the body can quickly become uncomfortable after staying stationary in one position for some time. While your first reaction may be to shift your position, scratch the itch, or rub the discomfort to alleviate the distraction, it is more helpful to your practice to simply notice the sensation and bring your attention back to your breath. These are simple physical sensations arising at the moment. There is no need to judge or engage them in any way—merely noticing them and gently bringing your attention back to the breath is the mindful strategy.

DISTRACTIONS, DISTRACTIONS, DISTRACTIONS

Jessica felt very discouraged during her first sitting meditation practice. While she was excited to begin mindfulness training, she was disheartened quickly about how often her intention of focusing on her breath was derailed with her attention pulled away to intrusive thoughts and feelings. She found that even after only two or three breaths, silly thoughts like old family memories, groceries she needed to pick up on the way home, the name of her high school English teacher, whom she had not seen in twenty years, and planning her sister's birthday, which was still three months away, kept flooding into her consciousness and pulling her attention away. Her discouragement about her perceived failure brought up feelings of sadness and shame. These feelings only added to her sense of incompetence, which triggered a tightness in her jaw and shoulders. By the end of twenty minutes of practice, Jessica convinced herself that she was a total failure and utterly incapable of being mindful!

Jessica's experiences of her initial mindfulness practice are not unusual. While this is not to take away from her felt experiences during the practice, all new meditators need to understand that Jessica's difficulties during her initial sitting practice are not unexpected. It is also important to emphasize that her experience was anything but a failure.

Remember that part of mindfulness's definition is that it is a process to regulate attention in the present moment. While mindfulness intends to hold your attention on the breath as your anchor, the reality is that this is an exceedingly difficult task to do. So let me share a little secret of mindfulness with you: It is fully expected that thoughts, feelings, and physical sensations will draw your attention from the stated goal of intentionally concentrating on your breath. This is simply the reality of being human!

Mindfulness is fully aware of this human tendency, but it does not alter its goal to be present with all the experiences that arise in each moment.

You want to be *aware* of a thought, feeling, or physical sensation that occurs. What you *do not* want to do is blindly and reactively follow every stimulus that enters your awareness. That is why you use the breath as your anchor of attention, a place always to return your focus.

What is critical is not that you have lost your connection to your anchor or even know what has grabbed your awareness, but that you are aware and notice this pulling away of your attention. As soon as you see your attention shifting away from the breath, the instructions are to, in a non-judgmental and gentle manner, bring your attention back to the breath. This noticing of your attention being pulled from the breath and then getting it back to the breath is what mindfulness is. Your meta-awareness recognized the intruding thought, feeling, or physical sensation, but you did not feel compelled to chase it as the cat automatically does with the laser beam. It is an "aha" moment when you realize that your attention is no longer centred on your breath. At that moment, you are fully aware of what drew your attention, which provides you with the opportunity to respond consciously and not merely react.

Therefore, Jessica's awareness of her concentration being drawn away from her breath to thoughts, feelings, or physical sensations is what mindfulness is precisely designed to do. She was aware that other stimuli crossed into her awareness, and at the moment she noticed the intruding interlopers, she had a decision as to what to do. She could reactively chase after whatever stimuli entered her awareness (picture the laser-obsessed cats!) or simply acknowledge the experiences and consciously respond by returning her awareness to the breath.

During meditation, the frequency of intrusions into your anchor of awareness varies, as does the amount of time that your attention is drawn away from the breath. The loss of awareness on your breath can be as short as seconds, or it could extend up to periods of one, three, five, fifteen, or twenty-five minutes or even more before you come to appreciate that your attention is no longer focused on the breath. Instead, your awareness has been snared into some thought, story, emotion, or physical sensation.

No matter how long your attention has been AWOL from the breath, the fact that you noticed this and your concentration returned to the breath is considered "a pretty good day" in the mindfulness way of being.

The reality is that your attention during any sitting practice is going to pull away from the breath ten times, 100 times, 1,000 times, 10,000 times, or whatever. The specific number is not important. Instead, it is the awareness you bring to *this* moment, knowing that your attention is focused no longer on the breath, and gently bringing your concentration back to the breath that makes for successful mindfulness moments. Seen in this light, the more often your attention is pulled from your anchor of the breath, the more opportunities you have to practise and learn the mindfulness way of being. So, in a somewhat weird way, be thankful to hijackers of your attention, for they are your teachers and gifting you with more opportunities to practise and learn mindfulness!

NOT SUPPRESSING THOUGHTS OR FEELINGS

It is also essential to know that when the instructions talk of letting go of your thoughts or feelings when you notice that your concentration has left the breath, it does not mean that you are trying to suppress them. Unfortunately, several in the group heard it this way and made the mistake of thinking that mindfulness requires them to shut off their thinking or their feeling. Others heard the instructions as meaning that if they are thinking, that is bad, and therefore, a good meditation is one in which there is little or no thinking. Still others had concluded that having feelings fouls the mindfulness practice, so therefore they should not experience any emotions. In addition, a couple more thought that having any discomfort in the body during mindfulness practice indicates personal failure. All of these perceptions represent misunderstandings about mindfulness.

As noted in Week One, mindfulness is not an attempt to become an empty-minded emotionless robot. Quite the opposite, mindfulness strives to be attentive and meet whatever thoughts, feelings, physical sensations, or other stimuli arise in any specific moment and have a healthy relationship to them.

At this point in the instructions, the emphasis is on the first part of the mindfulness definition—developing self-regulation of attention. Through practice, you need to learn that your attention can be focused and not scattered to any competing physical, cognitive, or emotional stimuli that come into your awareness. This ability to self-regulate your attention is a foundation for the second part of the mindfulness definition, which involves establishing your relationship to each moment.

DID I MENTION PRACTICE?

By even this early experience into mindfulness, you will undoubtedly recognize that it is a deceptively simple process. While one can learn basic instructions for mindfulness meditation in less than two minutes, practising it in a healthy and gratifying manner takes considerable discipline and practice. What makes it so tricky is that the mindfulness practice asks you to go against the usual expectations of meeting the physical, emotional, and cognitive demands and distractions of daily life. The feverish societal pace demanded of you to meet the often unrealistic expectations of what seemingly must be accomplished daily is a set-up to miss the individual moments that comprise your day.

Mindfulness is an antidote to the craziness of a frenetic daily way of life. To be clear, what mindfulness will not change is the number of hours, minutes, and seconds that comprise each day. However, mindfulness offers you a different and healthier way to *be with* those measurements, those moments of time. But to reap the benefits, mindfulness requires discipline and practice.

At this time in the learning process, recognizing the need for practice, it is recommended to focus again on the initial instructions for mindfulness meditation:

1. Sit quietly.

2. Use the breath as your anchor of attention.

3. Focus your awareness on the breath entering and leaving the body.

4. Take note when any thoughts, emotions, or physical sensations arise and vie for your attention.

5. Simply acknowledge the intrusions as thoughts, feelings, or physical sensations.

6. Gently return your focus to your breath as the anchor of awareness.

Repeat all the above as many times as needed during your practice session.

Learning any new skill can sometimes feel artificial, forced, or frustrating, so be gentle and caring with yourself. And difficult as it can be, try and leave the negative judgments about any assessment of your success or failure aside for the moment. Not only is a negative evaluation counterproductive to learning the structure of mindfulness, but it also is antithetical to meeting each moment in a non-judgmental manner. So, it makes sense when learning the form of mindfulness and developing a healthy relationship to the moment to simply notice such judgments ("Oh, there you are again!") but to refuse to get caught up or engage with them. They are merely judgments, stimuli similar to the cat's laser beam of light, to which you do not have to attend.

PRACTICE OF THE WEEK

Guidelines:

- This week, the assignment is to practise sitting meditation for **twenty minutes six days per week.** Ideally, you will practise each day of the week, but the reality of life is that this may not be realistic with unexpected intrusions. Therefore, instead of setting yourself up for failure by overcommitting every day, let's set a more realistic goal of practising six days each week. Remember, the goal is not to strive for perfection (not that I would even know what that would look like!) by setting unrealistic expectations on your practice schedule but rather to support a "good enough" schedule that will foster your commitment to establishing an effective and workable one. I also want to honour the "rebel" part that many of us carry who likes to have agency over our commitments, so *you* decide which day you will pass on!

- Set a timer (from your phone, tablet, computer, microwave, etc.) for twenty minutes so you do not have to be concerned with wondering when the time is up.

- If you found yourself feeling chilled during the body scan meditation, be sure to have a shawl or blanket available to keep yourself comfortable.

- Just as in the last session, you have the option of reading the instructions or listening to the audible presentation on the book's website, www.embracingagingmindfully.com.

- Be sure to record your daily sessions on your **Track Your Practice** log.

SITTING MEDITATION INSTRUCTIONS:

To practise sitting meditation, choose a time and place where you will not be interrupted for the entire twenty minutes. Sitting meditation is practised on either a chair or on the floor. Either way, it is recommended that you sit with your spine in a self-supported manner and not lean against the back of the chair, or if on the ground, against the wall. However, if you find you need to brace your back to be comfortable, leaning against the chair or wall's support is acceptable. While sitting on the floor can give you a reassuring feeling of being "grounded" and self-supporting in a meditation posture, it is not always the easiest thing to do with our aging bodies. However, should you decide to do that, sit on a thick cushion that raises your buttocks off the floor about three to six inches. This riser could be a pillow folded over once or twice, or you could purchase a meditation cushion called a Zafu specifically for sitting.

Whether you choose the floor or a chair, posture is important. It acts as outward support in cultivating an inner attitude of intention, patience, and self-acceptance. The main points to keep in mind about your posture are holding the back, neck, and head aligned in the vertical, relaxing the shoulders, and resting your hands comfortably in your lap or on your thighs.

Now that you are sitting, check in with your body. . . . Is it comfortable and aligned? . . . Take a second to make any adjustments needed. . . . Now bring your focus to your anchor of attention. . . . Decide where your anchor will be. . . . Recall that it needs to be a neutral point of focus that holds body sensations that you can track. . . .

Should you decide to use the breath as your anchor of awareness, choose the part of the body that allows you to feel the breath coming in and going out. . . . This could be through the nostrils, the mouth and back of the throat, the chest area, or on the belly. . . . Feeling the sensations of your breath becomes your anchor of awareness. . . .

Should you decide to use your hand as your anchor of awareness, place your hand on your thigh or belly or heart . . . anywhere that allows you to notice sensations through your hand and fingers. . . . The feel of your hand on your body is your anchor. . . . Be aware of any sensation that you notice from the contact of your thumb on where it is resting . . . on your first finger . . . on your middle finger . . . on your fourth finger . . . on your little finger . . . on the palm of your hand . . . not expecting or wanting any specific sensation or experience. . . . Just be curious . . . and notice. . . . Allow your mind to rest in the sensations. . . . Know that you can also slightly move your fingers or hand to enhance your awareness of any sensations. . . .

You can support the awareness of your hand sensations through making a mental note of the feeling. . . . You may note the feel as "rough" or "pressure" or "soft" . . . or the movement of the hand left or right or up or down. . . . Simply labelling the sensation to help sharpen your concentration . . . no need to analyze . . . or judge . . . or question what the sensation is. . . . It merely is a sensation that can anchor your awareness. . . .

If you are using your breath as your anchor of attention . . . allow your focus to be anchored on the breath and the part of the body you are using to hold your awareness. . . . Simply feel the in and out of breath through the nostrils . . . or mouth . . . or the gentle rising and falling of the belly . . . or the abdomen with each in-breath and out-breath . . . allowing the breath to be natural . . . noting its inflow and outflow, without trying to force or control it in any way . . . noting each in and out, each rising and falling, and settle into the breath's rhythm . . . allowing the mind to rest in the movement of the breath. . . .

While feeling the breath as your anchor, make a mental note to sharpen concentration . . . noting "in" while feeling the breath go in . . . and "out" while feeling it leaves . . . or saying only "rising" and "falling" with the sensations in the chest or the belly or the nostrils . . . very gently, very quietly in the mind . . . just supporting the awareness of the actual feelings . . . just noting in and out, or rising and falling. . . .

There is no need to make the breath special. . . . Each breath is simply unique in itself and is whatever it is. . . . It may be a deep or a long breath . . . or a short and shallow breath. . . . Whatever it is, it doesn't matter because it is merely a matter of noticing . . . noticing the breath as your anchor of awareness. . . .

You may notice as you are focusing on your anchor that your attention wanders . . . perhaps getting lost in a thought . . . maybe not consciously catching a breath or the sensation of your hand for quite some time. . . . Simply be aware that your attention has left your anchor and is drawn to a thought . . . no need to judge or analyze . . . no need to try to figure out how it slipped away. . . . It doesn't matter. . . . Perhaps give it a label, such as "planning" . . . or "thinking" . . . or "analyzing" . . . just noticing it as a thought and then just gently letting go of it and beginning again . . . letting go of the thought and returning attention to the breath's easy inflow and outflow . . . or your hand's sensations. . . . Once again, the breath or your hand becomes the anchor of your attention, of your awareness. . . .

Perhaps you will notice certain feelings or emotions arising as you are focusing on your anchor . . . your breath or your hand. . . . These could be positive feelings, such as excitement, expectation . . . or more challenging ones, such as worry . . . anger . . . fear. . . . Simply be aware that your awareness has left your anchor and is drawn to the feeling. . . . It again is not necessary to explore these feelings . . . not necessary to determine why they arose . . . not judging as to whether it is good or bad to have such a feeling . . . but to simply be aware of them . . . simply notice it. . . . Perhaps give it a label, such as "feeling" or "emotion," or more specific, such as "excitement" . . . or "sadness" . . . or "anger" . . . or "calmness." . . . No matter what it may be, let it go . . . and bring your attention gently back to your anchor of awareness . . . of the sensations in your fingers and hand . . . or your breath. . . .

You may find that while focusing on your anchor of attention, memories of the past or plans for the future arise. . . . Again, it is not necessary to judge these intrusions . . . nor to feed them through continuing to think about them. . . . Your task is simply to let them go . . . and bring your awareness back to your anchor . . . either your hand . . . or your breath. . . .

You may find that while focusing on your anchor of awareness, your attention will be drawn away by a physical sensation in your body . . . an itch . . . or a pressure . . . or an ache . . . or a discomfort . . . or a tingling . . . or a numbness. . . . When you notice your attention drawn to such sensations, it again is not necessary to judge as to whether it is good or bad . . . whether you should or should not have the feelings . . . .or why did the sensations arise. . . . It just is. . . . It is just a sensation. . . . Simply be aware that your attention has left your anchor and is drawn to the sensation. . . . Perhaps give it a label, such as "itch" . . . or "pressure" . . . or "discomfort" . . . or "numbness." . . . Simply notice the intrusion and then let it go. . . . Bring your attention gently back to your anchor of awareness . . . your breath . . . or your hand sensations. . . .

You may also find that your awareness is taken from your anchor through a sound . . . something you hear in your surroundings that pulls your attention away from your breath or your hand. . . . It could be a quiet and subtle sound . . . or a loud and intrusive one. . . . No matter how loud or quiet . . . no matter how pleasant or disturbing . . . no matter how long the sound is occurring . . . simply notice that you have lost contact with your anchor. . . . No need to judge yourself for losing touch with your anchor. . . . It just is a sound. . . . Perhaps give it a label, such as "sound" . . . or "music" . . . or "talking" . . . or "car" . . . or "construction." . . . Just notice. . . . Label the sound and then let it go. . . . Bring your attention gently back to your anchor . . . the sensation of your hand and fingers . . . or your breath . . . allowing your hand or your breath to be the anchor of your awareness and attention. . . .

No matter what arises that pulls your attention away from your anchor of awareness, it is merely a matter of noticing . . . noticing whether it be a thought . . . stories from the past . . . plans for the future . . . emotion . . . sensation in the body . . . sound. . . . Just notice your attention has been hijacked . . . and then bring your attention back to the anchor . . . no muss, no fuss. . . . Your anchor may be the sensations of your fingers and hand on your body. . . . If it is difficult to notice such hand sensations, then gently wiggle or slide an individual finger. . . . Any movement that allows you to feel sensations that you can use as your anchor of awareness . . . or your anchor may be sensing the breath . . . the awareness of the breath coming in . . . going out . . . the chest or belly rising . . . and falling . . . attention focused on whatever occurs. . . . There is no need to do anything else . . . just to be with the experience of sensing your anchor . . . using the sensations as the focus of your awareness . . . to notice when contact with your anchor is lost and simply returning again . . . and again . . . and again . . . beginning again . . . and again . . . and again . . . returning to your anchor of attention with patience and gentleness. . . .

And at the end of the session, when you hear the bells or your timer, slowly open your eyes and allow your attention to return to the room. . . . Allow yourself to see the room as if for the first time . . . quietly and gently allowing your gaze to move through the space that surrounds you. . . . Let your hearing receive whatever sounds are occurring in the room . . . and when you feel ready . . . gently and consciously arise from your seated meditation position . . . and continue practising to hold your awareness on just this present moment . . . setting the intention to maintain your sense of beginner's mind to whatever you will experience for the rest of your day.

MIDWEEK CUPPA...
REFLECTIONS ON
BEGINNER'S MIND
AND AGING

WEEK TWO

Welcome to your midweek review and exploration of the attitudinal foundation, beginner's mind. Each week will present this section as an opportunity to delve deeper into newly introduced attitudes and how they can assist your awareness, experience, and especially relationship to each moment. Recognizing that each week presents a wealth of mindfulness information and practices, "Midweek Cuppa . . ." offers a space for you to look at the attitude from another perspective, a lens offered through depth or Jungian psychology. Many obstacles to cultivating a mindfulness sensibility can arise from unconscious processes that act as a veil or filter obstructing your capacity to be present entirely in each moment. The examples portrayed will demonstrate reflections, insights, and exercises that you can apply to your own life in the service of investigating, exploring, and analyzing thoughts, feelings, and behaviours that act as troublesome issues that intrude into your life's ease, satisfaction, and well-being. Uncovering and developing a different relationship to both troubling characteristics and newly discovered aspects of yourself creates the unfolding potential of developing a new mindset to become a better friend to yourself. So, grab a "cuppa" of your favourite beverage and enjoy opening to further exploration of becoming you—all of who you can be!

The attitude of a beginner's mind is a powerful one that cultivates letting go of expectations as to what the next moment will bring. It opens the potential to more fully experience the richness of life that the unfolding of each moment has always offered, although not always accessible, because of our mistaken belief that we know what will occur next. To have lived so many years without a beginner's mind has been to miss the glorious adventure that living in each present moment provides. While beginner's mind is a gift at any time of one's life, as we age and embrace our time's finiteness, it can feel particularly gratifying to meet each unfolding moment with intention.

UNKNOWN FUTURE

However, a beginner's mind also brings to consciousness the often worrisome, if not feared, realization that you do not know what the future will bring. If you doubted this reality, the COVID-19 pandemic made it abundantly clear that moments change suddenly and without warning, critically affecting millions and millions of people in ways not expected. A single moment was all it took for "Patient 0" to become infected, unleashing consequences for the next moment and the next and the next to reverberate throughout the entire planet.

But you don't need the dramatic example of COVID-19 to understand the ever-changing moments of time and their subsequent effects. It takes only your conscious awareness to know that with every moment being "brand new," you are continually and relentlessly brought face-to-face with the unsettling reality that you do not know what the next moment and the next moment and the next moment will entail.

Some will complain that this can feel like an unexpected and shocking eye-opener—an abrupt awakening with flashing neon lights announcing, "The future is unknown!" What makes this realization so jolting is that not knowing what will happen is exceptionally troublesome for your ego. Remember that one of the ego's primary tasks during each waking moment is to maintain the fantasy that you are in control of your life and what will happen to you. To come face-to-face with such an opposing reality can figuratively and literally shake your world. The Buddhist teacher Pema Chödrön (2012) concludes that if you don't find some way to make friends with the unknown future, which she characterizes as a groundlessness and the ever-changing energy of life, you will always struggle to find stability in a shifting world.

However, let us be honest, for this seemingly jarring new reality that the future is unknown is, in fact, not a new insight. Deep down inside, you have always known that you cannot predict what is to come. Have you ever bought a lottery ticket? Not just any ticket, but the winning ticket? Your lost investment, most likely often repeated to reinforce the lesson, brings home the glaring reality that you cannot divine the future. But that has not been your only lesson—there have no doubt been countless other instances during your life where you have encountered but ignored, denied, avoided, or numbed yourself against this disturbing fact.

To acknowledge an unknown future is to realize that you are summoned by each moment to make life-defining choices with the outcome not known. While some of these choices are small and mundane (such as what to eat for dinner), others carry significant lifelong consequences (such as choosing a life partner). The fact that such daily choices, those that are big and those that are small, directly impacts how your future will unfold (which entails the next moment and next hour and next day and next year and next . . .) means that this present moment truly is the beginning of the rest of your life.

To acknowledge the existential reality that you do not know what the future brings means to accept there is no guarantee you will be alive for the next fifteen years, fifteen months, fifteen days, or even fifteen minutes. Not knowing the future means that you do not know if you will have a financially viable retirement. Not knowing the future means that you do not comprehend what your health will be like next year. Not knowing the future means that you do not know if you will lose someone close to you in the coming months.

It is always prudent to plan for the future and engage in activities that would support such plans as saving for retirement, living a healthy life-style, and so forth. However, you also know that many factors outside of your control, such as a global financial downturn, accidents, a pandemic, someone else's plans and so on can directly impact and potentially derail your expected life course.

SOOTHING CONTRACTS WITH THE UNIVERSE

To defend against these unsettling realities, as children/adolescences/young adults, we have all constructed what the Jungian analyst Dr. James Hollis (2005) calls "contracts" to provide a soothing belief system that pro-vides an illusory sense of control over the unpredictability of life. These contracts or personal mythologies are a form of magical thinking with you believing you can barter with the world or the universe or God to protect your vulnerable self. Thus, as a young person, you, like every one of us, began constructing a set of beliefs that you hoped would act as buffers or guardrails to make life more manageable and predictable and, therefore, psychologically safer. While these beliefs can change and are modified through the experiences of intervening years, as well as through influences from society, religion, significant others, and meaningful life events, they tend to be resilient and form our personal manifestos of "That's how my world works" and "That's how I will feel safe." Most importantly, your con-tracts shepherd you through life, providing the often unspoken but deeply believed playbook for how you should lead your life to avoid the unpleas-ant reality of an unknown future.

If you enjoy people watching as I do, you may be fascinated to observe the mass of humanity filtering through a busy and congested public space, such as an airport terminal or a metropolitan rapid transit station, and realize that no matter what their individual personal history, each one of them has created their personal contract, code, or rule book of how they need to interact with their world to be safe, satisfied, happy, and content. I like to imagine that each person has a cartoonlike bubble over their head in which are written their personal contracts.

While individual contracts are as numerous and variable as life stories, they are typically based on declarations of "If I . . . then . . . will happen." For example, Carlos believes that if he pleases those around him, then he will feel safe and happy. Bethany thinks that if her social circle includes prominent members of society, then she will feel worthy. Karl believes that having his children succeed at sports will testify to him being a good parent. Cindy thinks that working hard will guarantee her a secure and satisfying lifelong career no matter what job. Finally, Devon believes that eating a healthy diet will inoculate him from dementia in later years.

While the actual content of such contracts often provides kernels of truth and therefore can be of benefit to you, they fall apart when they provide you with an illusory sense of safety and security and become a dogmatic expectation of what life demands.

AGING AND THE BREAKDOWN OF CONTRACTS

Contracts are often not clearly enumerated or publicly declared until something happens that shakes, if not shatters, the constructed belief system. Therefore, you can always identify a contract under siege when you hear the disbelief in a person's voice as they lament, "It is not supposed to be this way"; "I did everything right"; "It's not fair"; "What did I do to deserve this?"; "Why is this happening to me?"

Who of us has not experienced feelings of disorientation or even betrayal when our assumed contract with the world or universe or God falls apart? While these experiences can happen at any time in life, as you age, the likelihood of the hollowness of such contracts becoming conscious increases. Aging brings to the glaring light of day contracts that cannot withstand the inevitable increased possibility of declining physical and cognitive functioning, the death of someone close, the financial adjustments accompanying retirement, the changes in marital or vocational status, or even the sad realization that "This is not the life that I planned." But aging, with a history of unfulfilled contracts, offers the opportunity to bring the wisdom and courage needed to now seriously question the integrity of your manifestos of how your world works.

WHAT EXACTLY IS MY CONTRACT?

While some contracts are so clear that they can be quickly and precisely enumerated, others feel hazier and elusive to grasp. If you are curious to clarify your contract, one method is through expressive arts by creating a visual picture that illustrates your contract's terms. For example, collage is a simple creative pursuit open to anyone without concern for artistic capabilities. While holding a question or issue in mind (such as concerning personal contracts, asking "What is my greatest fear?" and "How will I stay safe?"), collage involves flipping through magazines, finding pictures or words that address the issue at question, ripping or cutting them out, and then pasting them on a larger empty sheet of paper that presents a visual image, giving life to the issue.

Trusting one's intuition about which pictures or words speak to the story underlying the contract and trusting where they need to be placed on the blank paper can be very enlightening in providing access to your underlying constructed and long-held belief system. Take your time with this exercise. Stand back and open with curiosity to the entirety of the created picture. Explore what emotions arise by seeing this visual answer to your questions of greatest fears and safety strategies. Which images in your creation especially grab your attention? What associations do you have with specific images? How would you summarize the story held within your pictorial essay?

Another effective way of clarifying a contract is repeatedly asking the question "And then what . . . ?" to statements expressed through a stream-of-consciousness pattern addressing any issue that challenges your belief system. For example, Gary came to my psychotherapy consulting room with anxiety over his upcoming retirement. A physician looking forward to his retirement for many years, Gary developed a long bucket list of activities that he was interested in but had never taken the time to pursue. However, instead of feeling excitement as retirement inched closer, he felt a deep sense of anxiety and even dread about the future.

To help Gary explore what lay below this sense of anxiety and dread, I repeatedly asked "And then what?" to each of his stream-of-consciousness statements about his expected retirement experience. It is helpful not to question or analyze or debate your answers but rather to trust the initial response that arises into consciousness. For example, Gary first reported excitement about the possibility of having so much unstructured time with his retirement; then to knowing that it will probably feel a bit "weird" to not see patients as he has for the last forty-two years; to wondering how many of his long-term patients will fare in the future; to the recognition that he will miss many of his patients with whom he has developed close relationships over the years; to the enjoyment and satisfaction that he had with helping patients; to the respect he enjoyed in the community with his stature as a physician; to long-forgotten memories of feeling lost during his late adolescence; to remembering the pressure that he felt from his parents to do something meaningful and of service to others with his life; to his adolescent fears that he would never be able to meet his parents' expectations; to his ensuing period of acting out with drugs and alcohol; to the relief he felt when deciding on medicine as a career; to remembering the pride and joy that his extended family felt with his career choice; to wondering how will he fare not being a practising physician; to tearfully questioning, "So who am I now?"

The contract that Gary drew up as a young man that he would be accepted, loved, and respected by pursuing a professional career of service does not question or detract from his entering the medical profession, the good work he has done, or his satisfaction helping people. However, the contract implicitly offers a Faustian bargain that Gary would not experience the uncomfortableness of questioning his identity as long as he pursued such a career. Nevertheless, the contract falls apart with Gary's mistaken belief that his sense of self depends on his occupation—what he does, instead of who he is.

With the outer world circumstances changing (even though it is through his voluntary retirement), Gary is no longer protected from the anxiety associated with his questioning sense of self. At sixty-nine years of age, Gary again is forced to revisit his youth's central, troubling question that had never been resolved but simply held at bay. How to experience the unknown future without allegiance to his contract opens the floodgates to Gary's anxiety, never fully addressed. Like a knock on the door from a long-lost and unwanted relative, Gary's unresolved core identity issue has returned uninvited.

WHAT NOW?

With the conscious exploration of contracts developed and faithfully lived throughout the years, it is possible to decide the healthiest next step. In Gary's situation, he could simply continue his contract by finding some other service-oriented work (perhaps on a volunteer basis) that will again provide a shield against his identity anxiety. While this course of action will likely be successful not only by holding at least some of his anxiety at bay but also by being of benefit to the larger community, it only forestalls the inevitable confrontation that he will likely have to make in the future. Unfortunately, when Gary is no longer physically or cognitively or motivationally able to continue volunteering, his contract is again challenged with his same identity anxiety returning.

Mindfulness, with its emphasis on beginner's mind, presents an alternative course of action. Instead of continuing to defend against the unpredictability and lack of control over the future offered through your existing or even newly created contracts, know that you do have an option. Instead of creating a new (or, in Gary's case, extending his original) contract in an attempt to control the future (avoid anxiety), a healthier response would be accepting the inevitable unknown future that is your reality.

Mindfulness offers the potential to develop an alternative relationship to this existential conundrum on two fronts. First, the mindfulness practice's structural framework presents a conscious intention not to get lost in the future. Instead, the practice is to stay in the present moment and not allow yourself to squander it through quixotic and impossible quests to forecast and then live in the future. The future will arrive, but not at this moment. *Be Here Now* is the title of Ram Dass's 1971 book that aptly captures mindfulness's petition.

The second benefit offered through mindfulness is that you can also use the concept of a beginner's mind to change how you are with the reality that you don't know what the future will bring. You can courageously learn to *be with* the actuality that you have always known. Through the mindfulness experience, you can learn to hold whatever thoughts and feelings and physical sensations arise with acknowledgement and full recognition that you do not know what the next moment or the next moment or the next moment will bring. This change in relationship with the unknown provides the ground to live less in fear and enjoy more freedom to experience the present moment fully.

There is no getting around the fact that not knowing what the future holds can produce anxiety, but mindfulness teaches that you can meet and be with whatever arises in a healthy manner. But also remember that while the unfolding future moment may bring anxiety, it may, in fact, alternatively bring excitement, boredom, contentment, satisfaction, or many other experiences. You just don't know. Learning to hold the attitudinal foundation of beginner's mind means that you do not have to live in fear or deny or avoid or numb yourself to whatever thoughts, feelings, or physical sensations may arise in the unfolding future. You do not have to be held hostage to any potential emotional reactions. On the contrary, acknowledging a beginner's mind opens the door for a new foundation, for the confidence to develop a new relationship that allows you not just to endure but also enjoy living alongside an unknown future.

MINDFULNESS MEETS YOUR CONTRACT

Mindfulness practice presents a structured process to meet whatever arises in an open, receptive, and non-judgmental manner, including meeting the unknown future's anxiety. Our ability to change our relationship with unpredictability and lack of control is the reality of the outlook offered through the mindfulness instructions of holding our awareness on whatever arises in terms of thoughts, feelings, or physical sensations. To not ignore, avoid, or deny our human limitations or to alternatively fall into the grips of anxiety, enthusiastic abandonment, or any other emotional reaction associated with the unknown future presents a powerful alternative way of being. To adopt the attitude of beginner's mind is to meet each moment as the yet unknown one that it is. Thus, a beginner's mind expands your tolerance for whatever will arise, which in turn relinquishes your childlike innocence of ignoring the indisputable fact that you do not have complete knowledge or control over your future.

The complementary strategy that aging can offer to your mindfulness practice is through a conscious confrontation with your contracts—long-cherished undertakings that you developed with the understandable but erroneous intent of keeping yourself safe and secure. Exploring and challenging these belief systems takes away the artificial crutch upon which you have leaned in your attempt to predict and manage your future. However, to do so is not a nihilistic capitulation, nor does it leave you blind to the future. While it is vital that you continue making plans and looking forward with anticipation to your future, tearing up your personal contract only eliminates the fantasy that you will control the outcome. Letting go of private contracts is a declarative affirmation that you will embrace a beginner's mind.

Augmenting the mindfulness way of being through the Jungian psychological exercise of consciously exploring your constructed contracts can be of considerable benefit and assistance to your aging process. To consciously investigate your early belief system allows for a more informed attitude and, therefore, choice as to how you will meet the inevitable challenges that the unknown future presents to your aging life. Specifically, questioning the illusory beliefs by which you have lived your life allows for a more conscious response rather than an unconscious reaction to the unknown and unfolding future.

While during earlier years your contracts enabled you to avoid or delay (with varying degrees of success) anxiety associated with the unknown future, aging presents increasing challenges to this defence strategy. With advancing years, more experiences will likely challenge your safety and security contracts with the universe. Therefore, it will become increasingly more difficult to ignore or withstand the continuing assaults that reality presents. Knowing this to be the case, the question becomes, do you want to live in dread knowing that it is only a matter of time before another assault on your contract arrives unbidden, or do you want to confidently and courageously meet whatever the unknown future presents? You do have a choice. A choice about your relationship with not only the future but, more importantly, this present moment. Should your decision be an affirmation of living mindfully in the present moment, a follow-up question will inevitably arise: With advancing age, if not now, when?

"OUT, DAMNED NUISANCE—OUT, I SAY!" WORKING WITH PERSISTENT AND INTRUSIVE THOUGHTS, EMOTIONS AND PHYSICAL SENSATIONS

WEEK THREE

REVIEW SITTING MEDITATION PRACTICE

The atmosphere in the room before starting Week Three was difficult to read. I decided to ease into the session by acknowledging the obvious: "You have meditated, which by definition, makes you a meditator! More important than your new status—satisfying as that may be—is that you have begun to cultivate a new relationship to each moment during formal sitting meditation as you use your breath as a focus of awareness." (As mentioned in the last session, I will refer to only the breath as your anchor of awareness for ease of reading, knowing that you may be using your hand sensations.)

I also acknowledged another obvious, telling the group that while I am not clairvoyant (as my inability to pick winning lottery numbers will attest), I am willing to bet that most found instructions of this exercise deceptively simple. It is much easier to say, "Focus your attention on your breath," than it is to do, in part because as you begin to meditate numerous interruptions and intrusions force their way in! Despite your best efforts, a seemingly endless stream of unruly thoughts, emotions, or physical sensations draws your attention away from the breath. Nor does this happen just once or twice or three times during a sitting period. The multitude of interloping experiences feels like a never-ending assault, hijacking your focus from your breath to ANYTHING that wanders through your mind, body, and senses until you find yourself bouncing around from one thought, feeling, or physical sensation to another. Like the cat frenetically chasing the laser beam, your intended focus on your breath slips away on the fleeting moments.

Josie nodded enthusiastically and could hardly contain herself in her seat as she blurted: "I can't believe it! The sheer number and crazy content of intrusions that interrupted my focus of awareness on my breath was absolutely mindboggling! In just one session—one session!—this mind of mine just would not shut up! Listen to just a smidgen of what grabbed my attention:

- I wonder what is for dinner tonight.
- I hope that my supervisor liked my latest report.
- What will happen if a meteorite hits the earth?
- My left big toe feels itchy—really itchy!
- I shouldn't have been so snarky to my neighbour yesterday.
- How will I ever afford retirement?
- Why is the air conditioning system so loud?
- I'm bored. This meditation stuff is weird!
- Why has no one made a movie about three penguins living in a pink Cadillac?"

Bizarre though it may seem, Josie's experience is not unusual. Most new meditators experience such things as they begin the practice—thoughts, feelings, and physical sensations bounce around like a ping pong ball. Even holding your awareness on two or three breaths in a row can be a huge challenge. Who would have thought that the simple exercise of being still and focusing your attention on your breath would prove to be such a trial?

You may also find that you can become caught up in the stories attached to these thoughts, emotions, or physical sensations. This immersion in the mind's stories can be relatively short, no more than a few seconds, but it can also extend to many minutes. For example, Darnell related how a slight initial worry that his dog hadn't seemed to be his usual happy self that morning quickly led to wondering what an afterlife may be like; to feeling anxious about elephant poaching in Africa; and then becoming entranced by a lengthy (but pleasant) memory of watching the *Bambi* movie with his mother when he was six years old. All played out before he realized that his attention had wandered from the anchor of his breath!

Our minds are capable of generating stories that go on and on and on. New meditators often describe it being as if their mind has a mind of its own. It can feel like they are possessed by something that doesn't seem like them, which generates story after story after story. However discouraging this can be, it's also instructive. You learn the hard way that as long as the mind continues to be fed stories, it can feel like you are simply "along for the ride," as I related occurring during my first ride on my young horse Fionn.

And this, I believe, is one of the most important lessons to take away from this introduction to mindfulness: the recognition that the simple task of being fully aware of the breath in just this one moment is very challenging! It's not easy to be present, fully present, in each of the 54,000 seconds that comprise a waking day. However, I want to assure you that I do not mean to discourage you from mindfulness. Indeed, if that were the case, this would be the end of a very concise book! Mindfully living day to day is a practice and an achievable discipline—precisely what this book is all about.

CHATTY MIND

Given the mind's unlimited capacity to chatter away and generate story after story, it can be highly frustrating to learn how to focus your attention on just one thing like the breath. Should this happen as you meditate, don't take it as a negative reflection on your capabilities as a meditator. Instead, it is merely a recognition that the human mind's design continually generates thoughts, ideas, and plans with associated feelings and even physical sensations to accompany them. That's what your mind did yesterday; that's what it is doing now; that's what it is going to do tomorrow. This imaginative capacity of the mind has been enormously beneficial in developing creative advances in human civilization. Nevertheless, it can also be exasperating when all you want to do is be silent and focus on your breath, but your chatty mind just won't shut up.

However, remember that mindfulness's goal is to pay attention, on purpose, in each moment. Being present does *not* mean that you are attempting to empty your mind and body of all thoughts, feelings, and sensations. Instead, the objective is to be fully aware of whatever stimulus enters your consciousness but not get seduced into following it just because it has arrived.

Just as Josie in her initial meditation session reported myriad thoughts, emotions, and sensations during her meditation session, your experience will likely be similar. *Oh, here's a thought that sounds interesting. . . . But here is an itchy sensation that calls for my attention. . . . What is this emotion about?* etc. These intrusions go on and on as you get pulled away from being present in this moment by whatever images, thoughts, feelings, and perceptions scroll across your awareness.

When interlopers encroach, just notice your attention pulled from your breath as your anchor of awareness. Then gently return to your breath as the anchor, keeping your mind and body from being hijacked by the moment's latest flavour. Maintaining your awareness of your breath helps to stabilize your attention.

Of course, there is a time when it is appropriate to dance with thoughts, feelings, or physical sensations that arrive, but only when you willingly decide to *respond* to them rather than reflectively *react.*

It's important to know that the difficulty you experience when trying to focus your awareness doesn't arise because you are meditating. In other words, it's not the meditation that creates these mind stories, but instead that the meditation allowed you to clearly see what occurs on an ongoing basis as you move through your day. When you take a moment to think about this, it's pretty fascinating: your mind is churning all day long, generating "stuff" of which you are not always conscious. Who knew?

When you closely examine your wandering mind, you may find that the many intrusions feel disconcerting and often upsetting. Here's a brief sample of some of the reactions from students in my mindfulness class:

- Sanjay lamented, "It shouldn't be this way."
- Devon declared, "I don't like it."
- Helen quietly concluded, "It shouldn't be so hard.
- "I don't want it to be like this," scoffed Sam.
- Cindy sullenly confessed, "There must be something wrong with me."
- "Mindfulness is impossible and stupid," proclaimed George.
- Karl summed up many of the group's gloomy feelings with, "It is just not fair!"

Reactions such as these to the barrage of uninvited thoughts, emotions, and physical sensations are understandable but become barriers to what you are trying to accomplish. The common thread underlying reactions like these is rejection. Quite simply, you didn't ask for these intrusions, and therefore, they shouldn't be happening. It is a grown-up version of a two-year-old declaring that they are NOT tired when their eyelids are drooping, their head is nodding off, and everything you say soothingly is met with tears!

As you will recall, the definition of mindfulness is to pay attention, on purpose, in the present moment, non-judgmentally. You now know that this is not a piece of cake, so to do this, you'll need to find an attitude of acceptance.

ACCEPTING WHAT IS

One of the critical attitudes necessary to cultivate a mindfulness practice is acceptance—the act of acknowledging things the way they are without altering them. If you are cold, then you are cold. If you are lonely, then you are lonely. If you are bored, you are bored. There is no need, and it's of little use to ignore, deny, or avoid whatever is occurring at this moment. Acceptance is the "nod" or "tip of the hat" to the presently happening reality. It doesn't mean that you have to like what is occurring or feel helpless in its grip; it's just a conscious acceptance of this particular moment and whatever is happening in it.

This chapter's title is a riff on Shakespeare's Lady Macbeth and her inability to accept her reality—the deep guilt she suffered. Her demand that things should be different from the way they are ("Out, damned spot! Out, I say!") didn't work for her. Your similar order to the intrusive thoughts, feelings, or physical sensations ("Out, damned nuisance! Out, I say!") is just as impossible for you. Non-acceptance becomes an act of resistance to this world that you inhabit. To argue and fight against the reality of the moment ("I don't want this feeling. It shouldn't be happening! Why me?") only sets you up for failure. Denying the reality of the moment is a bit like fighting against gravity.

You probably know what I mean. Over the years, many times I've tried to convince myself that the reality of the moment *shouldn't* be happening. Well, I'm batting a perfect thousand in my failure to do this. Have you had any more success? I don't mean those momentary reprieves like having a drink or engaging in another distraction; I mean a sustained and long-term refutation of what is occurring. And what has been the cost—physically, emotionally, socially, economically—of engaging in this quixotic losing endeavour?

ACCEPTANCE DOES NOT MEAN INACTION

Non-acceptance drains your energy and focuses on a losing struggle to debate either what is occurring or whether it should occur. Non-acceptance demands an incredible amount of striving to try to make things different than they are. By not accepting the moment and whatever is arising, you don't clearly understand what you are dealing with, which means you have little hope of appropriately meeting the situation.

Acceptance, it must be noted, does not equate with passivity. It merely means that you see, feel, experience, and acknowledge the moment's reality as your initial response. Instructors in the mindfulness program at the University of Massachusetts Medical School found that before individuals could even begin to deal with their pain, they needed to accept it (Kabat-Zinn 1990). They describe acceptance as "putting out the welcome mat" to the pain; only then does it become possible to change one's relationship to the pain. As long as we resist even accepting that there is pain—"I don't want it! I never asked for it, and therefore it's not fair!"—we wage a continual fight with the experience occurring at that moment. And any dispute with reality is guaranteed to be a losing one.

Instead, it is possible to accept things as they are. Acknowledgement doesn't necessarily mean that you have to like everything that is occurring—merely accept it. Only then will you be able to fully participate in life to make changes that ultimately better your own life and the lives of those around us as well as the world. As the writer James Baldwin aptly noted: "Not everything that is faced can be changed, but nothing can be changed until it is faced."

Acceptance, therefore, is a very active process; there is nothing passive about it. I imagine acceptance as a pregnant pause, a moment in time, to recognize what is occurring before responding in any way objectively.

Mindfulness is an influential teacher of acceptance. In mindfulness meditation practice, you cultivate acceptance by experiencing each moment as it arrives, being whole with it, just as it is. You try not to impose your judgments, demands, critiques, commentary, or any other reactions to what you are thinking, feeling, or experiencing. Instead, the goal is simply to accept it. And why do we accept it? Because it just IS. It is occurring right now at this moment.

Don't be concerned if you struggle with acceptance. Just sit back, commit to focusing your attention on your breath, and watch and experience all that arises. Mindfulness practice generously provides ongoing ever-changing offerings to help you learn to be fully present, open, and accepting.

Ultimately, acceptance within the mindfulness paradigm bestows a gift, a willingness to see and experience things as they are. In addition, this attitude of acceptance lays a strong foundation for potentially changing your relationship to whatever is happening in you.

INTRUSIVE THOUGHTS, FEELINGS, AND PHYSICAL SENSATIONS

Henry had sat quietly in the group circle until now, when he leaned forward and said in an exasperated voice, "Yeah, I get it. Accept whatever shows up in your mind and body. But seriously, how do you learn acceptance when persistent and intrusive thoughts, feelings, and physical sensations test your patience and tolerance? They just never shut up!" At least half of the group nodded their agreement, revealing this to be a widespread concern.

As the initial instructions for sitting meditation suggest, when intrusions arise during meditation, do not judge them, fight them, or entertain them. Simply notice them, label them, and return to the breath as the anchor of your awareness. Intentionally practise accepting but not holding onto each thought, feeling, or body sensation that attempts to divert your attention, whether it feels crazy or insightful, important or trivial, pleasant or unpleasant. Observe them as they are, simply stimuli arising in this moment, and allow them to pass on.

REALLY PESKY INTRUSIONS

However, as you have found during your initial periods of sitting meditation, there are times when thoughts, feelings, or body sensations simply refuse to fade away. Despite your best efforts to note each one, label it, and bring your awareness back to the breath, these bothersome intrusions persist. The thoughts, feelings, and sensations continue to exert influence over your awareness, repeatedly and often forcefully pulling you away from the breath as your focus of attention. Persistent intrusions such as these seriously challenge your capacity to accept whatever is arising. So how do you deal with these irritating intruders?

Counterintuitive though it may seem, the strategy when dealing with highly persistent intrusions is to turn your attention toward them. That is, consciously move your attention from the breath as your anchor of awareness to the intrusive thought, feeling, or physical sensation, allowing it to become the new and temporary focus of your attention. Quite simply, consciously decide to allow the thought, feeling, or physical sensation to become the anchor of your awareness at that moment. It is like declaring, "Okay, you [thought, feeling or physical sensation] wanted my attention. You wouldn't allow me to focus my awareness on my breath. I accept that, so I'm all yours! Let's dance!"

Of course, the challenge is that as you focus on the intruding thought, feeling, or body sensation as your new anchor of awareness, it is far too easy to get pulled into the story surrounding it. The mind is highly creative and productive in terms of generating stories—any stories!—to fill your awareness of the thought, feeling, or physical sensation. However, the trick is that you can avoid getting pulled into the stories by using your awareness to locate where the intrusive thought or feeling manifests itself within the body. Ask yourself, "Where do I feel this thought?" or "Where do I feel this emotion?" While that may seem a bit strange, when you consciously put your awareness into your body, it is usually relatively easy to find the place where the thought or feeling resides. The reality is that thoughts or emotions strong enough to continually pull you away from the breath as the anchor of your attention will also live as a sensation somewhere in the body.

INTRUSIVE EMOTIONS

Let me give you some examples of how the process works when persistent and intrusive feelings pull your attention from your anchor of the breath.

Cassie knew from experience that she often felt her anxiety as tension within her stomach, jaw, neck, or shoulders. During one meditation, as worry and anxiety kept arising and pulling her attention away from the breath, she shifted her attention and did a quick body scan, searching for the place in her body where she presently experienced anxiety. She recognized that her anxiety's physical location changed over time and undertook to be open to the signs and signals her body offered in the present moment. Because her anxiety sometimes was situated in her stomach or neck or shoulders, she knew the importance of paying attention *in the present moment* to locate the body's current expression of a feeling. After a quick scan of her body, Cassie found that her jaw was tense and made that part of her jaw the new anchor of awareness.

Carlos found persistent feelings of sadness for his deceased mother as he meditated, pulling his attention from the breath as his anchor. Searching for his emotion's physical location, Carlos found a tight knot in the pit of his stomach. Rachel felt excitement in anticipation of her upcoming camping trip as tingling within her hands. An emotion's bodily location varies, not only within each person but also within each meditation session. You can never assume, in other words, that any personal feeling will always reside in a specific body location. In keeping with the essence of mindfulness, you can learn to scan your body openly and curiously whenever a feeling is strong enough to pull your anchor of attention.

CURIOUS EXPLORATION

Once you have shifted your awareness from your breath to your body, the aim is not only to be aware of the location but also to explore precisely how the body holds that particular feeling. For example, once Cassie had located her anxiety in her jaw, she learned to focus her awareness in a curious way to investigate precisely wherein the jaw it resided. Which side of the jaw—left or right or both sides? Was the sensation in the lower part of the jaw? In the upper part of the jaw? Did the sensation extend up toward the ears? Was it a tightness sensation? Was it a feeling of pressure? Did it have a sense of temperature, such as being hot or cold? Was there a numbness, a tingling, an aching sensation? Was it throbbing?

When assessing a body sensation's nuances in the present moment, the goal is not to relax the jaw or resolve the physical sense or emotion. Instead, simply *accept* that there is a body sensation connected with the feeling and allow a finely tuned exploration of it to become your new focus, a new anchor of your awareness. Your primary goal is to be present, sink into this moment, and apply your focus on the body sensation as your anchor of attention.

Most people find as they do this that the body sensation often changes. It can shift from where initially held to another area of the same body part or even a different part of the body. Sometimes the sensation's strength will change, the quality will change, or the sensation may simply dissipate and no longer hijack your anchor of attention. The objective is to merely hold your awareness on the physical sensation of the emotion, no matter its quality or location, as long as it has enough energy charge to maintain your awareness. When it no longer has the strength or power to hold your awareness, simply return to your breath as your primary anchor of attention.

The key to this process's success is to focus your awareness on the body sensation without judging it. If you experience feelings of resentment or anger toward the body part, and by extension, toward the original sense of anxiety, simply notice these feelings and bring your awareness back to the bare physical sensation.

INTRUSIVE THOUGHTS

Just as there are intrusive emotions when meditating, intrusive thoughts can also arise and pull your attention away from the breath. Handling intrusive thoughts is a similar process: Quietly shift your focus and utilize the thought's location in the body as the new anchor of attention.

George had been keen to begin a meditation practice as he hoped it would balance his busy work life. In his initial session, however, he noticed that thoughts of an upcoming business event he was in charge of planning kept intruding, thwarting his attempts to focus on his breath as his anchor of attention. At first, he tried to note the intruding thought, label it as "planning," and return to his breath as his anchor of attention. But his mind would have none of it, and he found himself drawn more and more into thoughts of the event's content, who would attend, and what it would mean to his career.

In the spirit of acceptance, George then made a conscious decision to move his anchor of attention from the breath to the thought of planning. He soon found, however, that as he focused on planning, his mind jumped from one idea to the next excitedly. It was as if, once the door was open to the thought of planning, his mind was only too eager to fill it with a thousand and one ideas and possibilities.

George's experience is common when meditating. In meditation, we often encounter thoughts with enough power to waylay the practice. An alternative and effective strategy is to shift focus again and search for the feeling tone associated with the thoughts when they arise. It can take time and experience to find the emotional content tangled up in intrusive thoughts, but it's worth the effort. A thought strong enough to repeatedly pull your awareness away from your breath generally has a considerable emotional charge attached to it. And powerfully charged thoughts are usually associated with an emotion located within the body.

In George's case, planning was an emotionally charged thought. It initially was a challenge for him to explore the emotion associated with it and discover where in the body he felt it. For example, his thought of planning a significant event could be accompanied by anxiety and even a sense of dread sensed as a tightness in the stomach. Alternatively, it could be associated with a sense of excitement and a physical sensation as the heart beats faster.

George identified his planning thought as primarily attached to a positive feeling of anticipation—he felt confident in his abilities and was ready to demonstrate his competency to his manager. While scanning the body for the location of his anticipation, George noticed a sensation of lightness within his chest. His anchor of attention then targeted this area, and he became an attentive and curious explorer. Where precisely in his chest did he feel this lightness? On the left side? On the right side? In the middle? Across his entire chest area? How high up his chest did this sensation extend? How low did it drop? Was it associated with quick and shallow breaths? Or with deeper and slower breaths? Was there a tingling? A fluttering sensation? Did it feel cool? Or warm?

George's meditation shifted to working with emotions felt in the body because this was what he was now dealing with. The thought (planning) attached to a feeling (anticipation), felt within the body (chest area), now became the focus and anchor of his awareness. The objective is to explore this body sensation in a very minute and exacting fashion in this present moment. George may well have had that same thought and associated feeling tone many times before, but he had never experienced it at *this* moment. Each moment is truly a brand-new moment in time that has never before existed. "Be truly curious" is the appropriate mantra to bring to each moment.

To review, put all your awareness into understanding what the body sensation is in that present moment. Explore its location, size, shape, sensation, temperature, and so on in the context of the total physical experience. If the body sensation attached to the feeling that originates with a thought shifts to a new location, then move the anchor of awareness to the new area. When the body sensation changes, either because its intensity has let up or dissipates, bring your awareness back to the breath. The breath once again becomes your anchor of attention.

INTRUSIVE PHYSICAL SENSATIONS

At times, the intruder can be a body sensation that continually pulls your attention away from the breath—a numbness in your buttocks, the pressure under your thigh, tightness in the shoulders, or an itchy left ear. When this happens, use that body sensation as the new object of awareness. Remember, however, that your initial primary response is to simply notice such sensations, label them, and return to the breath. However, if your awareness becomes hijacked by the physical sensation and you cannot quickly return to the breath, move your focus of attention to the body sensation itself. Then, follow the same pattern as noted above. Become a very mindful, curious explorer of what the sensation feels like. Explore its location, size, shape, sensation, temperature, the totality of its physical expression.

A seemingly innocuous but intensive itchy nose took over Bethany's attention. Following the mindfulness instructions, she initially noticed the itch, labelled it, and returned to her breath as her anchor of attention.

However, this seemingly slight body sensation was more robust than her ability to focus on her breath, so she accepted this and consciously moved her awareness to the itch itself, utilizing the itch as her new anchor of attention. She curiously examined its location, size, shape, sensation, and temperature in the entire physical experience context. The itch dissipated in short order, which allowed Bethany to return to her breath as her anchor of awareness.

IF THE PHYSICAL SENSATION IS TOO MUCH . . .

Of course, even with such mindful exploration, there may be times that the body sensation does not lessen or dissipate, in which case it's acceptable to decide to alleviate the body discomfort or distraction directly. However, the goal in this situation is to not give up too quickly on a curious exploration of the body sensation so that you can practise a different way of being with such intrusions.

Nevertheless, should the body sensation not dissipate and you decide to alleviate it directly, be aware that you have made this decision consciously. You are not just reflexively reacting to a sensation—instead, you are responding to it thoughtfully. Responding, not reacting, is an important distinction when being mindful.

Once you've decided to respond to the body sensation, before you start any actions, take a moment to be mindfully aware of how you will carry out the act. For example, if your buttock feels numb, before shifting your position on the cushion or chair, be aware of how you will do this. Are you going to put your hands down on the floor/chair and lift your buttocks off? Or are you just going to slide the buttocks to a different position on the cushion/chair? If your shoulders feel tight, are you going to raise both of them at the same time to stretch? Are you going to roll the shoulders forward or backward? To scratch the itch on your nose, are you going to reach your left or right hand? What finger on the hand are you going to use?

Try to be very specific. How are you going to *mindfully* make a move to deal with this intrusive body sensation? The underlying mindful message is that you are responding and not just reacting to the situation. After alleviating the invasive body sensation, gently bring your focus back to the breath as your anchor of awareness.

REWARDS AND BENEFITS

The critical mindful exploration of an intrusive and persistent feeling, thought, or physical sensation is valuable in many ways. First, it allows for the application of acceptance to whatever arises, which in this case is an emotion or thought or physical sensation that is powerful, intrusive, or persistent enough to draw your focus away from your breath. You don't have to want it, like it, or fight it—just use it to continue your mindfulness practice. It's just a thought, just a feeling, or just a physical sensation. Nothing special!

Secondly, it allows you to explore what happens to emotions, thoughts, and body sensations when you simply hold them in your awareness, withhold judgment, critique, and commentary, and do not feed them stories. This allows you to experience the ever-changing nature of your mind and to simply be a curious observer/participant of your experience in just this moment.

Third, a strategy of consciously moving your focus of awareness from the breath to the persistent and intrusive thought, emotion, or body sensation allows you to practise responding and not just reacting to whatever arises at the moment. Your tolerance to the various intrusive stimuli that you experience at any moment increases. Besides, as you learn to accept whatever arises and respond, not merely react, you begin to experience the ongoing changes occurring, and you begin to cultivate a new relationship to this moment . . . and then to this next moment . . . .and then to this next moment. . . .

PRACTICE OF THE WEEK

Guidelines:

- This week, the assignment is to practise sitting meditation for **twenty-five minutes six days per week** with the added instructions to work with intrusive thoughts, emotions, and physical sensations when they arise.

- Once again, choose a time and place where you will not be interrupted. Set a timer (from your phone, tablet, computer, microwave, etc.) for twenty-five minutes so you do not have to be concerned when time is up. By this point in your developing practice, you will likely have discovered whatever else you may need to comfortably engage in your sit (such as a shawl, cushions/boosters, pillow, etc.), so be sure to have them handy.

- Just as in the last session, you have the option of reading the instructions or listening to the audible presentation on the book's website, www.embracingagingmindfully.com.

- Be sure to record your daily sessions on your **Tracking Your Practice** sheet.

MEDITATING WITH PERSISTENT INTRUSIONS INSTRUCTIONS:

Assume the sitting posture that you have selected (either in a chair or on the floor). . . . Gently close your eyes. . . . Check in with your body. . . . Is it comfortable and aligned? . . . Take a moment to make any adjustments needed. . . . Decide where your anchor will be. . . . Recall that it needs to be a neutral point of focus that holds body sensations that you can track. . . .

Should you decide to use your breath as your anchor, choose the part of the body that allows you to feel the breath coming in and going out. . . . This could be through the nostrils . . . or mouth . . . or chest area . . . or belly. . . . Choose the place where you can most easily focus on the breath coming in and out as your anchor of awareness. . . .

Direct your focus to the breath in the part of the body you are using to hold your awareness. . . . Simply notice each in-breath . . . and each out-breath . . . allowing the breath to be natural . . . noting its inflow and outflow, without trying to force or control it in any way. . . . The breath knows what it is supposed to do. . . .

Note each breath's in and out, rising and falling, and allow a settling into your breath's rhythm. . . . Allow the mind to rest in that place . . . feeling the movement of your breath. . . .

While feeling the breath, you can make a mental note to sharpen concentration. . . . This can include noting "in" while sensing your breath go in . . . and "out" while feeling it leave . . . or saying simply "rising" and "falling" with the sensations in the chest or the belly or the nostrils or mouth . . . very gently, very quietly in your mind . . . just supporting the awareness of the actual sensations . . . just noting in and out . . . or rising and falling. . . .

There is no need to make the breath special. . . . Each breath is unique and is whatever it is. . . . It may be a deep and a long breath . . . or a short and shallow breath. . . . Whatever it is, it doesn't matter because it is merely a matter of noticing . . . noticing the breath. . . .

Should you decide to use your hand as your anchor of awareness, place your hand on your thigh or belly or heart . . . anywhere that allows you to notice sensations through your hand and fingers. . . . The feel of your hand on your body becomes your anchor. . . . Be aware of any sensation that you notice from the contact where it is resting . . . on your thumb . . . on your first finger . . . on your middle finger . . . on your fourth finger . . . on your little finger . . . on the palm of your hand . . . not expecting or wanting any specific sensation or experience. . . . Just be curious . . . and notice. . . . Allow your mind to rest in the sensations. . . . Know that you can also slightly move your fingers or hand to enhance your awareness of any sensations. . . .

You can support the awareness of your hand sensations through making a mental note of the feeling. . . . You may note the feel as "rough" or "pressure" or "soft" . . . or the movement of the hand "left" or "right" or "up" or "down." . . . Simply labelling the sensation to help sharpen your concentration. . . . No need to analyze . . . or judge . . . or question what the sensation is. . . . It merely is a sensation that can anchor your awareness. . . .

As you discovered during last week's meditations, while you are focusing on your anchor, your attention will wander . . . perhaps getting lost in a thought . . . or a feeling . . . or a physical sensation. . . . Simply be aware that your attention has left the breath or sensation of the hand and is now drawn to a thought, feeling, or body sensation. . . . No need to judge or analyze. . . . No need to try to figure out how it slipped away. . . . It doesn't matter . . . just accept that your attention has pulled away. . . .

Perhaps give it a label, such as "thinking" . . . "feeling" . . . "sensation" . . . or any other simple word to note the distraction. . . . No matter what it is, just noticing it as a thought, feeling, or sensation. . . . Then gently let go of it . . . letting go of the thought, feeling, or sensation and returning your attention to your anchor . . . the breath's easy inflow and outflow . . . or the sensations of your hand. . . . The breath or hand returns to be the primary anchor of your attention, of your awareness. . . .

No matter what arises that pulls your attention away from your anchor . . . it merely is a matter of noticing. . . . Whether it be a thought . . . stories from the past . . . plans for the future . . . emotions . . . sensations in the body . . . just notice and bring your attention back to your anchor. . . . If your anchor is the breath . . . bring your awareness back to the sensation of the breath coming in . . . going out . . . or perhaps your anchor is the sensations of your hand . . . movement of a finger . . . or feeling of clothing touching your hand. . . . Simply be with whatever is sensed with your anchor of awareness at this moment. . . . There is no need to do anything else . . . merely be with the experience of your anchor holding your attention . . . noticing the sensations of your breath or hand . . . and catching when your awareness has been hijacked . . . pulled away from your anchor . . . and with this realization, simply returning again . . . and again . . . beginning again . . . and again . . . returning to your anchor of attention with patience and gentleness again and again. . . .

However, there will be times when a thought, emotion, or body sensation is persistent and intrusive . . . when just noticing it, labelling it, and returning to your anchor is not successful. . . . When that occurs, you can use the invasive experience as your temporary focus of awareness . . . to consciously acknowledge that the thought, emotion, or body sensation demands your attention. . . .

If an emotion is strong enough to keep intruding into the focus on your anchor of awareness, just accept that this is the reality of this moment. . . . No need to become upset or frustrated. . . . Just consciously accept that the emotion will now become your anchor of attention. . . .

Holding the emotion, quickly scan your body to identify where you most strongly feel it. . . . It could be anywhere in your body. . . . It may take a few moments to locate it . . . but just know that if the emotion is strong enough to pull your attention from your anchor, it will be experienced somewhere in your body. . . .

The location of where you experience the persistent emotion now becomes your new, albeit temporary, anchor of attention. . . . Focus all of your attention on this body sensation. . . . Explore in a minute and finely tuned manner precisely what this body sensation that holds your emotion is like. . . . Be very curious as to exactly where in the body the sensation is . . . how large an area it is . . . diffuse and spread out . . . a micro point. . . . Does it have a sense of temperature? . . . Hot? . . . Cold? . . . Neutral? . . . Does it feel tight? . . . Relaxed? . . . Itchy? . . . Sense of pressure? . . . Persistent? . . . Throbbing? . . . Achy? . . . Sense of heaviness? . . . Lightness? . . .

Focus your awareness on exploring and identifying what that body sensation is like in the present moment. . . . The goal is not to try to change whatever the emotion or body sensation is. . . . Instead, it is merely a matter of accepting that there is a body sensation connected with the emotion and allowing the finely tuned exploration of it to become your new focus . . . your new anchor of awareness. . . . The primary goal is to be present in just this moment through applying your focus on the body sensation as your anchor of awareness. . . .

You may experience that by doing so, there is a change in the actual body sensation. . . . The quality of it may change. . . . The intensity of it may change. . . . The location of the body sensation that holds the emotion may change. . . . The physical sensations may dissipate completely . . . or the emotion itself may retreat. . . . Even if it is still noticeable, it may not hold the same charge or power that it once did. . . .

The goal is to simply maintain your awareness of the physical manifestations of the emotion as long as it is strong enough to pull your attention away from your usual anchor. . . . No matter the quality or location . . . keep your focus of awareness on the body sensations of the emotion as long as it is charged enough to hold your awareness. . . . When it no longer has the strength or power to keep your awareness . . . simply return to your primary anchor of attention, be it the breath or hand. . . .

In a similar manner to emotions, you may find that a recurring thought arises and pulls your attention away from the breath. . . . Should just noticing it not allow you to return your attention to your anchor of awareness, then the practice is to use the thought as the new, albeit temporary, anchor of attention. . . . Similar to working with recurring and intrusive emotions, persistent thoughts can now become your novel temporary anchor of awareness. . . .

In the spirit of acceptance of such intrusive and persistent thoughts, make the conscious decision to move your anchor of attention from the breath to the thought itself. . . . However, this is not as easy as working with emotions since the mind will often simply use the new anchor of awareness to generate ever more thoughts. . . . It is like you have opened the door to the thought, and your mind is only too willing to fill it with a thousand and one new ideas and concepts. . . .

To try and just hold the thought in and by itself as the new anchor of attention is not an easy task . . . so as an alternative strategy, it is better to link the thought to an emotional tone associated with it and, in turn, locate the emotion within the body. . . . What you will notice as you focus on the thought is that it will be associated with a feeling tone. . . . Over time and with experience, you will find that there will be some emotional content tied up with every thought. . . . If the thought is not strong enough to pull your awareness away from your anchor repeatedly, then it likely is not a thought that has much emotional power attached to it. . . .

Instead of focusing on the thought, explore what the emotion associated with the thought is . . . and then find where in the body you feel that emotion associated with the thought. . . . Whatever the thought is, it will be related to a feeling that can be located within the body. . . . When you find where the emotion is situated in the body, the strategy is the same as working with intrusive emotions because, in fact, that is what you are now focusing on. . . . The thought is attached to an emotion, which is felt within the body, which now becomes the focus of your awareness. . . .

As noted earlier, you become very interested in exploring in a very minute and exacting fashion what this thought/emotion/body sensation is like in the present moment. . . . Explore its location . . . size . . . shape . . . sensation . . . temperature . . . and overall physical impressions. . . . If the body sensation attached to the feeling that originates with a thought shifts to a new location, then move your anchor of awareness to the new area. . . . When the body sensation changes, either through the intensity of it letting up or in fact it dissipating, then bring your awareness back to your primary anchor of attention. . . . Your breath or hand sensation once again becomes your anchor of attention.

If you find that there is a body sensation in and of itself that is continually pulling your attention away from your anchor . . . such as an itchy nose . . . numbness in your buttocks . . . pressure under your thigh . . . tightness in the shoulders . . . or whatever . . . you can use that body sensation as the new, albeit temporary, anchor of awareness. . . . Remember, however, that your first response is just to notice the sensation, label it, and return to your primary anchor. . . .

However, if your awareness becomes hijacked by the physical sensation and you are not able to simply return to your anchor, then move your focus of awareness to the body sensation itself. . . . Then just as reviewed with intrusive and persistent emotions and thoughts, explore in a very mindful and curious manner what the sensation feels like. . . . Once again, explore its location . . . size . . . shape . . . sensation . . . temperature . . . as well as its overall physical impression. . . . Continue exploring the sensations as long as they are strong enough to hold your attention. . . . When the body sensation changes, either through the intensity of it letting up or it dissipating so that it no longer is strong enough to hijack your attention, then bring your awareness back to your anchor . . . the breath or hand sensations as once again your primary anchor of attention. . . .

However, suppose through doing this mindful exploration the body sensation does not lessen or dissipate. . . . In that case, it is certainly acceptable to decide to alleviate the body discomfort or distraction directly. . . .

The goal, though, is not to give up too quickly on the curious exploration of the body sensation. . . . This allows you to practise a different way of being with such intrusive body sensations . . . and to practise holding your attention exactly where you want it to be. . . .

Nevertheless, should the body sensation not dissipate and you decide to alleviate it directly, be aware that you have made this decision consciously. . . . You are not just reflexively reacting to a sensation. . . . Instead, you are responding to it, which is a crucial distinction concerning being mindful. . . . When the decision has been made and before you start any actions, take a moment to be mindfully aware of how you are going to carry out the activity. . . . For example, if your buttock is feeling numb and you are going to shift your position on the cushion or in the chair, be aware of how you are going to do this. . . . Are you going to put your hands down on the floor/chair and lift your buttocks off? . . . Or are you just going to slide your buttocks to a different position on the cushion/chair? . . . If your elbows feel tight, are you going to raise both of them at the same time to stretch? . . . Or extend the right one first . . . followed by the left one? . . . Are you going to stretch your arms up . . . or straight out in front? . . .

Try to be extremely specific as to how you are going to mindfully make a move to deal with this intrusive body sensation. . . . The underlying mindful message is that you are going to respond and not just react to the situation . . . and when you have alleviated the physical sensation, return your focus to your anchor of awareness. . . .

Know that you now have different strategies to work with distractions that take your attention off your anchor of awareness. . . . While the first response is to simply note that your attention has been pulled by a thought, emotion, or body sensation and return to your anchor, sometimes persistent intrusions will arise . . . intrusive thoughts . . . or emotions . . . or body sensations that are powerful enough to derail your intention to focus on your anchor of awareness. . . . You will know when they arrive. . . . Even with the best of intentions to hold your focus on your anchor, your attention will get hijacked. . . . When they do . . . and be sure that they will . . . know that you have a second level of response. . . . Consciously turn your focus of awareness to the body sensation associated with the thought, emotion, or physical sensation. . . . The body sensation then becomes your temporary

anchor of attention as you curiously and exactingly explore the sensations. . . . When the body sensation loses its power over your attention,
return to your breath or hand sensation anchor of awareness. . . .

Hijacking attention from your anchor could happen multiple times
during a meditation. . . . No matter how often it occurs, keep applying this
strategy. . . . With it, you will have consciously continued to direct your
focus where you want it. . . . If not on your primary anchor of attention,
then to the temporary site in your body that holds the pesky and intrusive
thoughts, emotions, or body sensations. . . . Your attention can later return
to your primary anchor when the power of the intrusion has lessened
or dissipated . . . either to your breath or to your hand sensation as your
primary anchor of attention. . . .

At the end of the session, when you hear your timer, slowly open your
eyes and allow your attention to return to the room. . . . Let yourself see
the room as if for the first time . . . quietly and gently allowing your gaze
to move through the space that surrounds you. . . . Allow your hearing to
receive whatever sounds are occurring in the area . . . and when you feel
ready . . . gently and consciously arise from your seated meditation position . . . and continue practising to hold your awareness on just this present
moment . . . setting the intention to maintain your sense of acceptance to
whatever you will experience for the rest of your day. . . .

MIDWEEK CUPPA...
REFLECTIONS ON
ACCEPTANCE AND AGING

WEEK THREE

Acceptance of the aging process is typically associated with losses. Like it or not, aging asks us (through some variation from a whisper to a shout) to accept that we are not as energetic, we are not as cognitively sharp or our skin is not as smooth and wrinkle-free as it used to be. The cultural emphasis on the consequences of aging is mirrored in the daily bombardment of advertising, tallying not only our losses (as if we haven't already noticed!) but also presenting the fantasy that in one easy step, it is possible to purchase reprieves painlessly. For example, a new cell phone automatically brings membership in the "in" group. A nightly skin cream has you dancing in the moonlight with the partner of your dreams. Buying the new red coupe makes you feel twenty years younger. Have you tried any of these? Are they working for you? I'm guessing that you probably would not be reading this book if such purchases had been successful!

Acceptance of aging is also a gift. It provides an opportunity to boldly let go of self-limiting beliefs that have lain unchallenged through the years, ones you have relied upon to define who you are. The Swiss psychiatrist Dr. Carl Jung noted a developmental imperative during the second half of life that pushes us to become the unique individuals we are—to become more than the limited sense of self we have often believed and embraced. Aging can summon new courage to greet unacknowledged personal attributes and capabilities laid dormant through the years. To reclaim or even claim for the first time a more realistic acceptance of what constitutes this life of yours is possible because you are older—hopefully wiser, but most definitely because you are more aware of the decreasing years available to you.

HOW DID WE GET SO SMALL?

How did we develop our initial, albeit limited, sense of self? To watch my three-year-old granddaughter running and playing in the sand on the Oregon coast beach is to witness pure, unbridled delight. Her laughter crescendos into squeals of joy as her little bare feet run into and then quickly away from the rising tide. Her unabashed pleasure and lack of self-consciousness just being in this moment make her oblivious to anything or anyone else. Watching her wondrous expression of elation that each of us is capable of is a joy in and of itself! But it also begs the question: What happened to us as adults that so often inhibits natural expressions of the raw emotion of joy? Or of wonder? Or of risk-taking?

The poet Robert Bly (1988) writes of the early developmental process wherein each learns what is acceptable and what is not "okay" about who they are. These dictums arise throughout your younger years from various sources: parents, friends, teachers, religious instructions, and societal norms. As a result, personal aspects that others initially judged unacceptable, and which you later judged the same, become stuffed into what Bly characterizes as an invisible bag that you then drag around behind you. Bly laments that this process is so powerful and effective that by the time he and his brother were twelve years old, they had each stuffed much of what was considered objectionable about themselves into their bags and became known as the "nice Bly boys." Which also meant, however, that their bags were already a mile long!

By the time you hit adulthood, the bag you drag around behind you is even longer, growing in size during subsequent years as the additional creeds demanded from relationships, work, and societal expectations regarding age and gender appropriateness are deposited. While I agree with Bly that each of us has created this invisible bag, we have also been responsible for maintaining the unwanted and disowned deposits. You have come to believe that an acceptable self-definition demands that this bag be preserved under lock and key.

But don't be fooled; your disowned aspects may not be consciously expressed, but they are not forgotten. Have you ever been shocked by an unexpected and unfounded judgment that you made about someone? By an abrupt, critical statement that you blurted out? By an erotic fantasy that made you blush? By an action that was followed by your quizzical admonition of "Where did that come from?" Well, it probably came from the contents of your long bag. Depth psychology deems these contents the shadow parts of ourselves, a metaphor for all we cannot or do not want to see of ourselves.

DISOWNED ASPECTS OF YOURSELF

Kate came to my psychotherapy office feeling listless and unexcited about her life. While she did acknowledge a sense of success and satisfaction, having parented her three now-grown daughters, built a robust social network over the years, and having been of service to her community through volunteer activities, a nagging unease would not be silenced. Although not self-diagnosed as depressed, at fifty-seven, Kate could no longer convince herself that she was happy and content with her life.

Therapy helped Kate explore the long bag she had been dragging around behind her. Starting with early childhood memories, she recalled the many messages she had received and internalized over the years. For example, she was not allowed to be too rambunctious, she had to always share, be responsible, and care for her younger siblings before playing herself, and she could never boast about her accomplishments. Marriage had taught Kate that she was not allowed to be angry, she must be upbeat no matter what was happening around her, and she must be supportive of her husband's career as well as sports interests. Her social circle demanded that she be content with her life and that she ought not to complain because clearly, others in the world were worse off.

Kate's learning and then internalizing what was acceptable and unacceptable is no different from our personal experiences. Each bag is, without doubt, a reflection of one's individual journey, although there probably are common deposits that most bags share. Attributes such as being greedy, selfish, unreliable, lazy, manipulative, narcissistic, inconsiderate, impulsive, untrustworthy, or deceitful are likely core aspects people do not characterize as positive. Who wants to have these characterizations? Likely no one, so they become unacceptable parts of yourself that you deposit into your personal bag.

Suppressing these negative personality attributes does have some limited benefit, as it probably allows for more harmonious social relationships, at least on a superficial level. And to be clear, Kate's goal to explore the shadow parts of herself didn't include pulling the disowned parts of herself from the bag and unleashing them on the world and those around her. Instead, the purpose was her understanding that many of her disowned aspects are shared by all humans. We each can demonstrate such attributes, but that doesn't mean that anyone, including Kate, need do so. However, denying even having the capacity for any can restrict and limit one's emotional well-being.

As she developed a mindfulness practice, Kate came to recognize that there were times when she was, in fact, angry, not feeling very charitable, wanting to do things just for herself, and feeling a deep sense of pride in her accomplishments. These were new revelations that percolated into her consciousness. With a developing sense of acceptance of all that makes her human, Kate developed a new and healthier relationship with these previously disowned aspects of herself. It didn't mean that she had to like all of them or act them out when they arose but rather initiate a process to broaden her sense of self. Acceptance of these previously unacknowledged feelings allowed Kate to expand her emotional life beyond the tight and unforgiving box that she had been inhabiting and, in fact, had created. Though she was not always skillful in expressing her newly accepted but previously disowned parts of herself, Kate began to experience what she characterized as a "larger life." She often felt like she was "coming home" to herself.

UNACKNOWLEDGED POSITIVE ASPECTS OF YOURSELF

Our long bags also contain unacknowledged positive traits, capabilities, and interests that we have not accepted as our own. By opening your long bag, you can allow yourself to discover unclaimed personal gifts, such as being more capable than you ever believed yourself to be; to travel on your own to near and far-off places; to build wooden children's toys; to succeed in learning a new language; to share yourself through volunteer activities; to run for elected office; to follow your long-buried and forgotten dream of playing the piano; to risk being vulnerable while loving another; and so on.

Kate came to acknowledge that she had a creative side that she had never developed or even explored. Once she realized this interest and accepted it as an unlived aspect of herself, she allowed herself to start delving into potential options for its expression. Kate was unsure what her creative outlet might entail, so she began drawing and painting classes at the local college. Nothing clicked, however, as she did not feel inspired or satisfied with these mediums. Not being easily discouraged, though, Kate continued her exploration and enrolled in an introduction to photography class, which proved to be a winner. Like a light bulb illuminating a darkened room, Kate found photography exciting and satisfying, so she continued taking further courses. Unacknowledged, her creative side had been long dormant. Still, by allowing and accepting the embryotic seed of the desire for creativity, she enlarged and enriched her life and enjoyed a newfound sense of self.

Kate's path to exploring her creativity is typical. Tentative exploration is how you go about embracing unacknowledged aspects of yourself. Kate's creative interests and capabilities were mainly unknown to her, so she couldn't quickly and confidently identify what medium would best satisfy them. The early path is often one of investigation through trial and error. Identifying a previously unacknowledged personal aspect requires taking a step toward what you believe and feel may be an option. When this forward movement meets with energy and motivation, try it out. It may be what you are looking for—or it may not. It may even feel difficult, as new skill development takes time. The only judge is yourself. If your emotional reaction and accompanying energy are compelling, continue taking steps toward the goal. If the energy and interest are not evident, switch gears and try a different avenue, task, or component of what you feel to be an unacknowledged aspect of who you are.

ACCEPTING AGING AS AN OPPORTUNITY

Aging provides an opportunity to look, however tentatively, into the bag that you have created—the bag that holds the shadow aspects of yourself. It takes considerable energy on emotional, physical, and psychic levels to keep the shadow bag closed, and as you age, it can become ever more constricting and intolerable. Acceptance of the disowned and unacknowledged parts of yourself begins the initiation into a new relationship with all that you are. Undertaken consciously and ethically, this exploration and acceptance of your disowned and unacknowledged inner constituents are incredibly freeing. It allows you to know on a visceral level what it is like to take off shoes that have been too small for you—shoes that you have mistakenly believed to be the only ones that you can wear. And by extension, it allows you to recognize that you have been living a life that was too small for you—a life you have mistakenly believed to be the only one for you. And by further extension, you have missed many moments that were available to you—missed because of your non-acceptance of all that you are.

Shadow work is a lifelong process. As you become more aware through living mindfully, you will continue to meet limitations you have imposed on yourself throughout your life, both consciously and unconsciously. Jungian psychology identifies shadow work as proffering one of the most significant paths to become the individual, the whole individual, that you genuinely are. There are many strategies for exploring your shadow; mindfulness represents a good entry into this process.

Engaging in the formal practice of sitting meditation (as well as others that we will identify in later sessions) allows you to see the thoughts and emotions that keep repetitively arising and become challenges to maintaining your awareness at this moment. Each of us has our unique "Top Ten" intrusions that play over and over, thwarting our good-faith attempts to focus attention purposefully. The formal mindfulness practice is not the place to further explore what these thoughts and emotions are since our emphasis is to train the mind to focus on just one anchor of attention. However, when you are off the cushion (not immersed in mindfulness practice), you can consciously explore more of these intrusions, when and where they arose, how realistic they are, and by extension, most importantly, whether you genuinely believe in them.

As we will discuss in later sessions, bringing mindful awareness to all aspects of your daily life will extend your capacity to pay attention, on purpose, in the present moment, non-judgmentally. This expanding awareness will allow you to see how your daily thoughts, beliefs, feelings, and actions limit your acceptance of all of who you are. For example, becoming aware of your fears and how they stop you from acting; your judgments of others and how they flare unexpectedly; the way your energy flags when presumed upon to meet someone else's expectations or needs; what's happening inside you when you feel the urge to punish someone; how you tend to shut down emotionally in the presence of others; the way your repetitive daydreams of a different life meet intense inner scorn and anger; when you just know that you could be happy if only . . . All are invitations to look inside the long bag you have been dragging behind you.

The essayist and poet David Whyte eloquently portrays that a life captured in personal shadows does not allow you to be all who you are in a poem called "Sweet Darkness":

> *When your eyes are tired*
> *the world is tired also.*
>
> *When your vision has gone*
> *no part of the world can find you.*

Time to go into the dark
where the night has eyes
to recognize its own.

There you can be sure
you are not beyond love.

The dark will be your womb
tonight.

The night will give you a horizon
further than you can see.

You must learn one thing.
The world was made to be free in.

Give up all the other worlds
except the one to which you belong.

Sometimes it takes darkness and the sweet
confinement of your aloneness
to learn

anything or anyone
that does not bring you alive

is too small for you.

(Whyte, "Sweet Darkness," 23)

This extended exploration of persistent and intrusive beliefs, feelings, and actions can help you consciously challenge the parameters of this life that you have created. You may find many beliefs and feelings that serve you well and that you want to keep. However, upon deeper reflection, there are likely others that you recognize, even tentatively, are not serving you well. What disowned and unacknowledged parts have you stuffed in your long bag? Which of those are impeding your ongoing development? What are you going to do with them? Such questions demand a conscious life, no matter what age you may be.

To explore your shadow sides is not an easy task. It takes courage. By this time in your aging life, you may have internalized the belief that these disowned and unacknowledged elements are not acceptable. And I don't mean to suggest that it is easy to accept previously unacceptable aspects of yourself. However, to begin meeting and then accepting these disowned portions of our shared humanity as well as unacknowledged aspects of our unique individuality is to start establishing a new and healthier relationship to our whole being at this very moment.

One reality of aging is that the time available to live this life is getting shorter. As the Catholic priest Father Alfred D'Souza observed: "For a long time it had seemed to me that life was about to begin—real life! But there was always some obstacle in the way, something to be got through first, some unfinished business, time still to be served, a debt to be paid. Then life would begin. At last, it dawned on me that these obstacles were my life . . . so treasure every moment you have and remember that time waits for no one."

Each of us has lived a long time in this constructed life that we believed was all there was. You have the capacity to at least explore, if not reshape, this life of yours. It must begin with an acceptance of you, every part of you, even those parts that were unacceptable for so long. With its acknowledgement of limited years to live, aging can be the gift to boldly and courageously ask: If not now, when?

STRETCH YOUR WINGS: EXTENDING MINDFULNESS INTO EVERYDAY LIFE

WEEK FOUR

REVIEW PERSISTENT INTRUSIONS PRACTICE

The group's animated discussions before beginning Week Four gave me hope that last week's discouraging experiences of intrusions into their attention self-regulation no longer seemed so bleak. Ken, who had said comparatively little the week before but whose body language suggested a disappointment and skepticism with his beginning meditation practice, was now eager to share his past week's adventure. He began by wryly informing the group that his dog, Charlie, had never taken a mindfulness class in his entire nine-year life and yet in the past week had become Ken's most influential meditation teacher!

Ken introduced Charlie as a good-natured golden retriever with a sweet face whose mild disposition allowed him to be poked and prodded by grandkids without expressing any retribution. However, when Charlie got a rawhide chew bone, he transformed into a possessive animal who jealously guarded his beloved and tasty new best friend. Even if a loud, startling noise erupted beside Charlie, he wouldn't take his attention off his task, which clearly was to savour every bite, softening the tough rawhide into a delicious white mushy pulp. Charlie's dogged (pun intended) tenacity was legion in the household, for there was no way to come between the dog and his bone until Charlie alone moved his attention to something else.

Ken explained that he felt discouraged by the sheer number of thoughts concerning the past that continually intruded into his sitting meditation practice last week. While he initially tried to notice them and return to his breath as his anchor of awareness, another new memory repeatedly arose out of nowhere to capture his attention. Therefore, Ken was pleased to learn the alternate strategy of temporarily relocating his anchor of awareness to the body region associated with the feelings attached to his memories and looked forward to testing its effectiveness.

During his sitting meditation the day after last week's session, Ken initially located the feelings associated with intrusive and persistent memories in his chest, and just as instructed, moved his attention to that area to explore its location, size, shape, temperature, etc. He found that these perceptions were across his entire chest and strongly associated with a cold heavy sensation. After a time focusing his awareness and exploration on the sensations, he suddenly noticed that they were no longer prominent enough to hold his awareness. Feeling confused with the sudden departure of the physical sensations in his chest, he briefly scanned his body and found there was now a sensation of tightness in his neck and across his shoulders.

Recognizing that these physical sensations of tightness were still associated with the emotions related to his memories, Ken therefore moved his anchor of attention to this new body location. The primary sensation Ken then found was a tightness particularly noticeable from his neck extending into his left shoulder. While he could feel pressure in his right shoulder, it was not as prominent as that on his left side. While settling into the exploration of these new sensations, Ken again noticed that they were gradually dissipating. While he still could feel the tension in his neck and left shoulder, it definitely had lessened along with the pull of his attention, and therefore he returned to the breath as his anchor of awareness.

Ken was pleased to address forceful memories through this new strategy of continually holding his attention on an identified anchor—if not his breath, then with the place in his body that held the feelings associated with his persistent intrusive memories. However, just as often as he experienced success in utilizing alternating anchors of awareness when old remembrances pulled his attention, another memory arose, which would not be alleviated by merely noticing its arrival. Not to be thwarted, though, Ken revelled in his newfound capabilities as he continued time and time again to find and explore the body area associated with the emotion attached to the memory as his new, albeit temporary, anchor of awareness.

This brings us back to Charlie's promotion to a venerable teacher status as Ken lightheartedly recounted to the group: "As I finished my sitting meditation, I opened my eyes to see Charlie contentedly munching on his rawhide bone. It suddenly dawned on me that just as nothing can separate Charlie from unrelenting possession of his favourite bone, I had become steadfast in maintaining my anchor of attention—nothing was going to come between my anchor and me, even if it meant surfing with it to new locations in my body! I ruffled the back of Charlie's head as I thanked him for his influential modelling of what loyal allegiance looks like and the realization that I too can be a faithful guard dog of my attention!"

While Ken's experience during the week resulted in self-satisfaction, not all new mindfulness students report this positive experience. Instead, working with just the structure of mindfulness meditation can be frustrating and can lead to early dropouts. Students sometimes say they feel a sense of failure when they cannot hold their attention on their anchor for any extended periods. Even though they understand the instructions that it is more important to just notice intrusions into their awareness rather than evaluate their capacity to monitor their breath or hand sensations, a decisive inner negative judgment of their capabilities and, more importantly, their sense of self can quickly kick in.

BETTER FRIEND TO YOURSELF

As noted in the Introduction chapter, mindfulness is at its heart a process of becoming a better friend to yourself. The instructions of mindfulness that you have been practising provide a structure or scaffolding to develop this new relationship. However, while these strategies of always having an anchor of awareness satisfy the first aspects of the mindfulness definition (paying attention in the present moment on purpose), deepening or even developing this self-friendship requires a conscious shift in attitude and sentiment. Furthermore, self-friendship requires you to hold and practise beliefs and characteristics emblematic and congruent of a positive relationship with yourself, especially for negative self-judging skeptics in the group like Ken.

The attitudinal foundations that we have begun identifying as beginner's mind and acceptance and the reflections on aging through world/self contracts and positive personal shadows that we have explored become critical components to nourish your self-friendship consciously. These elements or constituents of your self-friendship need to be tenderly realized, combined, and incorporated into the structure of mindfulness to give life to this healthier way of being. And since self-judgment has often intruded at this point in the mindfulness practice, we need to explore this powerful interloper that has the capacity to derail developing and deepening self-friendship.

NON-JUDGING

With the realization that holding your attention where you want it and when you want it is not easy, it is time to explore the third attitudinal foundation of mindfulness: non-judging. As you will remember, this, in fact, is part of the definition of mindfulness, which means to pay attention, on purpose, in the present moment, in a non-judgmental manner. Mindfulness is cultivated by assuming the stance of an impartial witness to your own experience. Therefore, when you start to practise, you will be paying particular attention to your own mind's activity and your relationship to whatever arises.

When beginning your mindfulness practice, it often surprising to become aware that you are constantly generating judgments about your experience. Almost everything you experience is identified and classified by the mind. You react to everything in terms of what you perceive its value is to you. Some events, people, and objects are quickly judged as "good" because they make you feel positive. Others are equally quickly condemned as "bad" because they are associated with negative feelings. The remainder are often categorized as "neutral" because you don't have any significant reactions to them. You may not even be consciously aware that the judgment is one of good or bad, but you will likely be aware that you want more or less of what you are experiencing at that moment. The desire for more or less is, in fact, another face of judgment!

What turns out to be particularly interesting is that there is often no conscious awareness of the evaluation process. Rather, this tendency of judging and classifying your experience locks you into automatic reactions that you are unaware of. They often have no objective basis, but these judgments tend to govern your mind, making it difficult for you to find any calm within yourself. Remember Dr. Jon Kabat-Zinn's comparison of the human mind to a yo-yo, going up and down on the string of your judging thoughts all day long.

Paying attention to the content of what arises in your mind and body as you focus your awareness on your anchor is, therefore, very instructive. You may not easily recognize the judgments that you make about each thought, feeling, or body sensation. Still, with practice and attentiveness, you will more readily be conscious of what is occurring. However, don't spend your time analyzing judgments about your thoughts, feelings, and physical sensations while engaging in your formal sitting meditation. This is counterproductive, as it takes you even further away from your goal, focusing your attention and awareness on just this moment with the breath or hand sensations as your anchor. In the mindfulness practice, simply notice such intrusions and return to your anchor of awareness.

However, outside of the formal sitting practice, pay more attention to the mind's judgments. Notice what you are drawn to and what you move away from; what you want more of and what you want less off; what you spend your time on and what you avoid. Be curious about your thoughts, feelings, physical sensations, and behaviours, especially about the continuously generated judgments. Get to know yourself better, no matter what age you may be.

What you will also likely find as you continue with developing mindfulness awareness, both during formal meditation practices and during your daily activities, is that many of these judgments are directed toward yourself. Not only do you judge the value of ideas, memories, plans, feelings, or body sensations, but you, as the central figure in your life's drama, are also continually being evaluated. Listen closely to what the mind decrees as the truth of who you are!

When asked for examples of self-judgment, the group erupted with a torrent of readily identifiable convictions. During the first few sessions, Helen told herself that she wasn't smart enough to master the mindfulness practice. Henry questioned his morality when erotic fantasies arose. Bernie felt inferior when comparing himself with his friends' career paths. Karl thought that he was a weak person because he could not hold his attention on his breath. Sybil decided there must be something wrong with her when she felt teary during a meditation sit. Beth continued to berate herself as an unworthy friend when recalling a disagreement she was involved with months ago. Finally, Sam wondered what was wrong with him when he felt disappointed about his retirement.

On and on, such self-judgments continue. Within the psychology field, these self-judgments are often characterized as an inner critic or parent or judge who cannot be satisfied. Indeed, you can never win the debate about your self-value as long as these negative self-judgments go unquestioned and you believe them to be true.

In the spirit of mindful awareness to explore your self-judgments, it can be instructive to spend a day or even half a day tracking conclusions you lay upon yourself as you go through daily activities. Just be curious about what emotional valence (generally characterized as good, bad, or neutral) is associated with thoughts, memories, plans for the future, behaviours, feelings, or body sensations that you experience. If you find it challenging to identify the judgment as good or bad or neutral, focus on whether you want more or less of what you are experiencing at that moment. Even basic activities, such as waiting in line for a coffee, will generate thoughts, feelings, or body sensations, which will likely also hold self-judgments if looked at more closely. Again, be curious as to what you are thinking and feeling about yourself.

However, even suggesting this exercise can be misconstrued as just another opportunity to beat up on yourself, to judge yourself negatively. Therefore, it is critical to emphasize that while the focus is on understanding your judgments as you go about your day, it is not to lay further negative assessments on yourself! This exercise is not about whether you are a good person or not—it is merely to pay attention to the judgments that your mind is making as you go through your day. These are JUST thoughts, feelings, or physical sensations that you like, don't like, or feel neutral toward—they are not any judgments about you as a person!

Mindfulness offers the opportunity to change your relationship with yourself, which to no small degree includes challenging ongoing self-judgments. As you have no doubt experienced with friendships, constantly (or even occasionally) feeling judged by another erodes trust and sabotages intimacy. Do you think that the outcome will be any different with a lifetime of judging yourself? As the American poet Ralph Waldo Emerson notes: "The roses under my window make no references to former roses or to better roses; they are what they are. . . . There is no time to them. There is simply the rose; it is perfect in every moment of its existence."

But you are not a rose. It is essential to recognize this human judging quality when it appears while practising mindfulness and intentionally assume the stance of an impartial witness by reminding yourself to merely observe it. When you find the mind judging, you don't have to beat up on yourself. You don't have to agree with the judgment. You don't have to debate the merits of the assessment. You don't have to get pulled down emotionally because of the verdict. You don't have to tense your body in reaction to the judgment. All that is required is to be aware of it happening. It is simply a judgment—a stimulus like any other phenomena that enters your field of awareness—there is no need to judge the judging and complicate or make matters even worse for yourself.

At frequent points with the meditation practice, you will no doubt find your mind saying things like "This is boring," or "This isn't working," or "I can't do this." But this negative self-judgment will arise not only with thoughts but also in terms of emotions as the mind can say that "This feeling isn't right," or "I shouldn't have this type of feeling," or "What's wrong with me for having these feelings?" And the mind, wanting to be an equal opportunity employer, will also graciously provide judgments that arise with physical sensations felt in the body. The mind can say that "I don't like this itchy nose," or "What did I do to deserve this ache?" or "I'm afraid of this discomfort—I have to get rid of it." These are all judgments—merely judgments of the mind.

When they come up—and don't be surprised when they do because they will—it is essential to recognize them as simply judgmental thinking, feeling, and physical sensations. Remind yourself that the practice involves suspending judgment and just watching whatever comes up, including your judging thoughts, feelings, and bodily sensations—without pursuing them or acting on them in any way. The mindfulness task is to just bring your awareness back to your breath or hand sensations as the anchor of your attention. No need to judge yourself or get caught up in trying to understand it—just let it go and bring your awareness back to your breath in a gentle manner. Marcus Aurelius, the first-century Roman emperor, had this figured out when he concluded: "If you are distressed by anything external, the pain is not due to the thing itself, but to your estimate of it; and this you have the power to revoke at any moment." You may consider yourself a "tough cookie," but no show of strength is needed—just *gently* bring your attention home to your anchor.

The idea of being an impartial witness to thoughts, feelings, and physical sensations that arise in your mind is an essential aspect of what you will be doing with mindfulness. With a change in your understanding and handling of persistent intrusions, the practice offers an opportunity to consciously respond to what is important to you rather than simply react and feel as though you were helplessly being dragged around by whatever stimuli pop into your awareness.

Mindfulness is not requesting a retreat from your life—rather, it offers the opportunity to more fully invest and experience all that your life presents. If there is a critical issue to contemplate or attend to, consciously invest your awareness in it. By all means, consider and devote the time and energy needed with problems that require solutions, plans for the future, and interpersonal difficulties that require attention. The goal, however, is to decide when you will do so consciously. To not get yanked around by such intrusions simply because they arise. To recognize that the vast majority of stimuli that occur and pull your attention from this moment are empty shiny objects that do not require immediate attention or add anything of value to your life, especially your self-friendship.

EXTENDING MINDFULNESS PRACTICE

This week, the goal is to extend your capacity of awareness beyond the body scan and sitting meditation practices. While both of these practices provide essential structure in terms of paying attention, on purpose, in the present moment, non-judgmentally, it is helpful to expand the catalogue of techniques available that can assist in learning mindfulness.

As you are learning these additional practices, it is crucial to hold the attitudinal foundations that we have reviewed (beginner's mind, acceptance, and non-judging) and additional ones to be introduced in later weeks, as essential components in the mindfulness way of being. Mindfulness is more than just holding your awareness on an identified anchor. Mindfulness is a way of learning to relate directly and consciously in a healthy manner to all that arises within your life. To assist in this goal, it is important to recognize that each attitudinal foundation is not independent. Each one relies on and influences the degree to which you can cultivate the others. Working on any one of them will assist your meditation practice. Together with the structural components of focusing your attention, they constitute the foundation upon which you will build a healthy meditation practice and, by extension, a robust mindfulness way of being—a home that you feel drawn to inhabit during your aging years.

WALKING MEDITATION

While many folks will find the sitting meditation practice a relaxing and welcome addition to their daily activities, others are not readily attracted to it. There are numerous potential reasons for this dislike. An individual's character may make it challenging to sit quietly or even find it physically uncomfortable, if not painful, to sit for extended periods. Walking meditation, therefore, provides a welcome alternative to those who find sitting meditation difficult or aversive. Even for those who have enjoyed sitting meditation, walking meditation offers a pleasant adjunct and alternative learning experience.

One of the things you find when practising mindfulness for a while is that nothing is quite as simple as it appears, which is as valid for walking as it is for anything. For example, when you walk, you know that you are primarily engaged in physical activity. However, you perhaps have also noticed that your mind, emotions, and body sensations don't need an invitation; they simply come with you. Have you noticed that you are usually absorbed in your thoughts or feelings to one extent or another when you walk? Have you noticed that when you walk, you are often not aware of the physical sensations involved? When you pay attention, you will find that you are hardly ever just walking, even if you declare that you are going out "just for a walk."

Usually, we walk for a reason. The most common one is to get from one place to another, and frequently, walking is how we can best do it. Of course, when walking, the mind is not left behind as it tends to think where it wants to go and what it will do there and so presses the body into service to deliver it. You will also find that there is an ongoing judgment about the walking in which you are engaged. You may enjoy the body's physical movements or may find the physical exertion to be a chore. You may revel in the sunshine warming your body as you are outside walking, or you may curse the rain or snow that is falling as you are trying to get from one place to another. Recognizing that thoughts, feelings, sensations, or judgments continue while walking, you can characterize the body as the chauffeur of the mind, willingly (or reluctantly) transporting it and doing its bidding.

Walking meditation involves intentionally attending to the experience of walking itself. It does not mean looking at your feet—instead, it means walking and *knowing* that you are walking. Specifically, it involves focusing on the sensations in your feet as the body is moving through space. You can also integrate awareness of your breathing with the walking experience, but we will first focus only on your feet's sensations. Your concentration on the senses in your feet while walking, therefore, becomes your new anchor of awareness.

You begin by making an effort to be fully aware as one foot contacts the ground, the body weight shifts onto it, your other foot lifts and moves ahead, and then it, in turn, comes down to make contact with the ground. You usually start slowly doing this to fully allow yourself to be with each movement from moment to moment. Sensing your feet moving slowly through space, therefore, becomes the focus of your awareness, your anchor of attention.

To deepen your concentration, do not look around at the sights but keep your gaze gently focused in front to see where you are going. You also don't need to look specifically at your feet—trust that they don't need your help, as they know how to walk quite well on their own. Instead, it is an internal observation cultivated, just the felt sensations of walking, nothing more. The sensed phenomena of your feet moving through space becomes your new anchor of awareness.

An additional strategy to increase your focus is to quietly or silently label each step by its function. For example, when lifting the first foot, say "lifting." You can hold it in the air for a moment or more, but when you decide to bring it forward, say "moving" to sharpen your concentration. And then when it is time to put the foot down, say "placing." These brief characterizations of your movements—lifting, moving, and placing—can be of additional assistance with focusing your awareness. You may decide that different words work better for you, such as simply "heel . . . toe . . . heel. . . ." Play with what works best for you!

Enjoy this physical embodiment of being fully present in the moment through feeling contact of the ground beneath you. As the Buddhist teacher Thich Nhat Hanh advises: "Walk as if you are kissing the earth with your feet."

What you find when focusing on walking in a very deliberate and conscious manner is that you may have often taken the ability to walk very much for granted. However, when you start paying more attention to it, you can appreciate it is an amazing balancing act given your feet's small surface area. Although we all know how to walk, if you are conscious of being observed by other people or even when you watch yourself, sometimes you can feel self-conscious and awkward, even to the point of losing your balance. When attempting to walk mindfully, you can also find that the mind wanders away from your feet into thoughts, feelings, or other body sensations. When this occurs, just as with the body scan and sitting meditation, you simply, in a very gentle manner, bring your awareness back to the focus of your feet, back to your new anchor of attention.

In strengthening your walking meditation practice, it is essential to recognize that you are not trying to get anywhere. To embody this intention, walk only about five or six feet, turn, and go back for five or six feet before once again turning and continuing back on that five- or six-foot stretch. With these restrictions, the mind can eventually grasp that there is no point in hurrying to get somewhere else. Nothing is interesting to grab your attention, and therefore, there is nothing to do except focus your awareness on the sensations of walking. This helps to put your mind to rest and relax into just being in each moment, using the felt sensations of your feet walking as the anchor of your attention.

Just as with the body scan and sitting meditation, the mind can generate judgments about the walking meditation activity. You may find the mind condemning the walking meditation, calling it stupid, useless, idiotic, or whatever. Or the mind can start playing games with the pace of the experience (such as speeding up) or beginning to look for any distractions that could be of interest. The mind can also just start thinking about the past or planning for the future.

You can be sure that any or all of these intrusions will occur—just as with the body scan and sitting meditation, it is not a matter of if they will happen but rather when and how often they arise. When this happens, the instructions are what you have already been putting into place—when you notice your attention pulled from your anchor, which is the sensations of your feet while walking—simply bring back your awareness. So again, there is no need to judge, analyze, debate, or engage in any way with whatever intrusions arose. It is simply a matter of noticing and then gently bringing your attention back to your anchor of awareness.

At this time, it is appropriate to point out (if this has not already become obvious) that walking in this prescribed manner can look very different than most people's walking experiences. To walk languidly and deliberately for only five to six feet before turning and returning those same five to six feet has been accurately and somewhat comically described as a "zombie walk" or "walk of the living dead!" Therefore, do not try this exercise at the mall or on a busy city street. Instead, it is best to practise this in a more private setting where your mindful allegiance to the walking meditation instructions does not bring unwanted attention from the authorities.

Walking meditation provides opportunities to explore your awareness capabilities in a relaxed and playful manner. For example, it is best to start walking meditation practice slowly to pay attention to your feet's movement in space. Over time, experiment with the speed of your walking pace. First, try going a bit faster and observe if you can still maintain the sensations of your feet moving in space. Then, continue to increase your walking pace to see if there is a point when it becomes at least tricky, if not impossible, to maintain this awareness as your anchor of attention.

Over time, it is also possible to link awareness of your breath with the sensations of your feet moving while walking. Connecting your breath with the feelings of your feet moving can create whole-body awareness. For example, you can be aware of breathing in as you lift your foot, hold the breath as you move it through space, and exhaling as you place your foot on the ground. I would encourage you to experiment with linking the breath and movements together as your anchor of attention, which can deepen your awareness of being in the moment as you engage in physical activity.

FORMAL MINDFULNESS PRACTICES

The body scan, sitting, and walking meditations in and of themselves are characterized as formal mindfulness practices for a couple of reasons. For one, they require a commitment to invest the time and hold your intention to learn and practise mindfulness skills. In addition, they also occur outside of your typical daily activities, which means exercising discipline to engage with them consistently and regularly. Therefore, formal meditation practices allow you, in an intentional and disciplined format, to learn and practise how you can focus your awareness, in the present moment, on purpose, in a non-judgmental manner.

These formal meditations are essential in learning the new mindfulness way of being. Just as with any new skill, you require practice, practice, practice. They not only provide a structure or scaffolding to learn such skills, but recent neuroscience research indicates that repetitive practice obtained during formal meditations also allows your brain to lay down new neural pathways that incorporate the new skills. That your brain can change through training, what scientists call "experience-dependent neuroplasticity," helps integrate mindfulness in daily life so that it is not just an isolated event but rather the foundation for a new and healthier way of being.

EASIER SAID THAN DONE

Formal meditation practices take time, as they are activities that you do not usually engage in during the day. Cassie tentatively raised her hand and described the difficulty she had finding time to participate in her daily practice sessions. She had diligently tracked her sessions on her practice log but had yet to find a structured time she could dedicate to regular practice. Finally, in frustration, she exclaimed, "I know it's important to do the practices, but my life is busy! I'm not a nun living a cloistered life—my life demands a lot of my time!"

Several others nodded in support of Cassie's struggles, which are, of course, realistic and understandable. The late head of the Sufi Order in the West, Pir Vilayat Khan, would also be sympathetic, as he notes: "Of so many great teachers that I've met in India and Asia, if you were to bring them to America, get them a house, two cars, a spouse, three kids, a job, insurance and taxes . . . they would all have a hard time!"

There is just no getting around it: learning mindfulness skills does require a commitment of your time. There is simply no way to short-circuit the time needed to realize a new way of being with your aging years. However, it is critical to recognize that the formal mindfulness practices that demand your time are not a waste of your time. Instead, engaging in these formal practices can be thought of as an exercise, similar to batting practice in baseball, that better prepares you for the actual game of life that each of you is playing. By intentionally and consciously committing to these formal meditation practices, you are setting the stage to more consciously experience your unfolding life in all its fullness, richness, and ever-changing nature.

INFORMAL MINDFULNESS PRACTICES

Notwithstanding the importance of investing your time and energy in formal meditation practice, it is not your only vehicle on this journey to embrace your aging years mindfully. Formal meditation practices are but one instrument that can take you closer to your eventual goal of mindfulness. Outside of the formal practice sessions, there are ample opportunities to continue learning to be more mindfully present. Cassie and many others in the group were pleased to hear that these informal practices arise out of daily activities that you are already doing, which means no additional time investment, and therefore, they are readily available to be of service to your learning process.

Informal mindfulness practices simply apply focused awareness on activities that you do regularly. While it is easy to identify many daily activities to which you can apply your burgeoning mindfulness skills, they all share a commonality of being ones to which you probably don't pay much attention. Instead, they are behaviours you have done so often that you do not even have to think about what you are doing—they have become rote operations completed mindlessly, which paradoxically makes them ripe for targets of your developing mindfulness training.

MINDFUL EATING

"One cannot think well, love well, sleep well if one has not dined well," extolled the writer, Virginia Woolf. Mindfulness must have heard her because one of the standard informal practices that mindfulness utilizes is eating. You know how to eat, as this is a daily activity carried out faithfully to nourish your body, mind, and spirit. However, it often is undertaken in such a hurried, thoughtless, and unobserving manner that it is not uncommon to come away from a meal oblivious to the discrete tastes, smells, and textures of the food just consumed. Since it is a given that you will need to continue eating to sustain your existence for the rest of your life, it provides a perfect informal practice toward your goal of being fully aware of whatever is occurring at the moment.

A typical entry into eating more mindfully is through the raisin exercise. Specific instructions for this exercise are outlined in the written and audible guided practice assignment accessed through the book's website, but as an overview, the idea is to take a single raisin and become mindfully curious, exploring all aspects of it. While you will likely have seen and tasted raisins on numerous other occasions in your life, try and experience this raisin as if for the very first time with a beginner's mind of curiosity, awareness, and observation.

You will explore this single little raisin, this morsel of food, slowly and deliberately, incorporating all your senses. That is, you will explore the raisin through sight, sound, texture, smell, and taste. While this may sound somewhat loopy, it never fails to open awareness to what actually occurs in the moments of eating!

As you will see, one of the central focuses of an informal practice is to slow the process down so that you can be fully aware and attend to whatever is occurring. The everyday practice of eating can, of course, apply to anything that you consume. For example, some would instead do this exercise with chocolate, and as a chocolate lover, I can certainly understand that preference. It is possible to extend this exercise beyond a simple raisin or piece of chocolate to an apple, snack food, or even an entire meal. However, a full meal will necessitate a considerable investment of time, so you need to plan accordingly. Therefore, I would not recommend beginning with an entire meal eaten in a slow and deliberate mindfulness manner with a house full of hungry grandkids! Over time, however, as your mindfulness skills develop, you will not have to take as much time to be attentive to the food and drink you consume. But for the moment, start small and very slowly.

Other daily activities ripe for use as informal practice exercises include brushing your teeth, washing the dishes (or even filling the dishwasher), raking leaves, weeding the garden, cleaning the bathroom, taking out the garbage, and so forth. The activity itself is not what is critical. Rather, any activity that allows you to slow down the process to experience it with your senses entirely is what makes it an informal mindfulness practice and, therefore, a good one to choose.

The instructions are the same for each activity:

1. Be aware of the steps involved.
2. Decide what the initial component of the first step will be.
3. Slowly begin working through each stage, focusing on your senses of sight, touch, hearing, smell, and (if appropriate) taste as these become your new, albeit temporary, anchor of awareness.

Be curious as to how you are experiencing each step through your senses. Take your time and be curious about this activity you could do in your sleep but want to approach with a beginner's mind as if undertaking it for the first time. Then, enjoy the process, knowing that it is another investment of your time and energy in becoming more mindful of your aging years.

INFORMAL BREATH AWARENESS

In addition to structured activities that provide tremendous opportunities for formal and informal mindfulness training, set an intention to be aware of your breath from time to time throughout the day. It does not have to entail lengthy periods but rather just a momentary noticing of your breath at that moment. Feel the breath rising and falling and be curious about what the breath feels like in that unique moment. It is also possible to use daily activities as triggers to remind yourself to notice your breath. This could entail when you get a coffee or tea, times when you are entering your home or office, times when you are stopped in your car at a red light. Again, the intent is not to take your full awareness off the situation you are in but rather to be curious about the breath in that particular moment.

Setting the intention to pay attention and be curious about the breath will strengthen your relationship with it at various times throughout the day.

PLEASANT EVENTS LOG

In addition to using formal and informal practices to deepen your mindfulness experience, it is vital to hone your awareness of recognizing that each moment throughout your day is an opportunity to be more fully attentive and conscious of what is occurring. One of the practice assignments for the coming week to emphasize this opportunity is to record at least one pleasant experience happening each day. Specifically, this exercise asks you to extend your awareness beyond formal and informal practices to your day-to-day existence. You will undoubtedly notice this is what the goal of mindfulness is—to be fully aware of what is occurring in your life on a moment-to-moment basis.

While you may initially believe this exercise to be a silly waste of your time since you, of course, know when pleasant events occur, I want to challenge your assumption. My experience as a psychologist working with clients is that the evolutionary imperative of focusing on the negative as a survival strategy is a compelling one that can often cause you to dismiss, diminish, or ignore positive experiences. While you no doubt are acutely aware of major positive events (such as the birth of a grandchild, the realization of a long-sought-after dream, acquisition of a significant object like a new car, etc.), there are likely many other, albeit more minor but still positive, events that occur daily.

Positive experiences can include an understanding look bestowed by a nurse during chemotherapy treatment, the invitation to go to the front of the checkout line because you only have a couple of items, a warm smile from a stranger, the cooing sound of a mourning dove, finding a long-sought-after item on sale, the sight of new buds on a tree, the laugh of a grandchild, and so on. So don't wait for the "big-ticket" happy events—be curious about what occurs in you, around you, and to you as you navigate through your day.

Since life encompasses 10,000 sorrows and 10,000 joys, you don't want to miss the good stuff! Neuroscientists tell us that being genuinely aware of the good things in life can affect the brain by generating positive neuroplasticity—laying down new neural pathways that carry a sense of inner happiness, strength, and resilience. Mindfulness provides an opportunity to be more consciously aware and better appreciate the small joys that can accrue daily.

The Pleasant Events log (accessed either at the end of this chapter or at the book's website) provides a convenient way to record such events during the following week. The log completed for the week is a vital extension of your formal and informal mindfulness practices. It is a reminder to pay attention to what you are experiencing as you go through your day. And it is imperative to be conscious and acknowledge that there are positive, albeit often tiny and transient, events that you experience.

PRACTICE OF THE WEEK

This week, as you expand your mindfulness awareness to other aspects of life, I invite you to try **three** different mindfulness exercises:

1. Formal Practice: Walking Meditation

Guidelines:

- Just as with the sitting meditation, choose a time that works for you—a time you know you will not be interrupted. Again, you may have to experiment with different times to find what works best for you.

- To keep the mindfulness strong, it is a good idea to focus your attention on one aspect of your walking rather than changing it repeatedly. So, if you decide to pay attention to your feet's sensation, stay with your feet for the entire walking meditation rather than partway through changing to focus on the legs' sense of moving.

- I recommend that you start walking slowly to focus your awareness on the specific sensations of movement in your feet. Then, over time, try different pacing to assess how strong your attention is.

- Walking meditation has often been called the "walk of the living dead" or "zombie walk." Since it looks weird to other people to just walk back and forth without any apparent purpose, especially if you are doing it slowly, you should do it someplace where you are not observed. Perhaps walk somewhere within your home or yard—I wouldn't recommend doing it at the local mall!

- I recommend exploring the different meditations by alternating the sitting and walking meditations for **thirty minutes, six days this week**. Spend the entire thirty minutes on either the walking or sitting meditation. Spending only a few minutes with one before changing to another makes it more difficult to stabilize the mind.

- However, if you find it physically challenging to do a full thirty minutes of walking meditation, by all means, split your meditation time between walking and sitting. I recommend that you decide in advance how many minutes you will do each rather than try and monitor your experience to inform your decision. If walking meditation is difficult, I would recommend only five or ten or fifteen minutes before changing to the sitting meditation.

- If your attention is pulled away from your anchor of awareness during your walking meditation, remember that your **first level of response** is to simply notice, label it, and return to your anchor of attention. However, if you experience intrusive and persistent thoughts, feelings, or physical sensations, then temporarily stop and use the **second level of response** strategy that you learned last week by temporarily moving your anchor of attention to the body sensation associated with the intrusion.

- Just as in the last session, you have the option of reading the instructions or listening to the audible presentation on the book's website www.embracingagingmindfully.com.

- Be sure to record your daily sessions on your **Tracking Your Practice** log under the Formal heading.

WALKING MEDITATION INSTRUCTIONS:

Begin by staking out your intended path. . . . You only need approximately five or six feet. . . . Stand comfortably at the beginning of your path. . . . Feel your body balanced while standing. . . . Bring to mind your intention before you start to walk . . . the intention to walk and be completely present and aware of knowing that you are walking . . . bringing to awareness the sensation of your feet moving through space as you navigate your short walking path. . . .

Hold your hands clasped either in front of you or behind the body. . . . The arms should not be swinging in counterpoise to the walking gait, as when walking to get somewhere. . . . Gaze out in front several paces with a soft focus to see without straining to look . . . not needing to gaze down at your feet . . . instead sensing where they are . . . knowing that your feet know how to walk. . . .

When clarity and focus are present, begin to take the first step sensing what is happening with your feet . . . start with focusing on your left foot. . . . Notice how the weight initially shifts onto your left foot. . . . Lift the right foot and hold it in the air . . . then move the right foot forward. . . . Before placing the right foot back down on the ground . . . hold that stance for a moment . . . then begin the next step with a shift of weight to your newly planted foot, your right foot. . . . Lift your left foot and hold it in the air . . . then move the left foot forward through space . . . before placing the left foot back down on the ground . . . attending to each step with openness, curiosity, and wonder . . . as if taking action is occurring for the very first time. . . .

To sharpen your concentration of focusing your attention on the sensation of your feet, when you lift the left foot, quietly say, "Lifting." . . . Hold your foot in the air for a moment and, when deciding to move it forward, say, "Moving." . . . Then when it is time to put your left foot down, say, "Placing." . . . The words typically used to sharpen your concentration are lifting . . . moving . . . placing. . . . However, you may decide there are different words that work better for you. . . . Experiment to see what is of assistance to maintain your anchor of attention. . . . The goal is to have your awareness focusing on the actual sensations of the body lifting, moving, and placing your feet. . . .

Continue to alternate each foot lifting . . . moving . . . placing . . . lifting . . . moving . . . placing . . . lifting . . . moving . . . placing . . . lifting . . . moving . . . placing. . . .

When you practise walking meditation, you are not trying to get anywhere. . . . To embody this intention, only walk for about five or six feet. . . .

This helps to put the mind to rest because it has no place to go. . . . Nothing interesting is happening to keep it entertained. . . .

On reaching the end of your defined path of five or six feet . . . stop. . . . Feel the sensation of resting on both feet . . . and after a moment or two, decide how you are going to make the turn. . . . There is no right or wrong way to make the turn. . . . It merely is a matter of being conscious and aware of the movements that you will engage in to do so. . . . Experiment. . . . Play with the actions. . . . Be mindful of the shift of weight from one foot to the other while turning. . . . Notice if your balance is challenged. . . . Just be aware of each movement during the turn . . . completing the turn to walk back down your short-defined path. . . .

Should your attention wander . . . apply your first level of response. . . . Simply notice this. . . . label it as a form of thinking, feeling, or body sensation . . . and without judgment, bring your awareness back again to the feeling of your feet . . . simply returning attention with your first level of response . . . beginning anew with the next step . . . and the next step. . . .

If during your meditation you experience intrusive and persistent thoughts, feelings, or physical sensations, use the second level of response by temporarily moving your anchor of attention to the body sensation associated with the intrusion. . . . Should you need to do this, stop walking and focus on the body sensation associated with the persistent intrusion. . . . In a curious manner, explore what body sensations are associated with the ongoing intrusion. . . . Take your time with this exploration and investigation. . . . When the intrusion has dissipated, bring your awareness back to the sensations in your feet. . . . Notice what it feels like to be held upright by standing on both of your feet . . . and when your attention is balanced and steady, return to your walking meditation practice. . . .

During the day, it would also be helpful to focus your attention while walking when going about your everyday business. . . . As noted earlier, it is not recommended that you would walk this slowly while in public . . . but even when walking at a more normal pace, you can bring your awareness and attention to the sensation of your body . . . to note your foot lifting . . . moving . . . placing . . . as you are walking with purpose to your destination. . . . It is this open awareness while engaged in daily activities that allow the mindfulness to not only strengthen but to also generalize to other areas of your life. . . .

Continue your walking practice until your timer signals the end of the session. . . .

2. Informal Practice: Mindful Eating

Guidelines:

- As an informal mindfulness practice, I invite you to eat mindfully. While you will likely benefit from eating mindfully through an entire meal, this can take quite a long time and may not be feasible in your home situation. Therefore, try it in different situations—perhaps while having a snack, or applying it to just part of a meal, or even just mindfully eating a few mouthfuls.

- No matter what you decide to eat while applying mindfulness, review these instructions before starting to remind yourself what you are looking to be mindful of—the different shapes, colours, textures, smells, sounds, and tastes of whatever you are putting in your mouth. Be curious as to whether the conscious food experience is any different from your usual eating patterns.

- You have the option of reading the instructions or listening to the audible presentation on the book's website, www.embracingaging-mindfully.com.

- Be sure to record your daily sessions on your **Tracking Your Practice** sheet under the Informal heading.

- Explore and enjoy!

MINDFUL EATING INSTRUCTIONS:

As a gentle reminder with all meditation practices, choose a time and place that works best for you. . . . Make sure you are comfortable and will be undisturbed for the duration of the meditation. . . .

Close your eyes for a few moments to prepare yourself for this meditation. . . . Become aware of your body . . . in this room . . . occupying this space . . . sitting on the chair . . . feeling the chair supporting and holding you . . . noticing your feet on the floor and the floor supporting your feet . . . and the earth supporting the floor . . . hands resting on your lap or your thighs. . . .

Pay attention to your breath as it flows in and out. . . . Allow your attention to be held by your breath. . . . These instructions will refer to a raisin as your object of awareness . . . but it could be any food that you choose to become your anchor of attention. . . .

Now open your eyes and take hold of one raisin or other food you will use. . . . Imagine that this is an object you have never seen before. . . . Allow your curiosity, awareness, and observation to be open to this new experience. . . .

Look at this raisin. . . . Pay close attention to see it. . . . Look at it carefully. . . . Perhaps hold it with your thumb and forefinger. . . . Notice the top and bottom . . . front and back. . . . What shape do you see? . . . Round? . . . Oblong? . . . What colour is it? . . . Perhaps brown? . . . Black? . . . Gold? . . . Maybe a combination of those colours. . . . Is it shiny or dull? . . . Do you see ridges or folds? . . . Maybe a stem? . . . Maybe not. . . .

Now let's close our eyes to see if that can enhance our other senses. . . .

Feel the raisin. . . . Is it squishy? . . . Dry? . . . Sticky? . . . Soft? . . . Hard? . . . Let your fingers fully sense what you are holding. . . . Explore its textures between your fingers. . . . Manipulate it with your fingers. . . . Do you notice any change in its shape or texture? . . . Does it feel cool . . . or warm . . . or maybe you feel no temperature? . . .

Notice what is going on in your mind while you are doing this. . . . Perhaps it is questioning . . . what is the point of this? . . . or judging that this is a strange thing I am doing . . . I'm not too fond of this or I like this. . . . Just note them as thoughts . . . and bring your awareness back to the object. . . .

Now smell the raisin. . . . Bring it up to your nose. . . . With each in-breath, thoroughly become aware of what you are noticing. . . . What do you smell? . . . Maybe earthy? . . . Sweet? . . . Salty? . . . Musty? . . . Maybe no smell at all. . . . Is there any reaction in your body to the scent of this object? . . . Perhaps you are starting to salivate. . . . Perhaps the smell brings up memories . . . pleasant . . . unpleasant. . . . No need to follow a memory . . . or a fantasy . . . just notice any reactions and then return to observe the raisin. . . .

Be curious about whether you can hear the raisin. . . . Bring it close to your ear. . . . Does it have a sound? . . . If you scrunch it near your ear . . . can you hear something? . . . Perhaps you feel silly listening to the raisin. . . . Just notice any sounds . . . thoughts . . . feelings . . . but not pulled into any story . . . just noticing and bring your awareness back to the item. . . .

Now gently place this food against your lips. . . . Is this felt sensation different from when you explored the raisin with your fingers? . . . When you are ready and without biting it, place this object in your mouth. . . . Resist the temptation to start chewing. . . . Just allow it to rest on your tongue. . . . Maybe move it to different parts of your mouth. . . . What do you notice? . . . Just explore the sensations of holding it in your mouth. . . .

Now, if you are ready and would like to . . . very slowly and gently bite into the raisin . . . just enough to break the skin of the raisin . . . and notice what happens. . . . What is the taste? . . . Sweet? . . . Tart? . . . Was it a burst or a gentle release of flavour? . . . Perhaps you like the taste . . . maybe not. . . . Slowly as you chew, become aware of your teeth coming together. . . . Notice the pieces of the raisin becoming smaller and smaller. . . . Notice the change of consistency of the raisin. . . .

And then consciously and with full attention, swallow the raisin. . . . Follow the sensations of ingesting as it enters the body. . . . Notice if the flavour lingers . . . then notice the absence of the food in your mouth. . . . Does the taste continue . . . or does the flavour dissipate? . . . What does the tongue do when the raisin is gone? . . .

Take a moment to savour the whole experience—all the senses that make up this one particular moment of eating just one single raisin!

3. Pleasant Events Log

Guidelines:

- To extend mindfulness beyond formal (such as sitting or walking) and informal practice sessions, I invite you to pay attention to your experiences each day. This week, the focus will be on pleasant events that you encounter.

- While you may initially believe this exercise to be a silly waste of your time since you, of course, know when pleasant events occur, I want to challenge your assumption.

- The goal of this exercise is to hone your awareness of small events that occur during your day.

- The log asks you to record the answers to the following questions:
    - What was your experience?
    - What physical sensations did you notice (if any) during this event?
    - What thoughts (if any) did you have at this time?
    - What emotions (if any) accompanied this occasion?
    - What made this a pleasant incident?

- I do **not** recommend that you record all this information as the event unfolds since this would take you out of the moment! Maintain your awareness and attention to the pleasant event itself as it evolves and hold the above questions in the back of your mind. Set your intention to put this information into your memory to be recorded later.

- There are no right or wrong events, thoughts, feelings, or body sensations you are mindful of. The purpose is to simply expand your awareness of the moments that arise each day and be consciously aware of those of a pleasant nature.

- The final box on the Pleasant Events log asks what may seem to be a rhetorical question but is a critical one—what made this a pleasant event? Was it the physical sensations? The thoughts? The emotions? Was it a combination of all of these? Was it a sense of being seen? Was it a sense of feeling appreciated? Was it a sense of accomplishment? You *did* make a judgment about this event, indicating that it was a positive one, so be curious to understand how you *know* that this was a pleasant event. This is not meant to question or undermine your judgment but rather to help you clarify how this judgment arose. It is an opportunity to explore and understand that you can respond instead of unconsciously react to whatever event presents itself to you.

- Try to avoid the easy and trite response ("Because it was pleasant!") and explore what specific aspects of this experience were pleasurable—expand your self-knowledge about how seemingly small and discreet events are part of your life. Life is made of 10,000 sorrows and 10,000 joys, so you do not want to miss the good stuff! Mindfulness provides an opportunity to be more consciously aware and better appreciate the small joys that can arise in each moment.

PLEASANT EVENTS

What was the experience?	What physical sensations (if any) did you notice in your body during this experience?	What thoughts (if any) did you have during this experience?	What emotions (if any) accompanied this event?	What made this a pleasant event?
MONDAY				
TUESDAY				
WEDNESDAY				
THURSDAY				

PLEASANT EVENTS

What was the experience?	What physical sensations (if any) did you notice in your body during this experience?	What thoughts (if any) did you have during this experience?	What emotions (if any) accompanied this event?	What made this a pleasant event?
FRIDAY				
SATURDAY				
SUNDAY				

MIDWEEK CUPPA... REFLECTIONS ON NON-JUDGING AND AGING

WEEK FOUR

William Shakespeare noted in his play, *As You Like It*, that in life "All the world's a stage," with old age bringing the "Last scene of all/ That ends this strange eventful history/Is second childishness and mere oblivion/Sans teeth, sans eyes, sans taste, sans everything" (2.7.166–169). While Shakespeare's summary is a theatrically bleak one, the reality is that diminishment of functioning is not easy to embrace, let alone accept.

As you may already have experienced, advancing years brings the possibility of a myriad of physical, cognitive, and emotional challenges that are not always readily welcomed. Nevertheless, the mindfulness focus on living in the present moment with an attitude of positive self-friendship can help take the sting out of such losses and is the continuing central focus of this book.

RIGIDITY AND CRITICALNESS

However, most of us have directly or indirectly encountered elders who seem to be experiencing a challenging time at this point in their life. Their agitated, perturbed, edgy, and restless countenance reflects the negative judgment that they bring to their world. Nothing seems right. They are easily critical of and quick to judge others' attitudes, beliefs, and behaviours. There is rigidity evident in the way they see and experience the world around them. There is less flexibility in understanding others because their beliefs and attitudes have seemingly ossified in their elder years. Their vitality dries up. Stereotypically, they are characterized as the "crotchety old man" or "withered old hag" of literature and film.

Unfortunately, such judging attitudes and behaviours may arise because of neurocognitive disease causing a confused awareness of reality and subsequent defensive rigidity, mistrust, and criticalness of others and the world. The fear that arises through diminishing cognitive capabilities can be incredibly distressing and frightening, resulting in the need for a compassionate caregiving environment.

However, outside of a neurocognitive disease etiology associated with older age, there are alternative understandings and explanations for an overly rigid and critical stance. For example, these severe and stern attitudes and behaviours can arise as a defence against accepting the inevitable changes—typically losses—that accompany advancing years. An angry assault toward life's "unfairness" quickly spills over to a rigid and critical stance directed toward everything and everyone encountered. As initially noted in Week Three and continuing throughout this book, the focus of mindfulness and its accompanying attitudinal foundations on a conscious acceptance of whatever arises presents a counterweight to negative self- and outer-directed judgments.

Week Three also introduced the personal shadow concept, the disowned or unacknowledged positive aspects of yourself that have laid buried beneath your consciousness. The exploration and acceptance of your disowned and unacknowledged inner constituents present the opportunity to expand your sense of self positively. To recognize that the life you have been living is mistakenly believed as the only one for you when, in fact, it is only a tiny and constricted version of your true potential.

PROJECTIONS

However, your personal shadow is more than the positive characteristics that were disowned or had gone unacknowledged. It also includes negative attributes, ones not considered worthy or ones that you would not be proud to own, and therefore, you do not even want to accept them as part of yourself. For example, rigidity and criticalness can be emblematic of your shadow, albeit aspects of a negative form. These negative shadow characteristics also live in the unconscious and therefore are ones that you do not recognize. Projecting these unwanted aspects of yourself onto others through emotionally charged rigid and critical reactions can protect these unwanted truths from consciousness. A recognition of engaging in critical and emotionally charged judgments about others provides the opportunity to assess what lies behind such seemingly "over the top" behaviours.

Examples of projections include Cleo being furious at the loud music coming from her neighbour's apartment. Jackson was livid with the congressman's negative characterization of his primary opponent. Liam was distressed that his friend did not show up as promised to help fix his car. Emma was enraged that the librarian did not let her know when her requested book became available. Finally, Sarah was fuming with the bus driver's dismissive and unhelpful directions about transfer points for connecting buses.

There may well be good reasons for emotional reactions to each of these behaviours. However, the degree of upset, the intensity of criticalness, and inflexible rigidity of the quick judgments flag each event as a potential projection of personal characteristics that you do not want to acknowledge. The passionate and vehement emotional reactions coupled with the quick and emphatic judgment of the neighbour to be inconsiderate, the politician to be intolerant, the friend to be unreliable, the librarian to be irresponsible, and the bus driver to be arrogant goes beyond the sting experienced at the moment by the other's behaviour. Instead, the "over the top" emotional reaction that lingers and will not quickly abate, fuelled by the dogmatic judgment of the other's inherent character flaws through a single behaviour, is usually a sign that a projection is alive and well.

WITHDRAWING PROJECTIONS

Withdrawing projections means, first of all, being aware that your reaction is beyond what the situation calls for. While the other's beliefs and actions can certainly arouse an emotional response, your felt and expressed rejoinder is simply too much. When you are aware of the inappropriate intensity and duration of your upset, the probing question to ask yourself is, "How am I like that? How am I inconsiderate/intolerant/irresponsible/arrogant or whatever your quick and pointed judgment of the other may have been?" An honest appraisal and self-reflection are the entry into exploring the unconscious negative shadow side of yourself.

While I've never met anyone who sincerely wants to be inconsiderate, intolerant, irresponsible, arrogant, or any of the thousand and one other negative character/behavioural attributes available to humans, the reality is that everyone does have the potential to act in such a manner. Like everyone else on this planet, you have the potential to hold such thoughts or express such actions, although just as noted in Week Three with Kate, this doesn't mean that you have to unleash them on others. Becoming aware of such beliefs or actions provides you with the gift of consciousness and the ability to respond instead of unconsciously react.

Meeting aspects of your negative shadow side can be humbling. The range of potential unsavoury, hurtful, and mean-spirited attributes that each of us possesses is not pleasant and, therefore, unwelcome. However, what is far worse is leaving them unexplored and thus submerged in your unconscious, as this only cultivates a fertile breeding ground for the lightning eruption of painfully critical reactions to others.

Recognizing that your negative shadow side is activated through your overcompensated reactions offers an opportunity to become aware of their existence. While the fallout from your unconscious negative shadow side can be evident at any age, holding and expressing such poisonous attitudes, beliefs, and actions can be incredibly destructive during your aging years. For example, the eruption of unconscious projections undermines your capacity to be present in this moment—it is like you are "possessed" by this defence mechanism that clouds your ability to fully experience each moment. In addition, the opportunity for more peaceful and harmonious relationships with others and especially with yourself, follow the conscious withdrawing of projections and the ongoing developing integration of all of who you are—the conscious and unconscious positive and negative shadow sides of your personality. Mindfulness, with its emphasis on non-judgment, supports this healthy personal development.

INTEGRATING YOUR SHADOW

Integrating shadow aspects of yourself is a lifelong process as there is a seemingly endless array of unconscious personal traits and qualities, including unwanted foibles, to uncover. However, after acknowledging and accepting that you have negative shadow characteristics, withdrawing projections presents a healthy inoculation against mindlessly unleashing rigid, critical, and potentially destructive words and actions. Knowing of the benefits accrued through withdrawing projections, the question becomes not should you do so, but rather if not now, when?

MINDFULNESS APPROACHES THE "WEIGHT AND PAIN OF LIFE"

WEEK FIVE

REVIEW LAST WEEK'S PRACTICES

It's impressive to see the difference seven days can make—at least in the mood generated by the mindfulness group as we met for Week Five. Almost halfway through the course, I could sense confidence coming alive in the room as I asked how their practice sessions had progressed. George was quick to recount that he thoroughly enjoyed the walking meditation, with it seeming easier to hold his anchor of attention while moving instead of sitting still. William liked walking in a wooded area, not because he focused on the surrounding beauty but merely through the sense of being held in the stillness of nature. Bernie echoed William's sentiment, often stopping before making his turn to close his eyes and become aware of the warm and satisfying deep inhale of a breath.

Even those who reported challenges with the exercise did so in a matter-of-fact, non-self-judging manner. For example, Betty noted that walking flared her arthritic hip pain, so she simply limited her walking time to ten minutes per session, followed by twenty minutes of sitting meditation.

Helen's childhood polio affecting her left leg made walking difficult, especially when she attempted to move slowly, so she found having her cane in hand proved critical for the slight off-balanced feelings that arose.

The difficulties reported with losing balance while walking slowly are common, so the remedy is to experiment to find the pace that allows you to move steadily while still able to notice the lifting, moving, and placing of each foot. The recommendation to slowly amble is simply to use your feet's sensation as your anchor of awareness—determining the specific speed is up to you. Be curious, however, as to what the awareness tipping point is: notice at what maximum speed you can maintain your attention on your feet's sensations and at what velocity you lose it.

However, the trophy for the most challenging week (if one were to be given) went to Sybil's dog, Cooper, who could not figure out what his owner was doing! As Sybil started her walking meditation, Cooper excitedly ran for the door expecting the treat of an outdoor walk only to have Sybil approach but then turn away from the door time and time again. Each day his hope and enthusiasm started expectantly high but gradually wore down to a resigned pout as Sybil's slow walk teasingly evaded the elusive door. Laying on the floor with his downcast eyes sadly tracking her every move, Cooper seemed unable to make sense of Sybil's behaviour. While Cooper eventually received his usual daily exercise, he likely continues to puzzle over what that slow walking was about!

Some in the group, echoing Cooper's apparent dislike, did not enjoy the walking meditation, while others preferred it over the sitting posture. These are only personal preferences so trust in what feels suitable for you. During longer meditation retreats, alternating sitting with walking meditations are the usual scheduled practice. The gift of sitting and walking meditations is that it provides you with options to participate in formal meditation practices.

What is so special about formal mindfulness practices? As previously mentioned, neuroscience has found that repetitively engaging in such practices lays down new neural pathways in the brain, positively affecting your developing mindfulness sensitivity. In other words, being mindful gets more accessible and rewarding with the more time you invest.

INFORMAL PRACTICES

Making the mindfulness practices work for you is what Betty did by reducing her walking time to manage her pain. If I had any doubts about whether others in the group would also take charge and flex their respective agency, I did not have to wait long, as they began sharing their informal mindfulness practices from the past week. While eating continued to be a popular exploration activity, with Beth noting that a simple lunch took just over an hour to consume mindfully, personal grooming was also trendy. This proved interesting because you will recall from the "Mind-Wandering" experiment reviewed in Week Two that personal grooming, such as showering, proved to be the most challenging activity to hold attention. Brushing teeth and washing hair, as well as luxuriously reclining in a hot bath, suddenly now became newfound experiences even though they had been undertaken thousands of times over the years.

However, Karl and Juanita independently discovered the winning informal activity of the week: mindful wine tasting! The smells and taste revealed through a focused awareness brought a cheeky chardonnay or a bold merlot to life in ways previously unnoticed by these self-described aficionados. By the nodding of heads, it was clear that many in the group made a mental note to "winefully" challenge their tastebuds in the weeks to come.

PLEASANT EVENTS

The playful spirit engendered within the group continued as they shared pleasant events captured during the past week. Sanjay spoke about receiving customer appreciation for going beyond what his job required; Malik enjoyed the sound of a woodpecker's determined quest for lunch; Cassie beamed with the laughter of her year-old grandson; Bethany chuckled heartily through her favourite TV sitcom; Darnell basked in the wonder of a full moon on a clear starry night; Carlos enjoyed his weekly bridge game night; Helen savoured a stranger's smile as they passed each other on the street; Josie welcomed a soft cool breeze on her face; and Karl delighted in a visit from an old friend.

However, the upbeat reporting of pleasant events gave way to a more sobering discussion, as many described the test to notice enjoyable events as they navigated personal difficulties. There was no denying that individual stresses, such as undergoing cancer treatment, grieving a spouse's loss after many years of marriage, adult children's addictions, financial insecurity, grandkids' school struggles, daily physical pain, loneliness, and depressed mood lived within the group. However, while undoubtedly a daunting task, holding the intention to notice the slightest positive experience was attainable. Notwithstanding meeting the assignment, Sam quickly pointed out that he never felt "over the moon" happy during the week, even as he could pinpoint pleasant moments. Ken spoke for others when he reported it felt "fake," seeking positive moments while struggling with his relationship issues.

The group concern was indeed valid—finding moments of pleasure is not a practical and long-term game plan to deny or avoid or numb yourself from difficult life experiences. But that is not what the pleasant event exercise and the more extensive process of mindfulness are offering—instead, this exercise and mindfulness itself is a reminder that life comprises 10,000 sorrows *and* 10,000 joys. Amid profound pain and suffering, life often presents what I call the "illusion of the moment," a false belief that the difficult time you are presently experiencing is all that is occurring and, in turn, available to you.

Instead, a grander array of thoughts, feelings, sights, sounds, sensations, and events continually play out alongside your present struggles. Some are positive, some are negative, and some are just neutral. Of course, you need to attend to the presenting issues of life—mindfulness is not petitioning you to abandon them in favour of a false cheeriness and good humour. Mindfulness is, however, offering you the awareness that life is not a dichotomous zero-sum game where everything is good or everything is terrible, life is fantastic or life is worthless. The middle path, the grey zone of life, is uncovered through mindfulness sensitivity by expanding your experience and awareness of what each moment offers.

For many in the group, the past week evoked considerable pain, loss, and sorrow. Yet, with the benefit of expanded and sharpened attention, they could experience at least one pleasant event each day. It may not sound like many—seven enjoyable moments in a week of difficulties—but it begins expanding your relationship to your life. It allows you to experience, not just read about, but experience the moments (albeit often quick and fleeting) of something other than ongoing struggles. Mindfulness did not create these pleasant moments, but it did help you to notice them.

This is not offered as a Pollyanna attitude; it is a realistic assessment that there is much playing out within you and around you that goes unnoticed. Mindfulness sensitivity allows you to begin expanding and developing trust to fully experience this life, all that this life of yours entails.

Therefore, this week's Pleasant Events exercise presented each group member the opportunity to meet time through the three invitations of awareness, experience, and relationship with discreet moments.

TRUST

In case you haven't noticed, it takes courage, a lot of courage, to meet each moment of your life in its entirety. Therefore, developing trust, a concept whose historical roots evoke images of confidence, reliance, and agreed-upon covenant becomes essential in honing a healthy stance to what arises in your awareness. Trust is so critical that it is one of the seven attitudinal foundations identified in establishing a non-judgmental relationship to each moment.

However, trust, especially trust in yourself, is a hard-won quest. As I'm sure you have all noticed, many, many voices are more than willing to tell you how to live your life! From parents, teachers, siblings, friends, supervisors, co-workers, authority figures, advertisements, and society in general, everyone seems to have an opinion about what you should do with this short life that is yours. Dictums as to what you should believe, pay attention to, feel, and perform run rampant through our Western culture.

And to be clear, it is imperative to listen and follow some of those views. As a society, we need to set and agree to abide by rules that allow for a more harmonious and safe existence. As a simple example, we all need to know and trust that drivers will stop at red lights. No matter how you may feel or what you would like to do as you approach a red light, the rest of us depend on you conforming to this agreed-upon rule of conduct. However, outside of society's regulations and laws, there can also seem like a chorus of voices petitioning distrust in yourself and bidding you to follow their dictates regarding living your everyday life.

Distrusting yourself can also live within the meditation field. Some schools of meditation are rigidly dogmatic that their way—and only their way—is the right way and must be followed. Some people who get involved in meditation believe their teacher's reputation and authority take precedent over their own beliefs, feelings, and behaviours. Submitting themselves to a teacher, belief system, or group dynamics can diminish their agency and control over their lives. Paradoxically, in an attempt to enjoy more freedom to be all of who they are, they end up losing themselves and, in the process, lose trust in their capacity to direct their lives.

An attitude of submission is antithetical to the spirit of mindfulness meditation and Jungian psychology, which emphasizes trusting that you can learn what it means to be yourself and that you can realize your potential. To give away your autonomy in a misguided attempt to find yourself is not a viable strategy.

Jungian psychology adamantly proffers that the reality of being human is that it is impossible to become like somebody else. Your life-long quest is to become more fully who you are, with much of that dependant upon your willingness to experience this life that is yours—that is the motivation for practising mindfulness meditation hand in hand with Jungian psychology. Know that teachers, books, and training retreats can be beneficial and supportive to your continuing development, but only as guides. As the philosopher Howard Thurman (1980) noted: "There is something in every one of you that waits and listens for the sound of the genuine in yourself. It is the only true guide you will ever have. And if you cannot hear it, you will all your life spend your days on the ends of strings that someone else pulls."

In developing mindfulness, you practise taking responsibility for being who you are as well as learning to listen to and trust in your own being. Each time you participate in formal and informal practices, you become your ongoing living experiment into your individuation, to become closer to who you are. Your awareness, experience, and relationship with all that arises within you and around you is your attending school. Is it easy? No! Does it go smoothly? No! Does it mean that you will do everything perfectly? Of course not! While I'm not even sure what "perfectly" looks like when it comes to living your life, learning any new skill means experiencing successes as well as failures. But to embrace the intention of developing a sense of trust in YOU, recognizing that this is not a static goal but a lifelong process, is worthy of pursuit.

YOUR RELATIONSHIP WITH TRUST

Through mindfulness and Jungian psychology, trust development is understood, supported, and shaped primarily in three ways. The first is that trust in yourself means learning to meet and hold thoughts, feelings, body sensations, and experiences healthily. Trust embodies the intention to become a better friend to yourself as you are more able to embrace the vulnerability that accompanies this life. Will this be easy—a walk in the park? No, it definitely won't! The 10,000 sorrows and challenges that we will each meet are not easy, including the mighty ones of grief and pain and sorrow. Accepting that this is part of life and learning that you can trust yourself to be *with* such challenges is a tremendous gift.

The second enrichment is through learning to trust that everything is changing. Through formal and informal mindfulness practices, you become aware and viscerally experience that you and the world and everything in it are in constant change, which helps generate a healthier relationship to all that you meet. Knowing through experience that everything does change, even though it can sometimes feel like the world is stuck on hold, makes it easier to be with the challenges that life presents since you are able to trust that even troublesome provocations will shift and alter over time. This embodied knowing strengthens your resilience and tolerance for the inevitable difficulties that will arise. As Jon Kabat-Zinn has said: "As long as you are breathing, there is more right to you than wrong!"

The third enhancement to your development is that cultivating trust in yourself naturally spills over to trust others. As you explored in Weeks Three and Four, trust in yourself means that you do not have to live under the influence of unconscious personal shadows, which also means withdrawing projections that you have placed on others. You can experience not only yourself but others with more clarity and integrity, leading to more harmonious and satisfying relationships.

Trust is, therefore, a critical attitudinal foundation to hold close while developing your mindfulness practice. And as you will soon learn, creating trust within yourself is essential when undergoing inevitable complex human experiences of physical and emotional pain.

THE EXPERIENCE OF PAIN

You will find as you move into the experience of pain with mindfulness meditation, all the attitudinal foundations that we have reviewed (acceptance, non-judging, beginner's mind, trust) are crucial to hold close. As noted in earlier sessions, Jon Kabat-Zinn's first mindfulness program at the University of Massachusetts Medical Center invited patients who had to endure and manage chronic conditions like untreatable pain, diabetes, or heart disease. Kabat-Zinn never claimed that he could cure such diseases. Instead, his mission was to improve the quality of patients' lives.

It is perhaps trite to say, but as a society, we seem to have an aversion to pain, even to the thought of pain or discomfort. This antipathy appears to be why we so quickly reach for medicine as soon as a headache comes on or why we shift our posture as soon as a slight muscle ache generates some discomfort. I have recently seen statistics indicate that the United States makes up only approximately five percent of the world's population and yet uses fifty percent of the prescription medication to treat pain.

STRATEGIES TO DEAL WITH PAIN

How to meet the "weight and pain of life," as the ancient Greek playwright Sophocles characterized our human existence, has been a topic of study for millennia. An overview of the more recent research indicates three main categories or strategies for dealing with ongoing physical pain. The first is *direct intervention*: medication to dull the pain, body movement (walk-off tightness or stiffness), massage, and so on. These are direct interventions through the body in an attempt to lessen pain. The second approach is *moving away* from the experience of pain. This would include distractions (doing another activity to try and get your awareness off the pain), imaginational interventions (guided meditations bringing to mind a different and more pleasant experience), or just trying not to experience what you are experiencing (ignoring pain). The third approach is *moving toward* the pain (holding an awareness of it), and this is where mindfulness comes in.

Contrary to the other two approaches, mindfulness embraces the third strategy by proposing that an effective method to deal with pain is being fully present with the experience. To meet pain directly is what C.S. Lewis observed as the only option: "Pain insists upon being attended to." To focus your awareness on the bare sensations of the pain, not indulging in the stories or judgments that you can generate about the pain, spawns a practical and effective attitude of being a curious explorer of this sensation.

There is a place for all three strategies dealing with chronic pain, but as usual, the key is holding the wisdom to know when each is utilized best. However, I should note that several laboratory experiments of acute pain found that more awareness strategies (moving toward) effectively achieve pain management in the long run. In contrast, distraction strategies (moving away) are less effective. It turns out that "tuning in trumps tuning out" is a successful long-term strategy. However, I still believe that sometimes distractions are beneficial, especially when starting to work with pain through a mindfulness strategy. It can feel empowering to have options when working with such a powerful experience as pain.

IT DOESN'T REMOVE THE BIOLOGICAL CAUSE

However, it is essential to recognize that no research to date has found that meditation produces clinical improvements in chronic pain by removing the biological cause of the pain. Instead, the relief comes in how people relate to the pain.

At this juncture, I could see more than one group member with a quizzical look wondering, if mindfulness meditation does not remove the biological cause of pain—the body's nerve receptors still fire in response to painful stimuli—how can this practice be of assistance? The short answer is we do not fully understand precisely why this turning toward the painful experience can produce a different response to the painful stimuli. But we do have some research that can open a few doors in our understanding of it.

A study done at the University of Wisconsin by Dr. Ritchie Davidson (Goleman 2017) brought together a group of experienced meditators (long-term practitioners with many years of training) as well as a meditation-naive group who over the course of a week learned an attentional stance of letting go of whatever experience arose. All subjects had a thermal stimulator attached to their wrist, which generates considerable burning pain without causing damage to the body. They were advised that the experiment was about pain and that they would get a ten-second warning (by feeling slight warming of the plate) before they received a ten-second blast from the fiery gadget. After the ten-second painful burning stimulus, the heat would subside and they would get a ten-second recovery period before starting again. In essence, ten seconds' warning, ten seconds' blast of unmistakable heat intensity, and ten seconds' recovery. All the subjects were in an MRI scanner to see how their brains would react.

When the plate warmed a bit with the control group, which was the cue that pain was coming, their brains showed activation throughout the brain's pain matrix (cognitive, sensory, and emotional), as if they were already feeling the severe heat. Their reaction to the "as if" pain—known as anticipatory anxiety—was so fierce that their pain matrix activation only became slightly more robust when the actual painful burning sensation began. Interestingly, after the heat subsided in the ten-second recovery period, that matrix remained almost as active, indicating no immediate recovery recorded in their brain even though the burning stimulus had stopped. Their brains were still registering pain even though the cause of the pain had been eliminated.

The experienced meditators, on the other hand, had a very different response in this cycle. For them, their pain matrix showed little change in activity when the plate warmed, even though they knew that severe pain was only ten seconds away. Their brains seemed to register that cue with no compelling reaction evoked. The meditators' brains showed enhanced responses through the actual moments of intense heat, mainly in the sensory areas that received stimuli, such as tingling, pressure, high heat, and so on, where the hot plate rested on their wrist. The pain matrix's emotional regions activated somewhat but not to the degree of the sensory circuits. After the heat stopped, all the areas of the experienced meditators' brain pain matrix quickly reverted to their levels before the pain cue, much more rapidly than was the case for the controls. For these experienced meditators, recovery from pain was strikingly swift, almost as though nothing much had happened at all.

So, what does this tell us about pain and the role that mindfulness can offer? It is clear that the meditators did feel the pain—it was not as though they had shut down their bodies to avoid experiencing the painful sensations. But what this suggests is that mindfulness can bring about a lessening of the psychological component—like the worry you feel in anticipation of pain—that accompanies a decrease in the intensity of the pain sensations themselves. The brain's pain receptors are still firing but without the added psychological components that can multiply this potentially distressing experience.

EMOTIONAL REGULATION AND PAIN

This sequence of anticipation-reactivity-recovery gives us a window on emotional regulation and the role it performs in your experience of painful stimuli. For example, intense worry about something like an upcoming painful medical procedure can cause you anticipatory suffering—just imagining how bad you will feel can get the brain's circuitry to fire as if the actual pain sensation was happening. As the control group experienced, you can also continue to be upset by what you have gone through after the real painful event. In this sense, your pain response can start well before and last well after the actual agonizing moments, which the control group experienced.

FEAR OF PAIN

One of the biggest obstacles to accepting pain is the fear that it will not only be unremitting but that it will also increase. I know this firsthand from what I experienced during my first ten-day silent meditation retreat over thirty years ago. After several days of alternating sitting and walking meditation, I could not ignore the considerable pain in my knees and hips. When I explored not only the physical sensations but also the thoughts that went with it, I found that my mind (just trying to be helpful, I'm sure!) expressed the concern that if the pain is this bad at this moment, what is it going to be like in the next five minutes? Or ten minutes? Or God forbid, even fifteen minutes? The fear of future pain experience added to the muscle tension and tightness that I was already experiencing. When I could let those thoughts go—to simply notice them but not fall into the story of anticipated spiralling discomfort, then the pain experience changed for the better. Not that it dissolved entirely, but the pain certainly lessened and left me with not only more comfort at the moment but a valuable lesson that I have never forgotten.

I am certainly not alone in this fear of pain, as evidenced by an interesting study investigating this concern. Researchers (Goleman 2017) inserted a subject's hand in ice water to induce pain—make no mistake, while this can be harmless, it can really hurt! When advised that they had to keep their hand in the water for ten minutes and asked to rate their pain after twenty seconds, most subjects reported that the pain was already intense and didn't think they could complete the experiment. Conversely, if the researchers told the subjects that they would have to keep their hand in the water for only thirty seconds and asked them to rate their pain after twenty seconds, most reported that the pain was relatively mild. The anxiety about being subjected to not only ongoing but increasing pain boosts the intensity of the present pain sensations.

The takeaway from these studies and my experience demonstrates that it is possible to change from a *reaction* to a *response* in reference to painful sensations. The long-term meditators were able to respond to pain as though it were a more neutral sensation. In more technical language, their brains showed a "functional decoupling" of the higher and lower brain regions that register pain—while their older, lower sensory circuitry felt the pain, their newer, higher brain functions did not react to it as much. Our expectations, fuelled by stories and emotions laying out the worst-case scenarios, are potent triggers to our experience of pain. This makes it clear that it is not just the actual pain sensory receptors that register what we are experiencing; it is the added cognitive and emotional components that can determine what we experience.

BRAIN NETWORKS

Another avenue of research that can help us understand what happens with mindfulness meditation is through the work of Dr. Norm Farb (2007) at the University of Toronto. His studies have shown various brain networks for different self-referencing styles and how you understand your moment-to-moment experience. One network termed the narrative focus (NF) is active when building a story based on your experience. It is a very chatty and busy network involving a considerable amount of thinking, wondering, analyzing, remembering what happened to you in the past, projecting what could happen to you in the future, and an array of emotions. A second network, termed the experiential network (EF), is active when grounded in what is experienced in the present moment. This network fires when you are very much in the body and attentive to the unfolding sensory experience without all the evaluations, memories, stories, and fantasies associated with the narrative network.

The difference in these networks can be related to viewing sports on TV. I grew up watching hockey on Saturday nights and understand the experiential focus to be aware of what is taking place on the ice through my sensory attention to the game itself. If I could turn the sound down on the commentators, I watch the players' movement of the puck from one end of the ice to the other, hear the crash of bodies into the boards, witness occasional fisticuffs when tempers flare, and behold the roar of the crowd and see the flash of a red light when a goal is scored. Suppose I turn up the volume on the TV to bring in the commentators. In that case, the narrative focus adds the non-stop overlay of information, including relaying the play-by-play happenings on the ice and judgments, side stories, projections, banter, and so on offered by the commentators. The narrative focus is the story generator; not satisfied with trusting your own experience of the game, it presents a never-ending cacophony of information.

Norm Farb's (2007, 2012) research found that people who train in mindfulness showed increased activity in the experiential focus network and decreased activity in the narrative focus network. It shows that mindfulness training can influence how the brain processes your moment-to-moment experience—how you experience your life unfolding and what you tell yourself about it. Mindfulness allows you to trust and rest in your experiences alone, not requiring the narrative focus's chatter through memories, fantasies, analysis, or judgments. The research found that this change in the brain's experience correlated with positive self-reports from the participants—overall, they reported improved emotional regulation and quality of life as they were calmer, happier, and felt more positively alive when spending more time in the experiential focus.

NEED FOR BOTH NETWORKS

But it's important to recognize that the experiential focus is not superior to the narrative focus—both are necessary to live an integrated and balanced life. However, when the narrative focus predominates—especially out of your awareness of it happening—it can hijack how and to what you attend, which in turn influences your awareness and understanding of moment-to-moment experience. It simply gets too loud, drowning out your actual sensory awareness of each moment. It is like an excessive focus on taking the perfect photograph so that you will recollect your holiday instead of attending to the actual moments as they unfold, trusting that these embodied memories will be of more value.

The narrative focus network has become the more prevalent of the two and therefore has been labelled as the default network. Some studies have identified the default network as the cerebral cortex area (newer part of the brain) that is most active when "not doing anything." Therefore, it is a misnomer to say that your mind is "blank" when you are just hanging out and not engaged in any task. Instead, underneath your conscious awareness, your narrative network is alive and firing a continuous stream of thoughts, feelings, and sensations, which, upon further exploration, turn out to be of little value. It fills the time and space of your life with judgments, commentary, fantasies, and memories. However, upon reflection, they are rightly seen only as worthless shiny objects, pulling your attention here and there like the laser beam's grip over the cat's uncontrollable behaviour.

The more you can train yourself to live your experience in the present moment without evaluating or judging it so quickly, the more you allow yourself to rest mindfully and trust in your own sensory experiences. There are, of course, times when you need your narrative focus to kick in, such as when you need to assess situations, solve a problem, plan for the future, or compensate for past actions. However, to be able to shift into the narrative network when it is appropriate and not have your life hijacked by it does appear to be a healthier way of being.

PAIN STUDIES

It is essential to preface the need for pain treatments by noting that debilitating pain is one of the most often reported fears of getting old since it can affect your independence. Therefore, pain is a significant issue to be conscious of as you age!

There have been numerous studies about pain treatment through mindfulness meditation, including with aging clients. The takeaway from the research is that mindfulness can have a positive effect on the experience of pain. Specifically, there is a lessening of the psychological components and the strength of pain sensations that makes the experience more tolerable. Mindfulness will not eliminate physical pain, but it does have a positive effect on your relationship to this unwanted experience. The importance of continuing practice became evident as the more often participants used mindfulness on their own, the better they did. While they continued to experience pain, their relationship to their pain changed for the better, which improved their quality of life. For a comprehensive review of the research, I would recommend the book titled *Altered Traits* by Daniel Goleman and Richard Davidson (2017) listed in the Reference and Resource section.

WORKING WITH PAINFUL SENSATIONS

As an instructor, it is imperative to "read the room," which means knowing when to stop recounting evidence to convince participants of the value of mindfulness and instead teach the skills needed for them to enjoy the benefits. So, when I asked the group if they were ready to experience the magic behind the science of mindfulness, I was not surprised when they responded with enthusiasm. While I used the word "magic" in jest, it was probably ill-conceived, for my extended thesis was to emphasize an opposite explanation for mindfulness's effectiveness. Instead of considering mindfulness to be some artifact of new-age mumbo-jumbo, it has a demonstrably solid foundation evidenced through neuroscience research. I believed that it was the appropriate time to provide the group with an understandable rationale supporting what they had been practising and what they were now entering with the experience of pain.

PAIN IS NOT GOING TO EVAPORATE

To set the stage for a mindfulness perspective, I began by emphasizing that it is not helpful to expect ongoing chronic pain to disappear. As reviewed above, there is no research indicating that mindfulness can take away the sensory experience of pain. Instead, it is more helpful to know several ways to *work with* painful sensations in the body. This perspective can have a beneficial effect on your relationship with, and therefore your experience, of pain.

Mindfulness meditative techniques vary depending upon the degree and chronicity of pain, but they all share this same basic premise of not expecting the pain to disappear. It is important to remember that the work of mindfulness is not meant to be a battle between you and your pain, and it doesn't have to be unless you make it into one. I may not be capable of picking winning lottery numbers, but I know that it will only make for greater tension and, therefore, likely more pain if you make it a struggle.

ACCEPTANCE OF WHAT?

Mindfulness involves a determined effort to *observe and accept* your physical discomfort and any attached agitated thoughts or emotions, moment by moment. The basic attitudinal foundation is an acceptance that, yes, you are experiencing a painful sensation but you can work with it. Your task is to explore your pain, learn from it, and know it better, rather than a misguided attempt to stop it or escape from it. A critical aspect of the mindfulness approach to pain is a lessening of the narrative we construct about it and an increase of the experiential experiences themselves. In other words, our relationship with pain changes with a corresponding alteration of our attention to the bare sensations we are experiencing.

The mindfulness programs for working with the pain experience express that you are "putting out the welcome mat" to describe your intended attitude with pain during meditation. Since the pain is already present in a particular moment, you do what you can to be receptive and accept it. It doesn't mean that you have to like it; instead, it means only that you acknowledge that there is a pain! We try to relate to it in as neutral a way as possible, observing it non-judgmentally, feeling what it viscerally feels like in great detail. This strategy involves opening to the raw sensations themselves, whatever they may be.

FIRST LEVEL RESPONSE

In terms of specific strategies that you can use with mindfulness for pain, you have already been doing the first level of response since Week Two. That is, to simply notice any discomfort in the body as a physical sensation, label it, and return your focus of attention to your anchor, whether that is your breath or hand sensation. The feelings of discomfort simply become another momentary experience that you can be aware of and not focus on.

SECOND LEVEL RESPONSE

When discomfort or pain becomes strong enough to pull your attention away from your anchor persistently—you essentially become hijacked by disturbances and pain can certainly be a powerful one—you can make a conscious decision to now use the intrusive painful body sensation as your temporary anchor of awareness. As you learned in Week Three, this second level of response means focusing your attention on the painful body area and allowing it to be your new but temporary focus of attention. You become very curious and precise about what the visceral experience is—you are not interested in thinking about the pain or your feelings about the pain, which is usually some version of "I don't want it—take it away."

Instead, your mission is to focus on the pain sensation's quality. As you learned in Week Three, explore whether it is tight, throbbing, aching, steady, pulsating, burning, stinging, itching, numbing, pins and needles, pulling, sharp, jabbing, shooting, electric, and so on. Is the temperature a hot or cold sensation? Is the pain dull, excruciating, gripping, inflamed? The goal is again to focus your attention in a laser-like manner on the pain sensation itself. Locating exactly where the pain is and with your attention focused on it, does the area of pain expand? Contract? Stay the same? Does the experience of the pain change with your focused awareness?

And what you will often experience is that the pain sensation lessens, moves to another part of the body, or dissipates. When pain is no longer hijacking your focus, simply bring your attention back to your primary anchor of awareness: your breath or hand sensation.

Notwithstanding the above-noted strategies, I have found that many people need to start their mindful relationship to the raw experience of pain in an even slower and gentle manner. Pain is powerful and needs to be respected but not feared.

THIRD LEVEL RESPONSE

In an accepting and considerate manner, the third level of response for working with intense pain sensations is to intentionally move your awareness from your usual anchor site (breath or hand sensation) to the area of the pain sensation itself. Once you know the place that holds the pain, direct the breath or hand sensation right into that region. For example, if you are using your breath as your anchor, with the in-breath, feel it coming through that painful area, and on the out-breath, feel it leaving from that same painful area. In this way, you are coupling the breath with the sensations in the region that is painful and allowing your awareness to hold them both simultaneously. Continue breathing in and out through the painful area, moment by moment, as best you can. You are allowing the breath to bathe that region with the incoming breath and then wash it away with the out-breath. The painful area and the breath become your anchor of awareness.

If using your hand sensation as your anchor, move your hand to the place in your body where you are feeling your pain. Once you have moved your hand to the body's area holding your pain, continue to use your hand sensations there as your anchor. Feel your fingers/hand on your body/ clothing at the pain site—experiment with alternating the pressure or movement to hold your awareness of both the pain and your hand sensations at the same time. You are coupling the hand sensations with the feelings in the painful region and allowing your awareness to hold them both simultaneously. Your attention is on your pain and hand sensations without judging, analyzing, or feeding them with stories.

It again is essential to recognize that you are *not trying to take the pain away.* You are utilizing a new, albeit temporary, anchor of attention to simply experience the sensation of the breath washing in and washing out like the waves of the ocean or your changing hand sensations against your body. As best you can, and with the lightest of touches, stay with this experience—watch what happens—see how it unfolds moment to moment.

This third level of response allows you to embody the process of befriending your pain. With time and practice, the pain will often slowly change and become more manageable. Yes, there may still be pain, but you learn that you can alter your relationship to it!

FOURTH LEVEL RESPONSE

When the pain experience is significant, a fourth level of response recognizes that it can be horribly difficult to hold any continuing focused awareness because of the sensations. Resorting to utilize the fourth level of response is not judging your capabilities; it simply accepts the pain experience's powerful and complicated nature. The degree of heightened pain is what it is at this moment.

The fourth level of response honours the experience by approaching your relationship to the pain very slowly. It starts with your intention to focus on only one half-breath or one sensation of your hand on your body. That is, knowing that the pain is so intense that it continuously pulls your attention away from attempting to use your anchor (for example, your breath), consciously decide that you are going to have your attention focused on only a singular moment. Specifically, you decide that your attention will focus on just the next in-breath—not the in-breath and out-breath, but only the in-breath. It is a recognition that severe pain requires small steps in your mindfulness practice. Your attention can then be drawn back to the pain, but it establishes that you could focus your attention on just one half-breath—just the in-breath—even with the significant pain you are experiencing.

If you can do this, try extending the focus to one whole breath. That is, knowing that the pain sensations can incessantly hijack your attention, make it your objective to now shift your focus to just one in-breath and one out-breath as your anchor of attention. We know that the powerful feelings can then pull your attention back to the pain, but you again have shown that you can focus your attention for just one breath. The goal is to continue then increasing the breaths on which you can concentrate. To not rush the process but to simply add a half-breath each time.

If you are using your hand on your body as your anchor of awareness and find the pain experience is significant, make it your intention to focus on only one sensation of your hand on your body. Knowing that the pain is so intense that it pulls your attention away from attempting to use your anchor (in this case, your hand on your body), consciously decide that you are going to have your attention focused on just that one hand sensation. Your attention may then be drawn back to the pain, but it establishes that you could focus your attention on one hand sensation, even with the significant pain you are experiencing.

When you can do this, try extending the focus to two hand sensations. Again, knowing that the pain captures your attention, make it your intention to shift that focus for just two hand sensations as your anchor of attention. We know that the powerful feelings can then pull your attention back to the pain, but you again have shown that you can focus your awareness on two hand sensations. The goal is to continue increasing the number of hand sensations that you can hold in your attention. To not rush the process but to simply add a hand sensation each time.

Over time, it also establishes more of a sense of trust in yourself, knowing that you can touch or be with—even for the briefest of moments—the experience of pain. Trust that this seemingly minor process can change your awareness, experience, and relationship with pain that will not disappear magically.

JUDGING MIND

As you work with pain in small incremental qualities of breath or hand sensations as the anchor of your attention, be aware of the thoughts and feelings that can arise. The judging mind can be especially punitive in beating you up for the limited breaths or hand sensations you could focus on. Again, as with other mindfulness practices, simply acknowledge and label "judging" and continue back to the practice. The intention is to be in this moment and experience the capacity to intentionally focus on the breath or hand sensation as your anchor of attention, even if only for one half-breath or one hand sensation.

BEFRIENDING YOUR PAIN

It is also essential to once again emphasize that you are not trying to take the pain away—you are just experiencing your anchor's sensation (breath or hand sensation) amid painful experiences. As best you can, and with the gentlest of effort, stay with this experience. Be curious as to what happens, seeing how the pain experience, and your relationship to it, unfolds moment to moment.

This process allows you to begin a process of befriending your pain, of putting out the welcome mat for unwanted sensations, even very intense ones, and see what happens when you invite them into your field of awareness along with your anchor. This practice is what the thirteenth century poet, Rumi (1995), invites you to do with all emotions in the poem, "The Guest House,": "A joy, a depression, a meanness, some momentary awareness comes as an unexpected visitor. Welcome and entertain them all!"

The mindfulness process becomes a marvellous opportunity of working with your pain rather than walling it off or ignoring it or being overwhelmed by it. It is the ideal opportunity to cultivate greater awareness and intimacy with the pain. And why is this important? Simply because the pain is already here in the form of intense and unwanted sensations, so turning away from it or even trying to distract yourself from it isn't an effective long-term strategy.

Over time, you might notice that your pain does not stay the same—that it is not a monolith, and changes in intensity, in quality, even in the body's location at times. Sometimes these changes are experienced moment to moment, hour by hour, or even day by day, in ways that you can become more sensitive to and learn from.

Strange as this may sound, studies have shown that a practical and effective approach, especially with intense pain sensations, is to go right *into* them with full awareness. Even if you can hold your full attention only for the briefest moment or glimpses—even for just one breath or hand sensation—whatever you can manage—you demonstrate to yourself that you can have a different relationship with painful experiences.

The research of mindfulness with pain experience indicates that having a method individuals can use on their own to ease their pain gave those patients a sense of "self-efficacy," a feeling that they can control their destiny to some extent. Having a process that you can use on your own, even to *touch* your pain—to be with it for even a brief time—can provide you with the realization that you can have a different relationship with your pain experience. This sense of agency over your life, in that you are not just a helpless recipient of the body's sensations, supports living better with pain that won't go away.

Mindfulness intervention with pain supports establishing a relationship of being a better friend to yourself. Through not only your increased capacity to be with pain but notably through the attitudinal foundations (acceptance, non-judging, beginner's mind, and trust) you have reviewed to date as well as the additional ones to be explored in later sessions, mindfulness provides you with a healthier and more resilient way of being.

PRACTICE OF THE WEEK

This week, I am again recommending **three mindfulness practices**: 1) Continue with the **formal meditation practice**; 2) Experiment with **informal practices**; 3) Use the **Unpleasant Events Log** to further strengthen your capacity to notice and hold whatever arises.

1. Formal Meditation Practice: Pain

Guidelines:

- This week, I recommend that you increase your daily formal meditation practice to **thirty-five minutes each day**. I encourage you to continue to try alternating sitting and walking meditations to see what works best for you. However, spend the entire thirty-five minutes on either the walking or sitting meditation. Spending only a few minutes with one before abruptly changing to another makes it more challenging to stabilize the mind.

- Pain is a compelling physical, emotional, and cognitive experience, so it is critical to approach it with respect and self-compassion. We have explored several mindfulness levels of response strategies these past few weeks, and today's practice will walk you through the process of trying all of them. As with all practices, simply allow yourself to experience what you experience without judgment or expectation. There is no right or wrong to what you experience.

- As with all the homework assignments, you can use either the written or audible guided instructions on the book's website before starting the practice. This week's instructions review all four response levels to remember and be comfortable knowing the optional responses you have to intrusive and persistent pain. However, utilizing either the written or audible instructions each day this week could be more than what is needed and prove intrusive if you do not require all four response levels.

- Therefore, as a suggestion, listen to the audible instructions or read the written ones enough times to feel confident that you know each level of response. Then, engage in your practice session on your own to be more in control of implementing specific strategies that you require. For example, you may meet pain with a Level One response or a Level Two. However, you may need to increase your responses to Levels Three or Four, depending upon your pain experience. Knowing your options and then engaging in your practice session provides the freedom to choose what is needed. You decide—play with how it best works for you!

- Remember to record your homework on your **Tracking Your Practice** log under the Formal heading. This will allow you to track your sessions and experiment with what time of the day works best for you and reinforce your efforts. Learning any new skill can be tricky, so use the tracking sheet as a motivator to pat yourself on the back for the investment of your commitment, time, and effort!

FORMAL MEDITATION INSTRUCTIONS (PAIN):

Let's begin. . . . Gently close your eyes. . . . Allow your attention to come into this space, letting go for a little while of your to-do lists, any expectations, and the need to change or alter what is happening at this moment. . . .

Now bring your attention to your body; notice your feet on the floor . . . notice where your hands are . . . maybe resting on the thighs, folded together on your lap, or at your sides. . . .

Now allow your attention to find your anchor. . . . It may be your breath. . . . Notice where in the body you feel it . . . perhaps the tip of the nose . . . the nostrils . . . the back of the throat . . . the chest . . . the belly. . . . Just notice that sensation. . . . Connect to the feeling of breath and the spot within your body where you feel it most. . . .

Or perhaps your anchor is the sensation of your hand where it touches your body . . . where you feel the texture of the fabric under your fingers . . . or the smoothness of your skin under your hand. . . . Allow this to become the anchor of your attention . . . recognizing the sensation of your fingers as they move against your skin or clothing . . . or the sensation of increasing pressure. . . .

Know that these sensations can support you as you travel through your days. . . . Know that at any time when your mind has wandered into thoughts, feelings, or body sensations, the breath or the touch of your hand will bring you back into this precious, present moment. . . .

. . . .

First Level of Response

If you find that your attention has been hijacked by a painful sensation or a thought or feeling associated with pain . . . and you have lost the breath or the touch of your hand as the anchor of attention . . . then notice it. . . . label it as just that . . . a thought, a feeling, or a physical sensation . . . and then gently and without judgment, bring your awareness back to your anchor of attention . . .

. . . .

Second Level of Response

If you find it difficult to return to your anchor because the physical sensation of pain or thought or feeling associated with pain has become too strong or too intrusive and has captivated your awareness, then allow your attention to temporarily find where in the body that intrusion resides. . . .

Locate the area of your body where you experience the pain. . . . The pain can, of course, be anywhere in this bag of bones that comprise your physical body, so be specific in identifying exactly where the pain resides. . . .

Without attaching a story to the physical sensation, just become curious as to where you feel it in the body. . . .

As you locate the body area that holds the pain, become very curious about the physical sensations. . . . What are they like? . . . Is there tightness? . . . Clenching? . . . Pressure? . . . Burning? . . . Throbbing? . . . Stabbing? . . . Is this sensation localized or does it radiate in a direction? . . . Outward? . . . Inward? . . . Is there a warmth or a coolness? . . . Is it big? . . . Small? . . . Can you sense a shape . . . or a density of the pain? . . . Continue to hold your attention and explore in minute detail the sensations associated with the pain in your body. . . .

As you explore the pain, perhaps you notice that it has moved. . . . sometimes in a dramatic manner to another part of the body or sometimes just a slight shift in location. . . . Continue to track and explore the pain sensations. . . . Like a dog who won't let go of a bone, hold on and don't let your attention be pulled away from your pain exploration, no matter where it may have migrated. . . .

Over time, as your attention has been exploring the painful body part . . . perhaps you notice that the sensation is somewhat dissipating . . . lessening in intensity. . . . If so, then once again, allow your breath or the pressure of your hand upon your body to become the anchor of your attention . . . the gentle in and out, rising and falling of the breath . . . or the movement or intensity of the pressure from your fingers or hand where they are in contact with your body. . . .

These Level Two strategies can also be applied to persistent and intrusive thoughts or emotions associated with pain. . . . Use the same process you learned last week to locate the thought or feeling in the body. . . . Become a curious explorer of the body sensations associated with the thought or feeling. . . . When you notice that the sensation is somewhat dissipating . . . lessening in intensity . . . once again, allow your breath or the pressure of your hand upon your body to become the anchor of your attention. . . .

Working with pain is similar to working with other compelling emotional and physical experiences. . . . While we use the above responses as our first and second responses to be with these experiences, we can also use additional ones when the emotional or physical experience is very strong. . . .

. . . .

Third Level of Response

If you are noticing a powerful, persistent intrusion of thoughts, emotions, or physical sensations in connection to pain . . . let's step for a moment into this space with the utmost love and compassion toward yourself. . . . Pain is a powerful experience that deserves your conscious respect . . . but not fear! . . . It is just another cognitive, emotional, and physical experience that we can befriend. . . .

Just notice whatever arises . . . a thought about your pain . . . an emotional reaction to having pain . . . or a physical sensation that is the pain experience itself. . . .

When the first and second response levels do not provide some relief, you can move to the third level of response. . . . You can now couple your usual anchor of attention with the place in your body where the pain sensation arises. . . .

Identify the area of your body where you are experiencing pain . . . if you are using your breath as your anchor, intentionally direct your breath right into that pain region with the in-breath. . . . Feel it coming through that painful area . . . and on the out-breath, feel it leaving from that painful area . . . breath in . . . and breath out . . . breath in . . . breath out . . . moment by moment . . . allowing the breath to bathe that painful region with the incoming breath and then to wash it away with the out-breath . . . allowing your awareness to hold both the pain and the breath simultaneously. . . .

If you are using your hand sensation as your anchor, allow yourself to move your hand to the place in your body where you are feeling pain. . . . Place your hand/fingers over that area. . . . Allow yourself to continue to feel the sensations of your hand over this area of your body. . . . Feel the pressure or slight movement of your hand over your painful body area. . . . Feel the texture of the fabric under your hand as it touches the pain. . . .

You are not trying to take the pain away . . . just directing your attention through your anchor (breath or hand sensations) to the painful area . . . using your anchor to focus on the painful site . . . experiencing the sensation of breath washing in and washing out like waves of the ocean . . . or the changing sensations of your hand on your body, where it is experiencing the pain . . . ever so gently touching the pain with your anchor . . . being curious . . . watching what happens . . . seeing how it unfolds moment by moment. . . .

If you find that the painful sensation lessens or dissipates . . . move your anchor away from the body area . . . and return to your usual focus on your anchor of awareness . . . using the breath or your hand sensations to hold your focus. . . .

. . . .

Fourth Level of Response

If you found the third level of response challenging to do because the pain experience is so strong that it continuously pulls your attention away from your anchor . . . or perhaps you feel like you can do nothing . . . you feel frozen with the degree of pain . . . then it is necessary to very gently and briefly approach your pain experience through the fourth level of response. . . .

Very gently notice if you can allow your attention to rest ever so briefly on your chosen anchor of awareness . . . to set your intention to hold your attention on only a small interlude of your anchor even in the face of pain that you are experiencing. . . .

If you are using your breath as your anchor, set your intention to focus on perhaps just one in-breath. . . . Nothing else needs to be done . . . just one in-breath. . . . Even during significant pain, you are setting a goal to hold your attention on only one in-breath. . . .

If you are using your hand sensation as your anchor, set your intention to rest for just a moment on the sensation of one finger pressing firmly into your thigh . . . or feeling for one moment the texture of the fabric under your finger as you gently rub it. . . . See if you can, just for one brief moment . . . allow your attention to return to the anchor even with the intensity of your pain experience. . . .

Knowing that the pain is strong enough to pull your attention away . . . make it your intention to return to your anchor even for just one brief moment. . . .

Then, if the attention is drawn back to the intensity of pain thoughts, feelings, or physical sensations . . . that is okay . . . knowing that you were able to focus your attention on your anchor—on one half-breath, or on a brief moment of tactile sensation in your hand or fingers . . . even with the raw pain you were experiencing . . . you were able to do this. . . .

Over time, try expanding your attention on your anchor for more extended moments . . . still only moments but increased moments . . . knowing that your attention is not able to rest on your anchor for long as it gets pulled into your pain experience. . . . Very gently, make it your intention to allow your awareness to rest on just one in-breath and one out-breath . . . or on the sensation of your fingers pressing twice firmly into your thigh . . . or feeling the fabric texture under your fingers on two occasions. . . .

Know that the powerful sensations of pain will likely pull your attention away from your anchor . . . but ever so gently and slowly, extend the moments that you can keep your attention on your anchor of awareness . . . perhaps one and a half breaths . . . or two breaths . . . or the sensation of your fingers on your body/clothing for three sensations . . . or four sensations . . . just setting your intention to focus your awareness on your anchor for slightly a bit longer. . . .

There is no rush in this practice. . . . It is a time to be compassionate and gentle toward what you are experiencing. . . . You may be noticing the judging mind. . . . It may be beating you up for the limited breaths that you were able to focus on . . . or on your ability to detect the pressure from your hand on your body. . . . Again, with the mindfulness sensitivity, simply acknowledge and label this as "judging" and allow yourself to continue back to the practice. . . .

As you set your intention for one or two breaths/hand sensations . . . notice how that felt . . . perhaps a sense of courage . . . a sense of accomplishment . . . a sense of hope that you *can* stay present to your experience without getting lost in it . . . knowing how powerful your pain experience is and yet you can stay with your anchor for moments . . . that even with the significant pain, you are able to direct your attention where you want it to be . . . on your anchor of awareness . . . that being your breath . . . or your hand sensations . . . for just a moment . . . and over time, to see if you can extend your capacity to be with this pain experience . . . for another moment . . . and later for another moment . . . not ruled by pain . . . but travelling alongside it . . . meeting it . . . changing your relationship to it as you focus your awareness on your anchor of attention. . . .

Perhaps you have found this very difficult to do. . . . Acknowledge that this is not easy. . . . It takes practice . . . and practice . . . and practice . . . coupled with your intention to hold the attitudinal foundations in this experience . . . acceptance . . . non-judging . . . beginner's mind . . . trust. . . . Be gentle and compassionate with yourself. . . . Allow your courage to declare: "I will try again later. . . . I will try again later." . . .

. . . .

However, you may find that even with utilizing all levels of response, the pain continues to be intrusive. . . . Maybe you feel you need to move your position . . . or scratch the itch . . . or rub the numbness . . . but before you act, become very mindful as to how you will move. . . . Remember from past sessions that the key idea is to respond and not to react to the physical sensation. . . .

. . . .

As you continue to meditate, remember that your intention with this mindfulness practice is to simply be in this moment . . . and, at this moment, to be able to experience your capacity of being able to focus on your anchor of awareness intentionally . . . the breath . . . or hand sensations . . . no matter what arises in the mind or body . . . to be able to befriend whatever arises . . . to travel alongside with whatever arises . . . even the more challenging and complex thoughts . . . feelings . . . and physical sensations that occur with pain . . . to develop a sense of confidence and trust in yourself that you can meet whatever arises . . . not that this will be easy . . . or painless . . . but to know that you do not have to hide . . . or avoid . . . or numb yourself to the 10,000 sorrows or challenges that are a part of this life that is yours . . . that you can learn to respond rather than just react to whatever arises . . . to be fully present in each moment. . . .

. . . .

I will soon bring your attention back to the room. . . . I will ring the bell three times. . . . Slowly and at your own pace . . . allow yourself to open your eyes . . . and bring your awareness back to the space while still being conscious of your anchor . . . of being able to hold attention of your anchor even as you are aware of your surroundings. . . . Offer yourself compassion for the courage to practice and to explore new ways of being present to yourself even in the midst of difficult experiences such as pain. . . .

2. Informal Mindfulness Practices

Guidelines:

- As we discussed last week, outside of the formal practice sessions, there are ample opportunities to continue learning to be more mindfully present. These informal practices arise out of the daily activities that comprise your life and are readily available to be of service to your learning process.

- This week, I invite you to continue exploring informal mindfulness practices daily. Be creative—try new ones outside of mindful eating.

- While it is easy to identify many daily activities to which you can apply your burgeoning mindfulness skills, they all share a commonality of being ones you probably don't pay much attention to. The project itself is not what is critical. Instead, any activity that allows you to slow down the process to experience it with your senses fully is what makes it an informal mindfulness practice and, therefore, a good one to choose.

- The instructions are the same for each activity: be aware of the steps involved; decide what the initial component of the first step will be; slowly begin working through each stage, focusing on your senses of sight, touch, hearing, smell, and (if appropriate) taste. Be curious as to how you are experiencing each step through your senses. Take your time and be curious about this activity that you could do in your sleep but want to approach with a beginner's mind as if undertaking it for the first time. Enjoy the process!

- In addition to structured activities that provide excellent opportunities for mindfulness training, it is also recommended that you set an intention to be aware of your anchor of attention (either your breath or hand sensations) from time to time throughout the day. This attending does not have to entail lengthy periods but rather just a momentary noticing of your anchor at that moment. Feel either the sensation of your breath or your hand sensations, and be curious about what this feels like in that unique moment. It is also possible to use daily activities as triggers to remind yourself to notice your anchor. The intent is not to take your full awareness off your situation but rather to be curious about your anchor in that particular moment. With practice, you will build a greater trust in your ability to be aware of your anchor of awareness and still be conscious and aware of activities in which you are involved.

- Be sure to again record your homework on your **Tracking Your Practice** log under the Informal heading.

3. Unpleasant Events Log

Guidelines:

- To extend mindfulness beyond formal (such as body scan, sitting, or walking) and informal practice sessions, I invite you to pay attention to experiences that you have each day.

- However, instead of being aware of pleasant events as you did last week, I invite you to be mindful of **unpleasant events**. Again, there are no right or wrong events, thoughts, feelings, or body sensations you are tracking. The purpose is to simply expand your awareness of the moments that arise each day and be consciously aware of unpleasant situations.

- In the spirit of being mindful of all that arises, being aware that these fleeting moments, unpleasant as they are, are an essential aspect of being fully engaged in this life that is yours.

- Life presents small (and sometimes large!) events that are not what you ask for, wish for, or even want. But even these unpleasant events are part of the fabric woven together on a moment-by-moment basis into something called "my life!" By being mindful with each moment, you can better experience the Clint Eastwood philosophy of life—that is, to experience "the good, the bad and the ugly!" You build confidence and trust that you can fully meet whatever arises on a moment-to-moment basis.

- Again, in terms of unpleasant experiences, do not wait for the "big bang" events of life to occur. The idea is to be mindful of any unpleasant events that you experience as you go about your day. However small (or significant) or short-lived (or extended) they may be doesn't matter as long as you intend to be aware of potential unpleasant events—both inside and outside of you—that occur during the day.

- The log asks you to record the answers to the following questions:
  - What was your experience?
  - What physical sensations did you notice (if any) during this experience?
  - What thoughts (if any) did you have during this experience?
  - What emotions (if any) accompanied this event?
  - What made this an unpleasant event?

- It is not recommended that you record all this information as the event unfolds since this would take you out of the moment! Keep your awareness and attention on the event itself and hold the above questions in the back of your mind. Set your intention to put this information into your memory to be recorded later.

- The final box on the Unpleasant Events log again asks what may seem to be a rhetorical question but nevertheless a significant one—what made this an unpleasant event? Was it the physical sensations? The thoughts? The emotions? Was it a combination of all of these? Did you feel judged? Did you feel unseen by another? Did you feel taken advantage of? Did you feel disappointed? Whatever it was, the purpose is to become more curious, understanding how you know that this was an unpleasant event. This exercise is not meant to question or undermine your judgment but rather to help you clarify how this verdict arose. It is an opportunity to explore and understand that you can respond instead of unconsciously react to whatever event presents itself to you.

- Remember, even though you are on the lookout for unpleasant events, don't forget that pleasant events are also occurring. So don't forget the pleasant ones—enjoy them fully! But the practice this week is to also meet and engage with unpleasant events in a conscious manner. Why? Because they will likely arise whether you want them to or not! Therefore, they are simply part of this life that is yours.

UNPLEASANT EVENTS

What was the experience?	What physical sensations (if any) did you notice in your body during this experience?	What thoughts (if any) did you have during this experience?	What emotions (if any) accompanied this event?	What made this an unpleasant event?
MONDAY				
TUESDAY				
WEDNESDAY				
THURSDAY				

UNPLEASANT EVENTS

What was the experience?	What physical sensations (if any) did you notice in your body during this experience?	What thoughts (if any) did you have during this experience?	What emotions (if any) accompanied this event?	What made this an unpleasant event?
FRIDAY				
SATURDAY				
SUNDAY				

MIDWEEK CUPPA...
REFLECTIONS ON
TRUST AND AGING

WEEK FIVE

There is no way to sugar-coat the reality that aging through your advancing years comes with losses. Getting older arrives with inevitable challenges to your physical, emotional, and social well-being. However, stereotyped images inflame the situation through ceaseless predictions of becoming dependent, frail, insecure, powerless, unprotected, weak, and defenceless. These images erode your sense of trust as aging has become synonymously poisoned with vulnerability.

VULNERABILITY

Vulnerability is a loaded concept, understandably clothed in fear because its definition includes susceptibility to physical or emotional attack or harm. To add to the frightening image, vulnerability carries a secondary definition of a person in need of special care, support or protection because of age, or disability. If there is any doubt about aversion toward the potential dangers of vulnerability, listen to the contrasting images offered to ward off perils that include being guarded, protected, safe, secure, strong, robust, defended, impenetrable, indomitable, and invincible. Maybe it's just me, but don't these characterizations foretell a high-pitched battle just for survival?

Fortunately, during recent years in the spirit of conflict de-escalation, Brené Brown has brought vulnerability out of the shadows to its rightful favourable position in human development. Dr. Brown champions vulnerability as the courage to "show up" when you cannot predict or control the outcome of a situation (Brown 2015). This view is a game-changer for it more accurately describes two key elements of vulnerability—what it is and how to meet it. Meeting vulnerability is the way to increase trust within yourself, to know that you can be with whatever arises. Not that this will always be easy, but that you are capable because of trusting yourself!

Dr. Brown makes clear that vulnerability is, by definition, an essential part of being human. This description will come as no surprise since your expanding awareness and experience throughout this course is premised on accepting that susceptibility to physical or emotional attacks is just part of your life. There is simply no way to completely defend against the pain, loss, and sorrows each of you has or will experience. Vulnerability comes as an unreturnable feature of your human package.

Establishing vulnerability as an undeniable human experience, along with acknowledgement of its power, means that you could probably use a little help to deal with it. And this is the second contribution that Dr. Brown offers, as she identifies a roadmap to navigate vulnerability by courageously showing up. Nothing more than simply "showing up." Sound familiar? Mindfulness is courageously showing up to whatever arises in your day-to-day moments, which means that at some point (likely every day!), you will get the opportunity to meet vulnerability.

TRUST SUPPORTS VULNERABILITY

With the ubiquitous nature of vulnerability coupled with its potential powerful challenges to your well-being, developing an attitude of trust within your mindfulness practice is an essential skill. Trust, riding along with the other attitudinal foundations, allows you to expand your tolerance and resilience to be with whatever arises in your awareness, which certainly includes physical and emotional "attacks." This developed capacity strengthens your resolve not only to be aware of what you are thinking or feeling but also to experience fully the ever-changing world that is yours. The resultant establishment of a relationship to vulnerability is no small feat, so pause to realize how transformative this shift in awareness, experience, and relationship is to the present moment's openness.

To be capable of meeting each moment is undoubtedly a practice that takes time. However, to even get small glimpses through your formal and informal meditations to date is to know—not read or wonder about—but viscerally know that you are more than what you previously envisioned as all of who you are. Your growing authenticity is witnessed through your expanding presence of each moment.

VULNERABILITY AND INDIVIDUATION

Vulnerability is at its core being true to yourself. While the quest to become who you are, your authentic self, can begin at any age, I found it frequently voiced with older clients. One of the aging gifts is that it can be a time to question previous long-held identities that no longer reflect your sense of self. Many clients had been aware of this inner drive over the years but had found it difficult to do the hard work required, so they have often met this inner impulse by mistakenly trying to find inner peace and happiness through outer world gambits. Within the psychology profession, this is commonly known as "rearranging the deck chairs on the Titanic"; that is, modifying life situations and events in the misguided hope that this would keep your ship, your self, afloat.

The list of attempted "deck chair" ploys is limitless but often includes the frantic but futile forecasts of "Maybe if I . . . change jobs; change life partners (or better yet stay in the relationship and have an affair); move across the country or ocean; buy a bigger house; downsize to a cabin in the woods; never retire; run away; etc." All valiant but inevitably impotent strategies for transforming the small limiting version of yourself to becoming the more extensive and authentic embodiment of who you are.

Genuine change to become more congruent with yourself requires strength, courage, and wisdom to meet the vulnerabilities that are inevitably part of the process of individuation. Your ego, while experiencing the pain of inauthenticity (you know deep in your bones that there has to be more to your life than this!), protests mightily against the demands required to meet unconscious aspects that encompass your greater identity, your true sense of self.

In addition to uncovering and integrating personal shadows and projections, as discussed during the last weeks, individuation also involves recognizing and exploring long-standing knotted challenges that interfere with your well-being. Mindfulness helps illuminate these troublesome obstructions as they repeatedly arise into consciousness when your busy and noisy inner cognitive and emotional chatter quiets. While mindfulness offers four levels of strategies to meet and be with these intrusions, recognizing persistent ongoing eruptions can indicate that additional intervention may sometimes be required outside mindfulness practice.

JUNGIAN PSYCHOLOGY MEETS VULNERABILITY

Jungian psychology envisions relentless reruns of stories, events, and emotions as a knock on your door of consciousness, invitations for further investigation into their nature and purpose. Rather than viewing such experiences as unwanted intrusions into your developing expansion of your authentic self, Jungian psychology understands them as signposts or symbols of unconscious aspects seeking the light of consciousness. In other words, they can be helpful if offered the opportunity! Opening to your vulnerability is not easy, so building trust in your capacity to do so is essential.

Ted's burgeoning mindfulness practice was a welcome addition to his new retirement life. However, being a physically active man whose time was always committed to work or home projects, he found the unscheduled and slower pace of retirement difficult to embrace. While enjoying the increased calm that he experienced with formal and informal mindfulness sensibility, he also became aware of a dissatisfied, low mood under the surface of his busyness. Mindfulness strategies to be with this feeling were helpful, but he became increasingly aware of its presence during most of his waking days. Ted trusted his realization that there was something to learn from this persistent, albeit unwanted, pesky low mood interference.

Ted expanded his relationship with this low mood by applying the Jungian strategy of active imagination, personifying the emotion to explore it better. He envisioned his low mood as an old hag; a witchy-like figure bent over with missing teeth and a crackly laugh, who taunted him for reasons initially unknown. Resting in his newfound mindfulness capacity of trusting that he could be with even this unwanted and unwelcomed aspect of himself, Ted became curious about who she was and what she wanted. Just as he would with a real-world figure that he had only met and was interested to know, Ted began dialoguing with the old hag.

Not just holding an internal conversation but physically writing the dialogue allowed Ted to give life to and track his unfolding exploration of her. This process is different from regular journaling *about* a situation as it rests upon a dialogue *with* this symbolic manifestation of the emotional life.

Ted started with the burning questions of "Who are you?" and "What do you want?" After writing the question, he listened for a response from his old hag. It may sound futile, but usually, some answers will come to you from your dialoguing figure. If nothing arrives, then try another question. Be honest with this new personified image of your emotion and express what you are thinking or feeling. Be angry or fearful or pleased or confused or exasperated or whatever. It is not the time to be clever or patronizing or submissive—it is time to be genuine and authentic with yourself by relating to this characteristic of who you are. You are not trying to appease or manipulate it into becoming your new best friend (remember, you already have a best friend—your anchor of awareness!). You may not like what your figure says, and if this is the case, then respond accordingly.

This process of meeting your internal emotional representations may sound crazy, but the reality is that you are already engaged in such inner dialogue on an ongoing basis. It already is part of your narrative focus, so the only difference is saying it out loud and transcribing your communication.

Active imagination can be a compelling entry into furthering your individuation, for it gives voice to unconscious parts of yourself—to further illuminate your quest for authenticity, wholeness, and psychological maturity. Not scripting the interaction ahead of time but curiously asking questions and being open to whatever the old hag responded allowed Ted to gain insight into this aspect of himself. Trust that your unconscious has wisdom that can be of benefit.

As with mindfulness, the goal from a Jungian psychological perspective is not to overpower or eradicate the experience (in Ted's situation, his low mood) but instead meet it through awareness and experiencing it fully, with the intent to develop an ongoing relationship. Over time, Ted's dialogue revealed that the old hag was, in fact, a benevolent figure who would make her presence known through him experiencing low mood when he was ignoring his genuine interests and desires.

Ted's lifelong pattern of keeping busy for busyness' sake proved to be counterproductive to what he genuinely wanted for this time in his life. However, old habits die hard, so when he found himself continuing to overcommit to projects that his heart was not in, especially those requested by others, the old hag made her dramatic appearance and grabbed his attention through an undeniable low mood. Therefore, when a low mood arrived, over time Ted became aware that it was his old hag nudging him to question his decision to take on new projects. The newfound awareness, experience, and relationship with his old hag became a boon to Ted's developing clarity of his true and authentic self. Ted's authenticity provided a new foundation for his enjoyment of retired life.

Mindfulness and Jungian psychology are two doors into awareness of complex parts of being human, providing a container to experience them fully and allowing for a different relationship to develop. Learning to do this with brief moments during mindfulness practice establishes confidence and trust to meet more significant, thornier issues that come into consciousness. Mindfulness moments are like batting practice for the game of life. Jungian psychology provides the additional avenue needed to courageously expand insight into often unconscious facets of your life that, until this time, have tripped your attempts to lead a more vital, satisfied, and contented life.

However, it is not easy meeting these troubling and challenging aspects of yourself, so why do it? The short answer is because they are already here, part of you, and cannot be magically exterminated. A long life lived can provide the confidence needed to drop into your vulnerability and trust that you can meet whatever arises. Trust, confidence, and courage open the possibility of insight, perspective, and personal growth offered through meeting and establishing a new relationship with all of yourself. Older clients often report that it feels like they have finally, after sixty or seventy or eighty years of living, "grown-up"! Without knowing your life expectancy, the obvious question knocking at your door of consciousness becomes, if not now, when?

"BEARING THE UNBEARABLE": MINDFULNESS MEETS GRIEF

WEEK SIX

REVIEW PAIN EXPERIENCE PRACTICES

Week Six arrived with the group ambience mirroring the warmer spring weather of early April. This original group of strangers with markedly different backgrounds and life circumstances had transformed into a supportive and trusting community, as evidenced by their review of last week's practices. Juanita shared that her shoulders' discomfort while in a sitting meditation "miraculously" disappeared with her Level Two response. Ken, Bernie, and Henry each echoed their pain's "Harry Houdini" act by applying Levels One through Three. Devon also found that his leg cramps while walking did dissipate when he applied Level Two response. However, relief took quite a while, definitely "not miraculously" as he teasingly reflected on Juanita's experience!

Jasmine sat silently during the good-natured review before quietly offering that her week's encounter with her chronic arthritic pain experience was quite different. When she attempted to apply her differing and escalating levels of response to her pain, her attention kept getting pulled into feelings of anger. She came to realize that while she had accommodated her knee pain over the years, she harboured considerable antagonism toward it! Since her attempts to be with the pain were hijacked by her angry feelings, Jasmine decided to use her anger as her focus of attention. Throughout the week, she deliberately monitored her anger and applied the levels of response to it directly. Jasmine found that her mindful awareness of the anger diminished it, although it did not eradicate it—she still felt upset but to a much lower degree. However, Jasmine surprisingly found that along with a diminution of her anger, her experience of pain also lessened.

The group sat silently, listening to Jasmine's recounting of her week's exploration before Jessica cautiously wondered aloud if she, too, had developed a different relationship with her pain without being conscious of it. Jessica found the mindfulness approach beneficial, although not eliminating her hand pain, and now questioned whether her daughter's comment that "Mom, you seem more relaxed and less angry" reflected a distinct shift in her relationship to pain. Many in the group nodded their approval of Jessica's explanation with comments affirming that they understood the effect that can occur with altering your relationship to whatever arises in moment-to-moment awareness. Inwardly, I was beaming with admiration, knowing that they got it, really understanding the power of both attention regulation and concomitant attitudes to change your relationship to present moment experience.

Working with pain mindfully is premised on the understanding that staying more within the mind's experiential focus rather than narrative network is a critical skill. The four levels of response you have learned to apply to painful physical stimuli open the door to your experiential network, permitting you to hold your attention within your senses. Coupled with the conscious application of attitudinal foundations, your relationship to pain can change. William laughingly agreed as he recounted that the image of his ongoing lower back pain has changed from a growling, spittle-spraying, and ferocious wolf to a yappy miniature lapdog barking incessantly—annoying, yes, but not menacing!

INFORMAL PRACTICES

Examples of informal mindfulness practices during the week continued to grow. While some expanded on previous personal care and savouring activities (including my favourites of Scotch sipping and chocolate tasting), Betty marvelled at the pleasure she received from simply wiping her kitchen counters. She spoke about her newly discovered enjoyment of observing the slow caress of the dishcloth over the counter. Initially drawn to the array of crumbs and food scraps littering the dull quartz counter surface, her hand gently took hold of the damp cloth to slowly sweep the leftovers into the sink, revealing behind a shiny clean finish. Breaking her reverence recounting this new experience, Betty estimated that during her sixty-eight years, she must have wiped counters at least 45,000 times and yet it took the intention to be fully present during the moment to appreciate its awe-inspiring capacity! However, while Betty was quick to point out that she was not planning on making a career of wiping counters, she did appreciate how ordinary daily activities hold the promise of discovery—the act itself did not change, only her awareness, experience, and relationship to it.

UNPLEASANT EVENTS

The group was unanimous that noticing unpleasant events during the week was more accessible than catching pleasant ones—no one reported difficulty identifying some degree of an unpleasant event on each of the previous seven days. Not that this self-report indicates that each life was miserable, but instead, it was indicative that their built-in hard-wired threat detection system was operable.

Those in the group experiencing ongoing physical pain mentioned that it was easy, too easy, to record discomfort as a daily unpleasant event since it was a constant companion. However, a few consciously stretched their awareness to identify other unpleasant events besides their ongoing pain and found no shortage of options. Offerings included disappointment with medical test results, being stood up on a coffee date, a long wait at the deli counter, a sharp rebuke from a family member, unexpected expenses, cancellation of a planned holiday, rude comments from a salesclerk, a pet's sickness, not being invited to a family gathering, a birthday forgotten, a near car accident because of the other driver's carelessness, and so on. Unasked-for moments that carried feelings of loss, uncertainty, invisibility, disappointment, fear, not receiving what was expected and uncared for.

Similar to pleasant events monitoring, mindfulness did not create unpleasant circumstances. Instead, it simply heightened your awareness that these undesirable events are part of life's adventure—the 10,000 joys and 10,000 sorrows that characterize a life lived. Mindfulness helps expand your awareness of events (pleasant, unpleasant, and neutral) in tandem with increasing your tolerance and resilience to meet them.

As you have been practising and learning during the past weeks, meeting whatever arises is the gift of mindfulness. Through attention regulation and realignment of your relationship to life's experiences, you can feel competent in living this life that is yours, which in turn provides increased satisfaction, contentment, and enjoyment.

You will perhaps notice that I didn't offer "bliss" as an intended outcome. As this past week has demonstrated, physical pain can be part of the package that you hold as your life. No sugar coating it or transcending this reality. However, as you have also experienced, even painful sensations can be approached and held in a qualitatively different manner. This week, you will get the opportunity to expand mindfulness from physical to emotional pain and see what it has to offer. Specifically, in the spirit of meeting the big-ticket items of life, let's explore what mindfulness can contribute to grief.

ATTITUDE OF NON-STRIVING

Moving into the grief experience brings us first to another attitude: non-striving, which is critical to hold during the mindfulness practice. You have no doubt noticed that almost everything you do in life is driven by a purpose, such as obtaining something or going somewhere, which is an aspect of the striving definition. However, striving evokes more than just having a goal, as the forceful action associated with striving reveals. Synonyms to striving include labour, plow, slave, strain, slog, struggle, sweat and toil, echoing its early meaning from words involving strife, such as contend, fight, or quarrel. Connotations of striving indicate there is an urgency or imperative to do something fervently.

However, with mindfulness, this attitude can be a real obstacle because meditation is different from most other human activities. Although it takes considerable effort and energy when beginning a meditation practice (as it is a new skill you are learning), meditation is ultimately a non-doing activity. It has no goal other than for you to experience yourself at this moment . . . and then at this moment . . . and then at this moment.

STRIVING FOR . . .

Striving, however, has other plans in mind for you. For example, when you begin a formal meditation and think, *I will get relaxed, or control my pain, or feel better about myself,* you have introduced an idea that is incongruent with your situation at the moment. That is, you have decided that this moment, with you in it, is not right. It is another judgment that the mind has created. Something must change to this moment to make it right or better or something! It is telling you to think, *If I were only smarter, or calmer, or a better meditator, or more disciplined, or more this or more that, then I would be satisfied. But right now, with things as they are, I am not acceptable.*

This judging attitude and accompanying striving to be different from how you are presently is antithetical to learning mindfulness, as this involves simply paying attention to whatever is occurring. As you have been practising, if you are upset, then you notice that there is unease. If you are in pain, then observe that there is pain. If you are worried about something in the future, then see the activity of worry in your mind. Just pay attention and learn; learn to observe whatever is occurring, and gently bring your attention back to your anchor of awareness.

Remember, you are simply allowing anything and everything you experience from moment to moment to be just as it is without being pulled into the scene. And why do you bear witness to what is occurring? Because it is happening. Why do you not chase whatever comes into your awareness? Because you are training your mind to become more stable, capable of focusing your attention where you want it, when you want it, and for as long as you want it. Mindfulness at its core!

RELATIONSHIP TO GOALS AND INTENTIONS

The reality is we all have goals, such that everyone is taking this course for a reason. The specific rationale will undoubtedly vary, but the likely essence is that you want to learn something that will be helpful, beneficial, and allow you to grow and develop in a positive direction during your aging years. To be clear, there is certainly nothing inherently wrong with holding an intention for your actions. However, the concern that is detrimental to your developing capacity to be present in the moment is the ongoing emphasis on what is *not* acceptable coupled with the continual monitoring as to whether the desired change has occurred.

During mindfulness retreats, there is an often-told story about the inherent impediment of striving to your intended goal of being fully present in each moment. The story begins with a young man who wanted to be the best martial artist in the world. For years, he travelled to all corners of the earth, seeking the teacher who would bring him to that lofty goal. At last, he found the teacher and was granted an interview with the elderly sensei. As the teacher poured the student a cup of tea, he asked, "What brings you here?" The student replied, "I want to be the best martial artist in the world, and you are the teacher who can assist me in my quest. How long do you think it will take me?" The old man thought about this desire and answered, "Probably ten years," to which the student immediately countered, "Ten years! What if I study day and night—how long will it take me?" The teacher closed his eyes, contemplated the question, and replied, "Probably fifteen years." The student was taken aback by this lengthening timeline, so he added, "But what if I work harder than any other student you have ever had—how long will it take me?" The teacher again thoughtfully considered the request and answered, "Probably twenty years." By now, the student was beside himself in disbelief and asked, "But how can that be—if I am willing to work day and night and harder than any of your students, why will it take me so long?" The wise old teacher calmly explained, "As long as you have one eye on your destination, you only have one eye open to find your way!"

BACK OFF FROM STRIVING

Similarly, when starting the mindfulness practice, it is important to back off from striving for results and instead stay focused on simply experiencing and accepting whatever is occurring at the moment. As an analogy, the goal of planting carrot seeds is to enjoy fresh carrots, but to impulsively pull up the new green shoots every day to see if they are yet ready interferes with the carrot's needed growing process.

SKEPTICISM OF NON-STRIVING

It doesn't take years of professional training to observe that many in the mindfulness group struggled to understand the concept of non-striving. I enjoy Richard's thoughtful skepticism, so I was pleased when he inquired, "Help me to understand what mindfulness is asking—I'm a little confused!"

Life goals are essential as your guiding star. Mindfulness is not asking you to relinquish them. Still, it suggests that the healthiest way to achieve them is to identify your intentions and then set aside the continuous impulse to monitor and assess whether they are complete. The young child's constant asking, "Are we there yet?" does not advance their desired goal and unfortunately detracts from their full awareness and presence of each moment.

Hold off striving to be different from what is happening at this moment. The reality is that with patience and regular practice, the movement toward the goals that you have set will likely take place by itself. Trust that this movement becomes an unfolding without your overpowering need to monitor, manipulate, and control constantly. While it may sound paradoxical, as you continue to develop your mindfulness practice, I would encourage you to back off the urge to strive for results.

To hold the attitude of simply being here now with whatever arises allows you to investigate what can occur with non-striving. Starting small with non-striving during meditation will enable you to experience what that is like. For just those thirty-five minutes of formal meditation or five minutes of informal meditation while washing dishes, let go of striving to be different or experience things another way, and be open to only whatever is occurring, which will help you understand non-striving better. As you discovered last week, non-striving is an essential attitude to hold when learning to be with physical pain; as you will soon see, it is also critical when meeting emotional distress such as grief.

HELLO, GRIEF!

With many shifting uncomfortably in their seats, the group fell silent when I introduced this week's topic of mindfulness meets grief. To enumerate our collective membership in this human experience, I asked how many had lost a loved one through death during the last five years. Eleven hands slowly rose. How many had lost a friend? Six hands went up. How many lost a pet? Four hands. How many experienced a medical diagnosis of a chronic or life-limiting illness? Five hands. Further questioning of how many lost trust in someone close, experienced a financial downturn, or lost faith in their spiritual beliefs were each met with solemn affirmations of loss.

By the time you have hit mid-life, if not before, you have most likely experienced a sense of grief and sorrow over a loss. Even if you have not faced the death of a loved one, as the group demonstrated, you have usually experienced a myriad of other grief experiences with losses associated with work, friendships, intimate relationships, pets, finances, health, trust, beliefs, faith, and so forth.

The language used to describe grief illustrates the magnitude of the emotional content. Bernie offered that "grief is like being hit by a freight train." Sanjay solemnly stated that "grief is like an arrow through the heart." Sam described grief "like waves on a violently churning sea." Others depicted grief "like losing your way in a dark forest" and "vicious, like a furious storm." The imagery associated with grief reflects the undeniable turbulent emotional substance that this experience generates.

I, too, am no stranger to loss on a personal level. On a professional level as a psychologist, my experience with grief had primarily been working with individuals experiencing what would be clinically characterized as "complicated grief," which involves grief that has become stuck or derailed in some way. Why usually just those with complicated grief? Within the psychotherapy field, it is still the case that people often enter psychotherapy only when they are in the throes of significant psychological distress. Not only does private practice psychotherapy require considerable financial outlay, but psychotherapy in general still has a negative connotation, with many people feeling that they must be "crazy" before seeking such intervention. Therefore, those arriving at my office were folks who not only had lost a loved one (including those gone through suicide or homicide) but who continued to struggle long after the event.

Bereavement concerns usually revolved around two issues: unfinished business with their departed continued to challenge their well-being long after the passing, or they were experiencing a lack of trust within themselves that they could survive their grief. Even with other clients whom I saw in psychotherapy whose presenting issues were not specifically about grief, many had significant unresolved relationship issues with a loved one that they lost.

But upon reflection over the years, I am not sure whether there is any other kind of grief, but that characterized as "complicated." Grief describes a big, messy, chaotic, unscheduled process that plays havoc with your emotional self! It can make you fearful, paralyzed, lonely, angry, confused, isolated, or all the above—often within ten minutes! It is painful—often incredibly so—there is just no getting around it.

When you think you are "over" grief, you often experience what has been called "re-grieving days." Days when acutely experienced grief re-emerges months, years, or even decades later during a special day, holidays, or without any particular cue or prompt. Grief demands your attention on its own schedule.

My approach to working with grief on a professional (and a personal level with my losses) is closely aligned with that understood through the hospice movement:

Grief is one of the most painful and challenging experiences
that each human can have.

Grief is not something to overcome.

Grief is not something to manage.

There is no manual, no playbook that allows us to skip painlessly through
the grief experience.

Grief needs to be lived, to be experienced, painful as it is!

MEETING GRIEF WITH TEARS

Working with grief is, as you know, a multifaceted process individualized for each person, although it is likely that most will experience tears. It is interesting and, to many people, somewhat surprising to note that the typical response of crying has been identified as a valuable way to meet your grief (Cacciatore 2017). Crying may act as a stress-relief valve because of its biochemical construction. Emotional tears are different from irritant tears that rinse the eye or irrigate it of foreign objects and are also different from lubricant tears that support blinking. Research has found that emotional tears contain higher protein concentrations, including the adrenocorticotropic hormone, which is a protein produced and then released in high doses during distress. This hormone signals the adrenal glands to release other hormones that then assist in regulating stress. Let it sink in how amazing it is that we have a built-in system designed to help us with our emotional pain! But also know that we can learn to work with our inevitable grief experiences in addition to this hard-wired support.

BREAK US OPEN

The intense emotional experience of grief is often said to "break us," but I believe a more apt and realistic perception is that "grief breaks us open" when understood through the process of mindfulness. And the gift of this broken-open experience is that we can consciously decide to turn toward it and not away from it. To turn in is a step in developing a different relationship, befriending this painful but inevitable human emotional experience.

BEFRIENDING GRIEF

In my experience, on both personal and professional levels, a critical aspect of meeting grief is through the concept of befriending it. This inner intention and attitude allow us to begin developing a new relationship to this painful human experience. When reflecting on my career as a psychologist, while turning toward our lives' painful experiences is a solid general therapeutic model, I believe it is imperative when working with your grief. I am, however, a pragmatist who believes that there is also a role for other responses to grief, including medication and times for distractions. To be clear, there is no definitive "playbook" as to the order of stages any one of us must go through to experience grief after a loss. But in my experience, at some point on the journey of grief, to not turn *toward* the suffering of grief simply forestalls this voyage, resulting in cumulative and long-standing challenges that are even more difficult to navigate.

It is, of course, acknowledged that grief exists on a spectrum from the milder sorrows of a friend moving away to the more gripping grief and loss experienced during the death of a partner, parent, or child. The death of someone we love shakes us or, in fact, feels like it shatters us when we are awash in feelings of sorrow, anguish, anger, and despair. These painful states can alternate with periods of emptiness, numbness, lifelessness, and paralysis. Everything feels like an effort that has often been described as the "lethargy of grief." Many writers have aptly observed that it is at these times that we recognize that we do not choose grief—it chooses us.

And while we do not have a choice in when the inevitable 10,000 sorrows present and their intensity, we do have a choice in how we deal with it.

MINDFULNESS EMBRACES GRIEF

Mindfulness can be of particular assistance when encountering emotional pain such as grief, just as it can be helpful with physical pain. Grief experiences will inevitably arise, so the challenge becomes how you meet them differently and more healthily. Learning to meet and be with emotional pain, coupled with changing your relationship to the complex and challenging experience of grief, remain the core goals of mindfulness. Let's first explore the effect that our relationship to grief has on our experience of it.

My early years working as a psychotherapist reflected my training: problems brought to the therapy room were to be solved, overcome, or somehow done away with as quickly as possible. It was primarily through my woundedness (including my own losses of loved ones), as well as exposure to Jungian psychology and spiritual explorations, that my relationship with whatever arrived in the consulting room changed over time from trying to eliminate such difficulties to one of helping the client *meet* whatever struggle had arisen in their life. This change in the relationship became one of how my client could meet their suffering—befriend their pain, resulting in more healthily being with it. There is a place for skill acquisition within psychotherapy. Still, our *relationship* to the challenges and struggles that we meet in life is what I came to believe of paramount importance when navigating this human existence.

GET OVER IT—NOW!

Unfortunately, as you all are aware, our culture is not interested in having each of you meet your suffering and develop a different relationship with it. This attitude certainly comes into play concerning grief. The frequent "helpful" advice is to assist the bereaved individual in avoiding, denying, and generally escaping the painful experience of grief—usually as soon as possible.

I'm sorry to report the cultural insistence that individuals should "get over" grief within a defined and short timeline has unfortunately been part of the psychology/psychiatric diagnostic culture. Until 2013, the reference text of diagnoses (*Diagnostic and Statistical Manual of Mental Disorders-IV*) recognized that depression and grief share many similar symptoms, especially in the immediate rawness after losing a loved one. However, it recommended that clinicians refrain from diagnosing Major Depression in individuals within the first two months following a loved one's death. Referred to as the "bereavement exclusion," it was believed that "normal" grief protected someone from the diagnosis of Major Depressive Disorder. However, this meant there was a time limit on how long suffering was *supposed* to be experienced—after two months, a grieving individual could be diagnosed with Major Depressive Disorder.

The more recent diagnostic manual (*DSM-V*), published in 2013, no longer has the bereavement exclusion. Instead, the manual does try to distinguish the differing emotional, cognitive, and physical qualities of depression from grief, which is a move in the right direction. However, by eliminating the bereavement exclusion, a diagnosis of Major Depressive Disorder can now be assigned after only two weeks, pathologizing a normal and expected emotional reaction to a catastrophic loss.

The latest diagnostic manual also presents what is called "Persistent Complex Bereavement Disorder" to be studied for potential future classification as a mental disorder. Several factors are associated with this possible diagnosis that we don't need to review, but what is noteworthy for our discussion is that the manual concludes this diagnosis is warranted if individuals continue to experience grief interfering with their lives. On the surface, this seems reasonable, but there is a built-in timeline. That is, the disorder is diagnosed if at least twelve months for adults and six months for children have elapsed since the death of someone with whom the bereaved had a close relationship. They specifically note that this timeline discriminates "normal grief" from "persistent grief." The cultural and professional imperative of grief having an acceptable specific lifespan clearly, but unfortunately, continues.

STRENGTHENING OUR CAPACITY TO COPE WITH GRIEF

Dr. Joanne Cacciatore lost her newborn daughter over twenty years ago and has devoted her personal and professional life to working with grief. She is an associate professor at Arizona State University and director of the Trauma and Bereavement Graduate Certificate program. In keeping with the belief that grief is not to be controlled or managed, she writes: "When I work with a bereaved person one-on-one . . . I do not try to induce a reduction of symptoms or a diminishment of grief. I have no agenda with my clients other than to be with them as they move with and between and through grief . . . I help them increase their ability to cope" (Cacciatore 2017).

Dr. Cacciatore uses the following scales to assist her clients in understanding the process of grief:

Grief Intensity (1 least to 10 most)
1 2 3 4 5 6 7 8 9 10

Ability to Cope with Grief (1 least to 10 most)
1 2 3 4 5 6 7 8 9 10

She notes that these tools highlight the fact that there are two separate issues at play with grief: 1) what you feel and 2) how able you are to cope with what you feel. For example, if you are feeling a grief intensity of 10 on a particular day—such as your lost one's birthday—and your ability to cope is high, such as 9, there is little strain between what you feel and what you trust you can feel. However, suppose you experience a 6–7 (medium-high) grief intensity and your ability to cope is only a 2 (relatively low). In that case, this divergence may give rise to intense anguish and psychological unrest. At such times, you are likely to doubt your capacity to be with your emotions and, consciously or unconsciously, choose to check out by whatever distraction means are available.

Dr. Cacciatore notes that within this model of meeting grief, the intention is not to cause the first number (grief intensity) to go down but rather to allow the second number (ability to cope with grief) to go up. The focus is on strengthening your personal and interpersonal resources rather than tempering the intensity of grief. This perspective allows grief intensity to rise and fall anywhere on the scale naturally, changing and fluctuating—as it inevitably will—according to life's ever-changing circumstances. Dr. Cacciatore rightly notes that "like love, grief can't be constrained by time and space." What is critical, however, is the development of trust within yourself to be with grief no matter when and where it arises.

ATTITUDINAL FOUNDATIONS TO BEFRIEND GRIEF

The attention regulation and attitudinal foundations reviewed over the past weeks that can strengthen your mindfulness practice equally pertain to Dr. Cacciatore's perspective to be with grief and enhance your capacity to cope with its associated roller-coaster emotions. As Dr. Cacciatore notes, "the more we practice staying with the emotions that we think may overcome us, the more we trust our ability to fully inhabit grief. The more we inhabit it, the more comfortable we are staying and allowing it to move through us" (Cacciatore 2017).

The concepts of acceptance, non-judging, non-striving, beginner's mind, and trust are essential in developing a healthy ongoing relationship with grief. As we have discussed, one of the foundations of mindfulness is that you can meet whatever arises in your life—which also includes the more challenging experiences such as grief over the loss of a loved one.

Dr. Cacciatore's perspective of not focusing on reducing the intensity of grief but rather increasing our capacity to be with grief is similar to the mindfulness concept of befriending grief. This point of view requires an *acceptance* and *non-judging* of suffering; *non-striving* to feel different from what is happening; a sense of *beginner's mind* to meet this experience like no other; all of which in turn can lead to a *trust* in developing your capacity to meet and hold the emotions of grief.

The attitude and openness to develop a relationship with grief are captured brilliantly in the poem "Talking to Grief" by Denise Levertov:

Ah, grief, I should not treat you
like a homeless dog
who comes to the back door
for a crust, for a meatless bone.
I should trust you.

I should coax you
into the house and give you
your own corner,
a warm mat to lie on,
your own water dish.

You think I don't know
you have been living
under my porch.

You long for your real place to be readied
before winter comes.

You need
your name,
your collar and tag.
You need
the right to warn off intruders,
to consider
my house your own
and me your person
and yourself
my own dog.
(Levertov, "Talking to Grief," 111)

Can you sense the difference in the relationship with grief? To meet it and not ignore it—to invite it in when it arises. As Rabbi Harold Kushner (2004) noted after losing his fifteen-year-old son: "Vulnerability to death is one of the conditions of life. We can't explain it any more than we can explain life itself. We can't control it, or sometimes even postpone it. All we can do is try to rise beyond the question, 'Why did it happen?' and begin asking the question "'What do I do now that it has happened?'"

WORKING WITH GRIEF

The psychotherapist Miriam Greenspan is a good teacher for working with complicated emotions. She became well-acquainted with grief when her son was born with a severe brain injury and died before he could even leave the hospital. Her book *Healing Through the Dark Emotions* (2003) compassionately addresses the experiences of fear, despair, and grief.

Ms. Greenspan reviews a three-step process in dealing with the "dark emotions":

1. Attending, which means feeling the emotions in the body, acknowledging their presence, and naming them;
2. Befriending, which means *allowing* the grief feelings to be present without trying to get rid of them, avoid them, or add to them by feeding them with stories of the past or projections into the future; and
3. Surrendering, which means allowing the emotions to simply be as emotions until they have run their course—not trying to change them or get rid of them before their time.

I could see many in the group nodding agreement when I asked if this reminded them of what they had been doing with their mindfulness practice. Of course, everyone has a personal manner of grieving. Still, Ms. Greenspan has identified a process that is consistent with the mindful attitude of developing a relationship with emotional pain.

Ms. Greenspan's process of attending, befriending, and surrendering provides a container that allows everyone to have their own grief experience. It also helpfully provides a map—not how to get out of grief—but critically, a model of *being with* grief.

BENEFITS OF AN ANCHOR OF AWARENESS

Mindfulness is of particular importance in a time of grief because of the significant disruption that grief brings to bear in our everyday life. This brings us to the second substantial area where I have found mindfulness to be of particular help with grief and bereavement. In addition to developing a different relationship with grief, mindfulness is of specific assistance by providing an anchor of awareness that allows you to be with powerful emotions.

Mindfulness practice does not offer an easy way out—but it does provide a strategy for you to hold these intense, volatile, and ever-changing emotional experiences. To my way of thinking, mindfulness provides that vital anchor for you to return to time and time again as you attempt to cope and be with the suffering that grief demands. Grief can feel like it is pulling you down, down, down a drain—swirling emotions that can leave you feeling disoriented and sometimes feel like you are going crazy!

So, to have an anchor—a place to come back to when you are feeling so disconnected or disoriented or ungrounded—is an essential companion through grief. To be with the grief that hits us like a rogue wave, unexpected and powerful enough to blow us over, is a significant challenge, but with a strong anchor, we can better meet and cope with the experience.

Over time and with practice, your anchor provides a place that feels safer and more grounded in reality at this moment. Many speak of this anchor being like shelter in a storm or oasis in an otherwise hostile environment. It is a place and a process that becomes available wherever and whenever grief makes an appearance. As Dr. Cacciatore noted earlier, the intention is not to cause the grief intensity to go down but rather to allow your ability to cope with grief to go up. The focus is on strengthening your personal and interpersonal resources rather than diluting the intensity of suffering. And your anchor is a critical tool to help in this process—it truly can feel like your new best friend.

APPLYING STRATEGIES TO WORK WITH GRIEF

Working with grief from a mindfulness perspective is the same as working with any powerful cognitive, emotional, and physical sensation that may arise. It involves explicitly accessing the four levels of response presented in last week's session on pain.

FIRST LEVEL OF RESPONSE

To review what we have been doing so far, the first level of response when thoughts, feelings, or body sensations associated with grief arise is simply noticing them, labelling them, and bringing your attention back to your anchor, which is usually either your breath or hand.

SECOND LEVEL OF RESPONSE

But suppose your mind repeatedly returns to the same kind of thought, feeling, or body sensation. In that case, your attention becomes hijacked—then we have a second level of response that moves your focus of attention to the body part corresponding with the thought, feeling, or sensation. It can sometimes be challenging to identify a specific body area that holds the emotion with grief. This challenge is especially tough when it feels like grief has descended over you like a heavy wet wool blanket that weighs you down. Should you have difficulty identifying a specific area where your sorrow is held, focus your exploration on your body from the stomach up the torso through the lungs and heart to the face areas. The vagus nerve runs through these regions and provides information to the brain when you feel stressed and under emotional or physical attack. If you still have difficulty locating where the grief is held even in these areas, then consciously use your heart area as the site for your temporary anchor of awareness.

The Level Two response practice then becomes using this body sensation as the temporary anchor—your focus of attention—through precisely examining what it is like. There is no need to analyze it or feed it with a story or judge whether you like it or don't like it, but instead simply to become the "curious explorer" of that particular body part in that specific moment. Explore its location, size, shape, sensation, temperature, and so on in the context of the total physical experience. Again, the goal is not to resolve whatever the thought/feeling/physical sensation is. Instead, it is simply a matter of noticing whatever the body sensations are. When the sensation lessens or dissipates, then bring the attention back to your anchor, which is your fallback focus of awareness that you will always have with you.

THIRD LEVEL OF RESPONSE

The third level of response for working with intense grief sensations is what we learned in Week Five, working with pain. That is, to now intentionally couple your usual anchor (breath or hand sensation) to the site of the grief sensation itself. If you are again having difficulty identifying a specific area where the grief is held, focus your exploration on your body from the stomach up the torso through the lungs and heart to the face areas. As noted earlier, the vagus nerve runs through these regions and provides information to the brain when you feel stressed and under threat. If you still have difficulty locating where the grief is held in these areas, then consciously use your heart area as the site for your temporary anchor of awareness.

If you use your breath as your anchor, direct the breath right into that body region that holds your grief. With the in-breath, feel it coming through that grief-stricken area and on the out-breath, feel it leaving from that grief-stricken zone. In this way, you are coupling the breath with the sensations in the region that is painful and allowing your awareness to hold them both simultaneously. Continue breathing in and out through that grief area moment by moment as best you can. You are allowing the breath to bathe that region with the incoming breath and to wash it away with the out-breath.

If you are using your hand sensation as your anchor, move your hand to the place in your body where you are feeling grief. Once you contact the site in your body holding your grief, continue to use your hand sensations as your anchor. You are coupling your hand sensations (your anchor) with the grief sensations in your body—your awareness is on your grief without judging it, analyzing it, or feeding it with stories.

It again is critical to recognize that you are not trying to take the grief away. You are utilizing a new site for your anchor of attention to experience the breath or hand sensation at the place that holds the grief. As best you can, and with the lightest of touches, staying with this experience, watching what happens and seeing how it unfolds moment to moment. This response again allows you to embody the process of befriending your grief. Instead of avoiding, numbing, or denying your sorrow, you are putting out the welcome mat for unwanted sensations, or as Denise Levertov talked about in the earlier poem, treating your grief like the warm, loving puppy that is your own.

FOURTH LEVEL OF RESPONSE

There are times, however, when grief demands a different kind of mindful attention. Just as we discussed in Week Five on pain, the fourth level of response when the experience is significant is to make it your intention to focus on only one limited aspect of your anchor of awareness. If you use your breath as your anchor, make it your intent to focus on just one half-breath. That is, knowing the grief is pulling your attention away, consciously decide that with only the next in-breath, you are going to have your attention focused on that breath experience, just for the in-breath. Your attention can then be pulled back to the grief, but it establishes that you can focus your attention on only one half-breath—just the in-breath— even with the significant grief you are experiencing.

When you can do this, then try extending it to one whole breath. Knowing that your attention focuses on powerful grief, make it your intention to shift that focus for just one in-breath and one out-breath; to bring your attention to the belly/chest rising and falling or the sensation of the breath in your nostrils or mouth for just one full breath. The painful feelings can then pull your attention back to the grief, but you again have shown that you can focus your attention for just one breath. The goal is to continue then increasing the breaths that you can focus on. To not rush the process but to simply add a half-breath each time.

If you are using your hand on your body as your anchor of awareness and find the grief experience is significant, make it your intention to focus on only one sensation of your hand on your body. Knowing that grief is so strong that it pulls your attention away from attempting to use your anchor (in this case, your hand on your body), consciously decide that you will have your attention focused on just that one hand sensation experience. Your attention can then be drawn back to the grief, but it establishes that you can focus your attention on one hand sensation—even with the significant grief you are experiencing.

If you can do this, then try extending the focus to two hand sensations. We know that the powerful feelings can then pull your attention back to the grief, but you again have shown that you can focus your attention on two hand sensations. The goal is to continue increasing the number of hand sensations you can attend to—not rushing the process but simply adding a hand sensation each time.

The fourth level of response provides you with the experience of knowing that even though grief's painful sensations are powerful, you can intentionally define your anchor of awareness. In the spirit of discovery, you are experiencing what you can do by moving your attention from the grief sensation back to your anchor for just the briefest of moments. This strategy may be only one or two or three breaths or hand sensations, but critically, you are experiencing a different approach to meeting the formidable emotion of grief.

PESKY JUDGING MIND

When working with these small incremental quantities of attention to your anchor (breath or hand sensations), be aware of the thoughts and feelings which can arise. The judging mind can be powerful in beating on you for the limited breaths or hand sensations you can focus on. Again, as with other mindfulness practices, simply acknowledge and label "judging" and continue back to the practice. The intention is to be in this moment and be able to experience your capacity of being able to focus on your anchor of attention intentionally.

EMBRACING GRIEF—"BEARING THE UNBEARABLE"

Bearing the Unbearable is the title of Dr. Cacciatore's (2017) book, and I can think of no phrase that more accurately captures the experience of grief. As you well know by this point in the course, these mindfulness strategies do not magically take away grief, nor is this the intended goal. Instead, it is a further development of your capacity to establish relationships with these most painful human emotional experiences through meeting them directly and consciously.

It is also not attempting to simply "hang on" by your fingertips with sorrow but rather "hold it" in awareness through the different mindfulness response levels. It allows you to increase your ability to cope with grief in a self-directed and healthy manner and learn that you can confidently tolerate what is commonly considered intolerable.

You have no doubt found that grief, like other powerful emotions, often comes in waves—usually when you least expect it! Recently I was shopping at Costco, minding my own business, when just as I rounded the frozen food aisle, I felt a lump land in the pit of my stomach. Like being hit with a gust of dusty wind, it caught my breath as the memory of my stillborn grandson swept through me. Even though it had been over two years since he passed and with no triggers like babies in sight, little Bowen's memory arrived unbidden. Stopping my shopping cart in the aisle (which draws no attention as everybody does it at Costco!), I imagined my breath coming in and out through my stomach area (Level Three response). Holding awareness of both the gripping tension in my lower abdomen coupled with my breath washing in and out, I allowed my grief memory to just be. In no more than a minute, I felt the tension easing. The feeling did not completely go away, but it lessened as I continued to be aware of my breath, using it as my anchor in this mini storm of mourning. Continuing to hold Bowen's memory in my mind with a felt sorrow in my heart, I was able to continue shopping, confident that I could hold and be with this bittersweet experience of being human.

By holding a mindfulness sensibility to meet sorrow, over time you will notice that your grief does not stay the same and, in fact, changes in intensity, in quality, and even in the location within the body. Sometimes these changes are experienced moment to moment, sometimes hour by hour, or day by day, or even week by week in ways that you can become more sensitive to and develop an openness to meet. But also have patience with yourself—grief cannot and will not be rushed! Mindfulness, therefore, establishes over time more of a sense of trust in yourself—that you can touch or be with, even for the briefest of moments, the experience of grief.

Difficult as it often is, to be with grief is a challenging but necessary human experience. There is no escaping the loss experience, so the question becomes, how you will meet it? The therapist Megan Devine wisely concludes: "That's the real work of grief recovery . . . finding ways to live alongside your loss, building a life around the edges of what will always be a vacancy . . . Recovery in grief is a process of moving with what was, what might have been, and what still remains. None of this is easy" (Devine 2017).

"None of this is easy" is so true! And because it is not easy, it also takes courage to meet and develop a different relationship with grief and bereavement. But as the writer and artist Mary Anne Radmacher stated, "Courage does not always roar. Sometimes courage is the quiet voice at the end of the day saying, 'I will try again tomorrow.'"

That, too, is courage!

PRACTICE OF THE WEEK

This week, I recommend that you continue with **two daily exercises** to support your developing mindfulness practice: 1) a **formal meditation** and 2) an **informal meditation**.

1. Formal Meditation Practice: Grief

Guidelines:

- I recommend you continue your formal meditation practice for **forty minutes each day** during this coming week. I encourage you to continue to try alternating sitting and walking meditations to see what works best for you. However, spend the entire forty minutes on either the walking or sitting meditation. Spending a few minutes with one before changing to another does not help stabilize the mind.

- Grief is a compelling physical, emotional, and cognitive experience, so it is essential to approach it with respect and self-compassion. As with all practices, simply allow yourself to experience what you experience without judgment or expectation. There is no right or wrong to what you encounter.

- We have explored several mindfulness strategies these past few weeks, and today's practice, similar to last week's, will walk you through the process of trying all of them. As with all the homework assignments, you can either use the audible guided instructions or just read them to yourself before starting the practice.

- This week's instructions review all four response levels to remember and be comfortable knowing the optional responses you have to meet grief. However, utilizing either the written or audible instructions each day this week could be more than what is needed and prove intrusive if you do not require all four response levels.

- Therefore, as a suggestion, listen to the audible instructions or read the written ones enough times to feel confident that you know each level of response. Then, engage in your practice session on your own to be more in control of implementing specific strategies that you require. For example, you may meet grief with a Level One response or a Level Two. However, you may need to increase your responses to Levels Three or Four, depending upon your grief experience. Knowing your options and then engaging in your practice session provides the freedom to choose what is needed. You decide—play with how it best works for you!

- Remember to record your homework on your **Tracking Your Practice** log under the Formal heading. The recording will allow you to track your sessions and experiment with what time of the day works best for you and reinforce your efforts!

FORMAL MEDITATION INSTRUCTIONS (GRIEF)

Please allow your attention to come into this space. . . . Sense the whole space in this room. . . . Perceive the space around you . . . feeling whatever there is to feel. . . .

Now bring your attention to your body. . . . Notice your feet on the floor . . . your buttocks on the chair or cushion . . . your hands resting on your thighs or folded together on your lap or at your sides. . . .

Now allow your attention to find your anchor. . . . If it is your breath . . . notice where in the body you feel it . . . perhaps the tip of the nose . . . the nostrils . . . the back of the throat . . . the chest . . . the belly. . . . Just notice the sensation of breathing. . . . Connect the feeling of breath to the spot within your body where you feel it most. . . .

Or perhaps your anchor is the sensation of your hand where it touches your body . . . where you feel the texture of the fabric under your fingers . . . or the smoothness of your skin under your hand. . . . Allow this to become the anchor of your attention . . . recognizing the sensation of your fingers as they move against your skin or clothing . . . or the sensation of increasing pressure. . . .

Know that these sensations can support you as you travel through your days. . . . Know that at any time when your mind has wandered into thoughts, feelings, or body sensations, the breath or the touch of your hand will bring you back into this precious, present moment. . . .

. . . .

Each of you has experienced losses . . . perhaps losses of many kinds . . . the loss of someone who has had meaning in your life . . . the loss of a beloved pet . . . the loss of a relationship . . . the loss of a job . . . the loss of your health . . . the loss of a dream. . . . By the time you have hit mid-life and beyond, you have each likely experienced a number of losses . . . and accompanying those losses are often the feelings of grief . . . sadness . . . anger . . . emptiness . . . confusion . . . numbness . . . fear . . . and sometimes a mixture of all of them at once.

While grief over your losses is not something that you can harness . . . or manage . . . or manipulate for it to be painless . . . it is possible to establish a different relationship with the complex emotions associated with your losses . . . not that these strategies will miraculously inoculate you against the inevitable pain that lies within grief . . . because nothing will . . . but there are ways to establish a healthier way of being with this challenging human experience. . . . Mindfulness offers you a way to accompany grief as it demands your attention. . . .

If you are aware of a rising of thoughts, emotions, or physical sensations connected to your loss and grief, step into this space consciously, mindfully, and with love and compassion toward yourself . . . to practice holding and walking with grief moment by moment. . . .

. . . .

First Level of Response

If you find that your attention has been hijacked by grief or sorrow . . . a painful thought or memory or feeling or sensation associated with grief . . . and you have lost the breath or the touch of your hand as your anchor of attention . . . then notice it. . . . Label it as just that . . . a thought, a memory, a feeling, or a physical sensation. . . . Then gently and without judgment, bring your awareness back to your anchor of attention. . . .

. . . .

Second Level of Response

If you find it difficult to return to your anchor because the grief memory, thought, feeling, or physical sensation has become too strong or too intrusive and has hijacked your awareness, then allow your attention to find where in the body that intrusion resides temporarily. . . .

If the grief is a thought or memory, explore what emotion accompanies it. . . . Perhaps it is anger . . . or sadness . . . or aloneness . . . or longing. . . . Whatever it may be, find where in your body the feeling is held. . . .

If the grief as a persistent intrusion is an emotion . . . perhaps sadness . . . anger . . . disappointment . . . confusion . . . or whatever it may be . . . locate where in your body you feel it. . . .

If the grief is a physical sensation on its own . . . a tightness . . . numbness . . . tension . . . tingling . . . whatever it may be, be aware of its location. . . .

The grief can, of course, be anywhere in this bag of bones that comprise your physical body, so be specific in identifying exactly where the grief resides. . . . Become curious as to where you feel it in the body. . . . If you have difficulty finding a particular area in your body where it is held, then choose your heart region as the place to focus your attention. . . . Use the heart area as the place where your grief is located. . . .

As you locate the body area that holds the grief, become very curious about the physical sensations. . . . What are they like? . . . Is there tightness? . . . Clenching? . . . Pressure? . . . Burning? . . . Throbbing? . . . Stabbing? . . . Is this sensation localized or does it radiate in a direction? . . .

Outward? . . . Inward? . . . Is there a warmth or a coolness? . . . Is it big? . . . Small? . . . Can you sense a shape . . . or a density of the grief? . . . Continue to hold your attention and explore in minute detail the sensations associated with the suffering in your body. . . .

As you explore the grief sensations, perhaps you notice that it has moved . . . sometimes in a dramatic manner to another part of the body or sometimes just a slight shift in location. . . . Continue to track and explore the grief sensations. . . . Don't let your attention be pulled away from your grief exploration, no matter where it may have migrated. . . .

Over time, as your attention has been exploring the body area holding the grief . . . perhaps you notice that the sensation is somewhat dissipating . . . lessening in intensity. . . . If so, then once again, allow your breath or the pressure of your hand upon your body to become the anchor of your attention . . . the gentle in and out, rising and falling of the breath . . . or the movement or intensity of the pressure from your fingers or hand where they are in contact with your body. . . .

While your first and second responses to intrusions that take your attention away from your anchor are powerful strategies that can be very effective, there are also times when strong emotional experiences associated with loss and grief require more attention. . . . That is, even with the application of the first two responses, you can find it challenging to continue to focus on your anchor of awareness. . . .

. . . .

Third Level of Response

The third level of response available is to introduce a new way to relate to the persistent intrusions of grief. . . . It is another way to be with the difficulties and challenges that grief presents . . . to be mindfully present with the strong thoughts, emotions, and physical sensations. . . .

If you continue to notice a rising of thoughts, emotions, or physical sensations in connection to your grief . . . and the first two responses have not proven effective . . . know that you do not have to run from them, numb yourself to them, or implement any other escape strategies that are available to you. . . .

Instead, it is possible to mindfully step for a moment into this difficult space with the utmost love and compassion toward yourself. . . . Recognize how powerful and challenging grief experiences can be. . . . They are among the most difficult human experiences that you will ever meet. . . . Grief is big . . . messy . . . chaotic . . . and seems to have a mind of its own. . . . Grief is a powerful experience that deserves our conscious respect . . . but not fear. . . . It is just another cognitive, emotional, and physical experience that we can befriend. . . .

When the first and second response levels do not provide some relief, move to the third level of response. . . . Allow your attention to find the area in the body where you feel the grief. . . . It may be in your jaw . . . stomach . . . chest . . . arms . . . hands. . . . As noted earlier, if the suffering is difficult to isolate in your body, consciously choose your heart region as the one to hold your grief. . . . The new strategy is to now couple your usual anchor of attention with the place in your body where the grief sensation arises. . . .

If you are using your breath as your anchor, now intentionally direct your breath right into that grief region with the in-breath. . . . Feel it coming through that grief area . . . and on the out-breath, feel it leaving from that grief area. . . . Breath in . . . and breath out . . . breath in . . . breath out . . . moment by moment . . . allowing the breath to bathe that region with the incoming breath and then to wash it away with the out-breath . . . allowing your awareness to hold both the grief and the breath simultaneously. . . .

If you are using your hand sensation as your anchor, allow yourself to move your hand to the place in your body where you are feeling grief. . . . Place your hand/fingers over that area. . . . Allow yourself to continue to feel the sensations of your hand over this area of your body. . . . Feel the pressure or slight movement of your hand over your painful body area. . . . Feel the texture of the fabric under your hand as it touches the grief . . . recognizing your anchor of awareness at the site of grief in your body. . . .

You are not trying to take the grief and sorrow away . . . just directing your attention through your anchor (breath or hand sensations) to the grief area directly . . . using your anchor to focus on the grief site . . . experiencing the sensation of breath washing in and washing out like waves of the ocean . . . or the changing sensations of your hand on your body, where it is experiencing the grief . . . ever so gently touching the grief with your anchor . . . being curious . . . watching what happens . . . seeing how it unfolds moment by moment . . . knowing that you are touching the grief that you are experiencing. . . . .

If you find that the grief sensation lessens or dissipates . . . move your anchor away from the body area . . . and return to your usual focus on your anchor of awareness . . . using the breath or your hand sensations to hold your focus. . . .

. . . .

Fourth Level of Response

If you found the third level of response challenging to do because the grief experience is so strong that it continuously pulls your attention away from your anchor . . . or perhaps you feel like you can do nothing . . . you feel frozen with the degree of grief you are experiencing . . . then it is necessary to very gently and briefly approach your grief experience through the fourth level of response. . . .

Very gently notice if you can allow your attention to rest ever so briefly on your chosen anchor of awareness . . . to set your intention to hold your attention on only a small interlude of your anchor even in the face of grief you are experiencing. . . .

If you are using your breath as your anchor, set your intention to focus on perhaps just one in-breath. . . . Nothing else needs to be done . . . just one in-breath. . . . Even during significant grief, you are developing a goal to hold your attention on only one in-breath. . . .

If you are using your hand sensation as your anchor, set your intention to rest for just a moment on the sensation of one finger pressing firmly into your thigh . . . or feeling for one moment the texture of the fabric under your finger as you gently rub it. . . . See if you can, just for one brief moment . . . allow your attention to return to your anchor of awareness even with the intensity of your grief experience . . . knowing that the grief is strong enough to pull your attention away. . . . Make it your intention to return to your anchor even for just one brief moment. . . .

Then, if your attention is drawn back to the intensity of grief thoughts, feelings, or physical sensations . . . that is okay . . . knowing that you can focus your attention on your anchor—on one half a breath, or on a brief moment of tactile sensation in your hand or fingers. . . . Even with the raw grief you are experiencing . . . you can do this. . . .

Over time, try expanding your attention on your anchor for more extended moments . . . still only moments but increased moments . . . knowing that your attention is not able to rest in your anchor for long as it gets pulled into your grief experience. . . . Very gently, make it your intention to allow your awareness to rest on just one in-breath and one out-breath . . . or on the sensation of your fingers pressing twice firmly into your thigh . . . or feeling the fabric texture under your fingers on two occasions. . . .

Know that the powerful sensations of grief will likely pull your attention away from your anchor . . . but ever so gently and slowly extending the moments that you can keep your attention on your anchor of awareness . . . perhaps one and a half breaths . . . or two breaths . . . or the sensation of your fingers on your body/clothing for three sensations . . . or four sensations . . . just setting your intention to focus your awareness on your anchor for slightly a bit longer . . . just a little bit longer . . . not trying to change the grief experience . . . instead, just learning to be with the grief experience even when it is strong. . . .

There is no rush in this practice. . . . It is a time to be compassionate and gentle toward what you are experiencing. . . . You may be noticing the judging mind. . . . It may be beating you up for the limited breaths that you were able to focus on . . . or on your ability to detect the pressure from your hand on your body. . . . Again, with mindfulness sensitivity, simply acknowledge and label this as "judging" and allow yourself to continue back to the practice. . . .

As you set your intention for one or two breaths/hand sensations . . . notice how that felt . . . perhaps a sense of courage . . . a sense of accomplishment . . . a sense of hope that you can stay present in your grief experience without getting lost in it . . . knowing how powerful your grief experience is and yet you can stay with your anchor for moments . . . that even with the significant grief, you can direct your attention where you want it to be . . . on your anchor of awareness . . . that being your breath . . . or your hand sensations . . . for just a moment . . . and over time, to see if you can extend your capacity to be with this grief experience . . . for another moment . . . and later for another moment . . . not ruled by grief . . . but travelling alongside it . . . meeting it . . . changing your relationship to it as you focus your awareness on your anchor of attention. . . .

. . . .

Perhaps you have found this very difficult to do. . . . Acknowledge that this is not easy. . . . It takes practice . . . and practice . . . and practice . . . coupled with your intention to hold the attitudinal foundations in this experience . . . acceptance . . . non-judging . . . beginner's mind . . . trust . . . non-striving. . . . Be gentle and compassionate with yourself. . . . Allow your courage to declare: "I will try again later . . . I will try again later" . . .

. . . .

As you continue to meditate, remember that your intention with this mindfulness practice is to be in this moment simply . . . and, at this moment, to be able to experience your capacity of being able to focus on your anchor of awareness intentionally . . . the breath . . . or hand sensations . . . no matter what arises in the mind or body . . . to be able to befriend whatever arises . . . to travel alongside with whatever arises . . . even the more challenging and complex thoughts . . . feelings . . . and physical sensations that occur with grief . . . to develop a sense of confidence and trust in yourself that you can meet whatever arises. . . . Not that this will be easy . . . or painless . . . but to know that you do not have to hide . . . or avoid . . . or numb yourself to the 10,000 sorrows or challenges that are a part of this life that is yours . . . that you can learn to respond rather than just react to whatever arises . . . to be fully present in each moment. . . .

. . . .

Take these next few moments to keep practising. . . . Be gentle with yourself. . . .

. . . .

I will soon bring your attention back to the room. . . . I will ring the bell three times. . . . Slowly and at your own pace . . . allow yourself to open your eyes . . . and bring your awareness back to the space while still being conscious of your anchor . . . of being able to hold attention of your anchor even as you are aware of your surroundings. . . . Offer yourself compassion and loving-kindness for the courage to practise and to explore new ways of being present to yourself even amid difficult experiences such as grief. . . .

2. Informal Mindfulness Practices

Guidelines:

- As we have discussed in past weeks, outside of the formal practice sessions, there are ample opportunities to continue learning to be more mindfully present. These informal practices arise out of the daily activities that comprise your life and therefore are readily available to be of service to your learning process.

- This week, I invite you to continue exploring informal mindfulness practices daily. Be creative—try new ones.

- While it is easy to identify many daily activities to which you can apply your burgeoning mindfulness skills, they all share a commonality of being ones you probably don't pay much attention to. The activity itself is not what is critical. Instead, any activity that allows you to slow down the process to experience it with your senses entirely is what makes it an informal mindfulness practice and, therefore, a good one to choose.

- The instructions are the same for each activity: be aware of the steps involved; decide what the initial component of the first step will be; and slowly begin working through each stage, focusing on your senses of sight, touch, hearing, smell, and (if appropriate) taste. Be curious as to how you are experiencing each step through your senses. Take your time and be curious about this activity that you could do in your sleep but want to approach with a beginner's mind as if undertaking it for the first time. Enjoy the process!

- Again, be sure to record your activity on the **Tracking Your Practice** log under the Informal heading.

- In addition to structured activities that provide tremendous opportunities for mindfulness training, I also recommend that you set an intention to be aware of your anchor of attention (either your breath or hand sensations) from time to time throughout the day. This awareness does not have to entail lengthy periods but rather just a momentary noticing of your anchor at that moment. Feel the sensation of either your breath rising and falling or your hand sensations. Be curious about what this feels like in this unique moment.

- It is also possible to use daily activities as triggers to remind yourself to notice your breath. The intent is not to take your full awareness off the situation you are in but rather to be curious about your anchor in that particular moment. For example, check in with your anchor when you get a coffee or tea, when you stop at a red light, when you leave your home or work, and so forth. With practice, you will build a greater trust in your ability to be aware of your anchor of awareness and still be conscious and aware of activities you are involved in.

MIDWEEK CUPPA... REFLECTIONS ON NON-STRIVING AND AGING

WEEK SIX

Desiring to be rid of intrusive troublesome personal foibles arises throughout a lifetime. Still, my psychotherapy practice found that aging years often act as an incentive to confront the most troubling ones. The recognition of limited years remaining is a forceful motivator to address long-held beliefs and behaviours that limit life's happiness and contentment.

However, while striving for personal growth and development is a laudable goal, achieving positive change is often unsuccessful through fierce, gritty determination and action. Paradoxically, change can often come about through the gentler and self-compassion course of non-striving.

SHAME'S POISON

Reid slumped in the chair in my office, head bowed with eyes cast to the floor as he tentatively shared a long-held but closely guarded secret: "I feel like an imposter that no one would love if they really knew me!" While this concern frequently is experienced by adolescents struggling with identity formation when entering young adulthood, Reid was seventy-three years old when I first met him. He had a successful career as a skilled tradesman (now retired), a long-term marriage, and had raised a loving family of four kids. He was admired in the community for his volunteer work, active in a service club, and proud of maintaining friendships formed in his high school days. And yet, even with these impressive life accomplishments, Reid's inner world was racked with self-doubt and recriminations. During our first hour together, he acknowledged that his life from an early age had relentlessly been haunted by a destructive inner voice condemning him as unworthy and inadequate. Through tears of despair, Reid sobbed that he had lived a life of shame!

Shame is a self-conscious emotion typically associated with a negative evaluation of yourself, a virtual laundry list of what you lack. The varieties of shame are numerous, with examples being that you are not smart enough, beautiful enough, moral enough, competent enough, lovable enough, or sufficient enough in some way that defines your inner belief in who you should be. Shame is a critical inner voice concluding that some essential characteristic is absent at your core, resulting in what Dr. Tara Brach characterized as a persistent "trance of unworthiness" (Brach 2016).

In my psychotherapy practice, I found the incidence of shame to be considerable. It is a powerfully damaging tenet that unchecked undermines the ability to find satisfaction and contentment in life. An early researcher on shame, Gershen Kaufman, went so far as to declare: "Shame is without parallel—a sickness of the soul. It is a violation of our essential dignity."

While the common perception is that a shame-based identity will result in a defeated, poorly functioning attachment to society, I have found just the opposite—many clients have spent a lifetime attempting to outrun or overpower the punishing inner judge through enduring overcompensation. Striving mightily becomes their pervasive and unquestioned mantra!

Many high-functioning and accomplished individuals are ironically driven to their success by an underlying sense of inferiority. While the striving to prove to themselves that they are worthy by way of triumphs and achievements may result in career, financial, and personal success, paradoxically, it spectacularly fails to quiet the inner critic, only resulting in a new round of striving. With shame, as with mindfulness meditation, striving proves to be a losing strategy. As the nineteenth-century philosopher Arthur Schopenhauer accurately describes: "All striving comes from lack, from a dissatisfaction with one's condition, and is thus suffering as long as it is not satisfied; but no satisfaction is lasting; instead, it is only the beginning of a new striving" (Schopenhauer 1969).

Aging often arrives with weariness to the ongoing and failed strivings to silence the punitive inner judge. While mindfulness can often help change your relationship to the experience of shame, its powerful destructive quality is not to be underestimated. Shame can be a vicious and damaging emotion, requiring a more structured and direct treatment. Jungian psychology presents a practical and effective treatment addition with its equivalent goal of developing a relationship with all aspects of yourself.

JUNGIAN PSYCHOLOGY MEETS SHAME

A Jungian psychological perspective on shame concludes that it is often borne in early childhood. If there has been stunting of positive beliefs or incorporation of false/misperceived ideas regarding your self-worth, it usually has roots in the initial phases of life. Attention spent in therapy exploring your early years is not undertaken as an intellectual exercise nor a "witch hunt" to blame others. Instead, it attempts to reduce the effects of early childhood interferences and begin fostering an attitude facilitating a more realistic self-concept foundation.

Jungian psychology rejects any semblance of perfection within human life. Instead, it seeks wholeness and acceptance of all of who you are, which includes limitations and inadequacies echoed by Suzuki Roshi's famous dictum: "You are perfect the way you are—and you could use a little improvement"!

Over the years, while working with my own and many clients holding shame-based identities, I have developed a treatment protocol that has proven fruitful. Combining aspects of mindfulness with Jungian psychology, a four-step treatment practice of shame shreds its powerful, destructive force allowing it to be incorporated into an expanded and healthier sense of self.

Reid's exhaustion of a lifetime's struggle to overcome his perceived shame was palatable. With retirement, he no longer had an outlet of work accomplishments that offered the false hope, as he had clung to so many times during his life, that maybe *this* time, with a new goal or project, he would be able to satisfy his inner judge. However, even Reid recognized from his history that outer world accomplishments proved impotent, only providing a band-aid with limited and fleeting relief to his painful inner life. Reid felt trapped and did not want to waste his years continuing to hide from his punitive inner tyrant, so he was ready to try a new way of meeting his painful lifelong companion of shame.

FIRST STEP—AWARENESS

Your entry into mindfulness has vividly unearthed a cacophony of emotions that you experience on an ongoing basis. Reid, however, had not been exposed to this mindfulness reality, so the first step in changing his relationship to shame was to become aware of when it arose. This may sound trite—of course he knows when shame shows up! However, your mindfulness experience has demonstrated that it can be confusing to identify any particular emotion with so many feelings swirling around.

However, as learned in the mindfulness practice, an effective strategy to identify feelings is to pay attention to what emotions feel like in the body. Learning to recognize that painful emotions are often expressed through a tight chest, shallow breathing, constricted throat, tense muscles, frozen jaw, furrowed brow, and so forth, Reid became a curious explorer focusing on feelings of shame. Over time, he recognized the arrival of shame-based feelings through tightness somewhere in his body. While this tightness often showed in his chest, at other times, he also found it occurring in his face and throat. Tightness became Reid's knock on the door—a sign that shame was likely activated.

In addition to exploring body sensations, he also tracked any impulse to hide as a complementary method to identify shame feelings. The impulse to hide with shame may sound peculiar but is an essential factor to explore. One of shame's core features is an attempt to conceal what you believe about yourself from others; you think you are unworthy and you do not want others to recognize this "truth," so a desire to become invisible rides shotgun with shame. Trying to force the world to look away to keep your shameful situation from being seen becomes a pressing imperative.

Understanding and becoming aware of this time-worn strategy of hiding allowed Reid to directly identify his long-held shame and begin changing his relationship to it. No longer striving to escape from this feeling as quickly as possible, Reid learned that he could meet and hold shame through his body exploration of tightness.

STEP TWO—COMPASSION

Since Reid's shame-based feelings likely initially arose during early childhood years, it is essential to understand that he is not emotionally operating on an adult level when they are presently activated. Instead, at the present moment, when shame erupts, Reid is emotionally feeling like a young child. While this may not sound rational, it is the way that our emotional life operates.

Since Reid's present painful experience of shame is a powerfully problematic one, he needs to take the next self-soothing step. This is done on an imaginal level, with Reid seeing himself as a young boy who feels scared, hurt, sad, in pain, or whatever he experiences. Using his mind's eye, he sees himself as an adult soothing his young child self by holding his hand, having him sit on his lap, holding him close, telling him that he is safe and will be all right. Whatever Reid would do in the outer world to comfort his own children is what he now needs to do for himself.

The intention is to reduce the emotional valence that Reid is presently experiencing. The goal is not to completely eradicate the charged emotions (while this would be welcomed, it is not likely to occur) but, instead, take the heightened emotional functioning down a notch or two. I've found that the increased emotional charge of shameful feelings negatively interferes with the following steps' implementation without this self-soothing.

Neuroscience confirms that rational cognitive capabilities to learn a new way of being are taken off-line when shame is actively present.

In addition, the other benefit of compassion at this step is through Reid's understanding that when shame-based feelings initially began, he, as a young child, was not capable of fully understanding what was happening. He simply did not have the intellectual capacity to evaluate the situation and understand what other factors led to his unworthy and unlovable feelings. Without reasoning capacity to consider alternate hypotheses, Reid's child-centred fallback position of concluding that there must be something *wrong with him* inevitably laid the foundation for a shame-based identity. To now comprehend that, as a child, Reid did not have any other option to make sense of his world except to conclude that he was unworthy led to a new sense of compassion for himself.

STEP THREE—RIGHT THINKING

With the emotional charge of shame-based emotions dampened, Reid was now ready to meet shame directly. While his inner judge may sound like someone from his past (such as a parent, sibling, teacher, religious figure, etc.) who was critical, harsh, or abusive, the reality is that maintenance of shame over Reid's lifetime has required his active participation. The shift from Reid hearing destructive negative judgments coming from others to understanding that they perpetuate from within himself is a significant step necessary to alter these sinister accusations. This is not meant to blame Reid for having these beliefs, for this would only continue his feelings of shame; instead, with the recognition that the hostile inner critic comes from within himself, he can take responsibility to now challenge and change it. This alteration in awareness facilitates Reid's understanding that he holds more agency over his life than earlier believed.

Reid's mindful awareness of his inner self-judgments illuminated a core theme running through his shame-based identity. While experiencing school challenges with a likely undiagnosed dyslexia condition, Reid had, nevertheless, been able to graduate from high school and complete an electrical apprenticeship through sheer determination and creative strategies. However, his fear of being seen as "stupid" remained throughout the years, even though his hard-won successes would realistically negate that characterization.

An essential key to working with Reid's inner judge recognized that its pronouncements are of a generalized nature. The inner judge dogmatically declares that Reid is *always* stupid or is *never* smart enough—there is no middle ground to the critic's black-and-white world assessments. Reid's task was to challenge his judge's overarching negative assertions just as a good lawyer during cross-examination of a witness needs to pick holes in their testimony. This required examining Reid's life story to collect details that counter the judge's dogmatic negative declarations.

Reid was able to take inventory of past actions and identify many instances of precisely the opposite to what the judge so condescendingly hurled at him. Countering the supposition that Reid was stupid was, in fact, easy to accomplish with his completion of school, earning his journeyman trades qualification, working successfully at his career for over forty-four years, financially providing for his family, responsibly and lovingly raising his children, participating in multiple benevolent community projects, etc. All activities incongruent with being "stupid"!

One of the trickier aspects of this step recognizes that some of what the judge says is most likely true. Like all of us, Reid could not say that every decision made over his long life had been the absolute best, most appropriate, and "smartest." Clearly, that would be considered a life of perfection to which none of us can claim. Any attempt to present yourself as the mirror opposite to what your critic promotes is only a desperate defence continually rooted in shame.

The skillful approach to meeting the judge's negative declarations is not attempting to prove that you are perfect but instead to refute the claim that you are *always* or *never* one way or another. Yes, you have likely acted or thought in ways for which the judge criticizes you. Still, the reality is that you have also demonstrated the capacity to exhibit healthier decisions and actions, which means that the judge's condemning assertions are patently false! Reid's goal at this step is to develop a more flexible and realistic self-assessment.

STEP FOUR—RIGHT ACTION

After Reid successfully refuted the false generalized beliefs driven by his shame-based identity, the next step, and perhaps most difficult, is to act in a non-shame-based manner. As reviewed earlier, shame desperately wants you to hide from the world whenever a potential shame-inducing experience occurs. This continual attempt to avoid others seeing you for who you mistakenly believe you are not only takes considerable time and energy to implement but also reinforces your shame beliefs.

Therefore, an essential step in Reid's development of a different relationship with shame is to not fall into this reflexive avoidance pit; instead, a critical healing strategy is for Reid to act in a healthy, non-shame-based manner. Reid's challenge is to be honest and genuine when he makes a mistake or behaves in a less-than-skillful way by owning his misstep. This doesn't mean that Reid needs to take out a full-page ad in his local newspaper or openly "confess" his failure on Facebook, declaring his error for all to see; however, it does ask Reid to stand up and be his authentic self, which includes owning his mistake.

Learning to hold uncomfortable emotions that will undoubtedly arise when Reid makes an error takes courage and strength. The capacity to develop tolerance and resilience through mindfulness practice facilitates acceptance and a demonstration of your changed relationship to yourself, a new camaraderie befriending yourself.

Meeting your shame head-on does not mean that this is a one-and-done treatment. Shame beliefs and avoidance actions did not become habituated overnight, so do not expect them to retreat in the blink of an eye. My experience is that unhealthy shame thoughts are simply never going to evaporate completely! To believe that you will never have another shame thought cross your awareness is to continue to hold to perfection's erroneous goal. So, when shame pokes its head out of the shadows (as it inevitably will!), confidently know that you can meet this old irritant for what it is—just a thought, a feeling, or an action that you can meet, hold, and transform into your unfolding life journey.

As you age with the awareness of time inexorably passing, the imperative to shake intrusive self-limiting annoyances grows stronger. It is a gift to meet the moment when corrective action can no longer be postponed, for with limited time available to fully live this life that is yours, if not now, when?

TOUCHING THE END: MINDFULNESS ENCOUNTERS CHRONIC/ LIFE-LIMITING ILLNESS

WEEK SEVEN

MEETING GRIEF'S MULTIPLE LAYERS

A palpable heaviness was evident in the room as the seventh mindfulness session began with a review of the past week's practice sessions. After a long silence, Darnell quietly recounted that during the week, when he started to work mindfully with his grief over his mother's passing, he found his attention was repeatedly pulled to several conflicting feelings, including not only sadness, but also guilt and anger. His attempts to be in the moment by focusing his attention on his breath frequently were interrupted by memories of the care his mother received during her last months and his questioning as to whether there was more that he could have done to alleviate her suffering. While he rationally understood that he was very attentive to her needs and therefore unable to identify anything more he could have done, nevertheless, feelings of guilt continued to wash over him.

To confuse the matter even more, though, Darnell also felt intrusive feelings of anger toward his mother for having left him! While he understood that these were not rational thoughts, he still found it challenging to work with them effectively both during his mindfulness practice and throughout his day.

Over the coming days, however, Darnell's diligent application of the mindfulness strategies, including using the identified intrusive thought, emotional tone and associated physical body sensation as the new anchor of his awareness, proved helpful. The feelings of guilt gradually receded as he simply held them in his attention, not judging or criticizing or analyzing or trying to make them go away—just being with the feeling of guilt when it arose. He was aware that the feeling did not have any basis in reality and therefore was just a feeling that could arise and fall away.

The feelings of anger also gradually reduced but continued to intrude into his daily life. While reading the Midweek Cuppa section, Darnell readily identified with the powerful feelings of shame he had been carrying. This allowed him to unravel his feelings of anger toward his mother and found that they were actually concealing his underlying feelings of shame. That is, Darnell came to realize that his anger toward his mother for passing masked his deep-seated core belief of "not being good enough," and that he, even at fifty-seven years of age, would not be capable of successfully living his life without his mother's presence and support. Uncovering this deep-seated feeling of shame allowed Darnell to realize that his central work with anger was not about his grief as he mistakenly believed, but rather to address his core identity beliefs and feelings appropriately.

Darnell's experience of letting go of thoughts, feelings, and physical sensations is a terrific example of mindfulness's benefits. His guilt experience demonstrated that since there was no rational basis for believing that he did not do enough for his dying mother, he could just be with the feeling, allow it to arise without a struggle, and then just let it go as it receded. Not that this was a quick or easy process, but through perseverance and commitment to the mindfulness strategies, he was able to develop a different and healthier relationship to his feeling of guilt.

Darnell's experience with anger also is instructive. While these feelings did diminish over time with mindfulness practice and the treatment protocol addressing his shame beliefs proved helpful, Darnell realized that he had been hiding from his life. With his sense of self-identity feeling quite shaken, he decided to proactively confront whatever else may be undermining his enjoyment of life and therefore sought additional professional counselling. While some may interpret this as a weakness of mindfulness, I believe it demonstrates a positive and powerful gift that mindfulness holds. When thoughts, feelings, or body sensations prove resistant to mindfulness interventions over time, or when you intuitively know that there is considerably more psychological baggage to be sorted, it is advisable to seek additional professional assistance. Whether this further intervention is of a psychological or medical nature, mindfulness can help you identify issues that require more than what the practice can offer.

REVIEW GRIEF PRACTICE

Working with grief during the past week has reinforced your known experience that it is undeniably a big, messy, and chaotic process that forcibly resists any attempts to be tamed or mastered. While a mindfulness approach can be beneficial, it is, of course, no magic bullet that effortlessly eradicates all your pain and sorrow associated with personal losses. However, this comes as no surprise because, as noted throughout this course, you know that nothing will protect you from the inevitable pain, loss, and sorrow that each life encounters!

However, what mindfulness does offer is a means to change your awareness, experience, and relationship with the difficulties associated with loss and sorrow. To meet grief in this way is to turn toward it, befriend it, and establish a different affinity with this challenging human experience.

MINDFULNESS PLUS

Darnell's experience makes clear that mindfulness is not a panacea for all that interferes in your life. In the spirit of developing consciousness, sometimes meditation is not sufficient. Additional intervention, such as psychotherapy, can be beneficial, especially when dealing with a history of past traumatic experiences or incomplete developmental tasks of your emotional life.

While some may see this as a weakness of mindfulness practice, I see it as a strength in that letting go of denial or adversarial attitudes to moment-to-moment experience allows you to understand better whatever is arising and be able to respond rather than reflexively react. There is no absolute rule on how long mindfulness practice should continue before seeking additional professional assistance, so this is left as an individual decision.

As a guide, however, should such thoughts, feelings, or physical sensations continue even with the conscious application of attitudinal foundations such as acceptance, non-judging, non-striving, beginner's mind, and trust, it is probably wise to seek additional professional intervention. Darnell is a good example, as while increased consciousness allowed him to let go of his cover-up anger toward his mother and address his long-standing underlying issues more appropriately, his need to address his more pervasive misperceived sense of identity required additional intervention.

PATIENCE

Darnell's attitudes of beginner's mind, acceptance, non-judging, non-striving, and trust helped meet and establish a healthier relationship with his experience of grief. His recently revealed unsteady sense of identity will require a process of change over time necessitating patience, which is the sixth attitudinal foundation to review.

There is a useful illustration of the crucial nature of patience, in the classic example of a child trying to help a butterfly's entry into the world by breaking open its chrysalis. Unfortunately, the butterfly doesn't benefit from this because it is only through the butterfly's struggle to remove itself from the chrysalis on its timeline that its wings become strong enough to fly away. The process simply cannot be hurried. As the ancient philosopher, Lao Tzu, summed up this important lesson, "Nature does not hurry, yet everything is accomplished."

Patience is a form of wisdom indicating that you understand and accept that life will evolve in its own time, which is diametrically opposed to your likely repeated demands of what and when life should be. A close cousin to non-striving, the word patience comes from the Old French language meaning "calm endurance," with later additions clarifying that this tolerant perseverance response is needed to meet hardship, provocation, pain, delay, and so on. Therefore, patience refers to not only the action of waiting with resolve and determination but also includes a critical companion attitude invoking images of tolerance, self-control, and steadiness—the stereotypic image of being unflappable, solid, and firm as the Rock of Gibraltar!

In the same way, practising mindfulness makes it abundantly clear that you cannot rush the learning process of paying attention, on purpose, in the present moment, non-judgmentally. I'm sure that by now, you have had at least one moment of feeling impatient when attempting to focus your attention on your anchor of awareness! Okay, I'm facetious about there being only one occasion—a more realistic record would likely be more moments of impatience than you can remember, perhaps even during your last formal forty-minute meditation session! Patience, simple as it is to understand, is not easy to muster. An old Moroccan saying that "At the gate of patience there is no crowding" fittingly applies to early mindfulness training.

Precisely because your patience will be tested, it presents as an essential attitude to nurture during mindfulness. The attitude of patience supports accepting the mind's wandering tendency by remembering that it is just what the mind has always done and will continue to do. You don't have to react reflexively but rather can consciously respond, and there is no benefit to vilifying yourself when your attention wanders. To be patient is simply to be curious of each moment, meeting and holding it as it is, trusting that you can gently return to your anchor of awareness and, through this process, live fully in this unfolding moment. You are knowing and developing trust that these moments patiently knit together, advancing the story of your life. Patience enables you to live more fully in the moment in service of becoming a better friend to yourself.

The gift of patience is through engendering self-confidence. Over time and with practice (lots of it, to be sure), there is no need to become anxious or question your capacity to meet and hold whatever arises. Patience, in conjunction with trust, non-striving, acceptance, non-judging and beginner's mind, generates a foundational belief in your capacity to be with the moment. This does not mean that you will blissfully float above the situation, for its content can still be painfully challenging—remember, this is life! Instead, patience provides a container to support your capacity to respond mindfully to all that crosses your awareness.

With its increased potential of experiencing new challenges such as chronic/life-limiting illness, aging will certainly trial your attitudinal capabilities to be with each moment in a patient and healthy manner. But as you have done throughout this course, let's not just talk about it. Let's get personal and put mindfulness to the test with chronic/life-limiting illnesses!

CHRONIC/LIFE-LIMITING ILLNESS

Studies of Western industrialized countries indicate that only approximately ten percent of us will die suddenly—therefore, the rest of us will face many choices about how to live with illness and, by extension, how we live with our dying. Even if you question the accuracy of statistics or that figure is off by a few percentage points, it does indicate that most of us will likely have to live with chronic/life-limiting illnesses.

HELLO, ILLNESS

"There is nothing like a serious illness to blow down our fragile houses of sticks and straw," concludes the writer Kat Duff (1993), who experienced chronic fatigue syndrome. It may be cliché to say, but coming so close to an incurable or life-shortening illness can be crushing in every aspect. From a physical perspective, everyday life activities may require more energy, and even with your best efforts, you may not be able to do what you used to do when you wanted to do it. Illness can often bring the demoralizing reality that you may need help from others. Unpleasant physical discomforts like fatigue, nausea, and pain can become your new roommates.

Mentally, you may battle with feeling unwell from the illness or treatment. You may wrestle with the diagnostic statistics signalling that this illness may be prolonged or even that it is unlikely you will recover from it. When your health deteriorates through illness, you can feel diminished, whittled away by loss after loss. Dr. Jung described his experience following a heart attack as a "painful process of defoliation" (Jung 1973).

And emotions—a flood of cascading feelings can easily overwhelm you! Fear and anxiety are compelling, powerful emotions that can be aroused through chronic/life-limiting illnesses. The fear of the unknown future with such an illness can be disabling in and of itself. Regret for things you have done or yet to complete can also plague your waking (and sometimes dreaming) moments. Anxiety about running out of time before you have accomplished what you wanted to accomplish or experience what you wanted to encounter with family and friends can be distressing. Recognizing the enormity of adjustments and losses to come can be disheartening and saddening.

Socially, you may notice that your relationship with loved ones and friends is shifting. Sometimes they become closer, illness propelling you to acknowledge and not miss the passing moments, while other connections may be growing more distant. Illness has a way to acutely underscore which relationships are the important ones and which are not. Your connection with your work life can change dramatically, often ending in a manner not expected or planned.

The writer Kat Duff (1993) noted: "We drop out of the game when we get sick, leave the field, and desert the cause. I often feel like a ghost, the slight shade of a person, floating through the world, but not of it. The rules and parameters of my world are different altogether."

Spiritually, you may try to come to terms with your understanding of the universe and what has happened to you. If not already explored, you may be prodded to investigate the meaning of life and, relatedly, wonder about death and what it will be like. As Mary Oliver (1992) muses in her poem titled *When Death Comes:* ". . .when death comes. . .I want to step through the door full of curiosity, wondering:/ what is it going to be like, that cottage of darkness?"

A chronic/life-limiting illness diagnosis can also prove a positive motivation to review your life and discern what is profoundly important. Illness can push you to strip away the negative self-judgments that you so often carry, the frantic pace of "doing" that you have until now believed to be necessary and to cherish those in your life who truly matter. As a result, you become ever more real and authentic. While not usually identified when a diagnosis first arrives, over time, individuals report that experiencing a chronic or life-limiting illness can, in some ways, be seen as a gift. But if that change in relationship to our illness does occur, it usually follows a period of upset, unrest, fear, and turmoil.

PROBLEMS PREDICTING THE FUTURE

As discussed in Week Two, an unsettling reality of life is that you do not know what the future will bring, notwithstanding your personal mythology incorporating contracts you made with the world, universe, God, and so on to create an illusory sense of control. While the immediate consequence of a chronic/life-limiting illness will vary, one of its characteristic effects is that it forces you to come face-to-face with this reality—your future is unknown! However long it may be, your future is now undeniably dependent on more than what you alone can affect. The unknown future becomes consuming as your primary lens through which your thoughts, emotions, and actions unfold. If ever there was a cause for upset, unrest, fear, and turmoil, this has to be a strong contender! In addition to the negative impacts of the illness itself, this undeniable confrontation with your inability to know what your future holds feels disorienting and destabilizing—it can feel like you are going crazy!

While not trying to be Pollyanna concerning a chronic or life-limiting illness, it is nevertheless vital to be aware that your ability to foretell how your life will be in the future, while a dominating focus, is not very strong.

As reviewed in Week One, future time travel is based on your brilliant capacity to make predictions about future events you have never experienced before. In essence, you generate mental simulations or previews of coming events that cause you to have emotional reactions, which you then use as a basis for your predictions about your anticipated emotional quality of life if they were to happen. Receiving a diagnosis of a chronic or life-limiting illness now makes the situation very real; it is no longer a simulation.

This diagnostic reality now opens the floodgates of your imagination to generate more future consequences, often ever wilder and usually bleaker than previously created. At times like this, you appreciate just how creative your mind can be with creating frightening worst-case scenarios; your creative capacity rivals the best of Hollywood scriptwriters.

However, in the area of emotional prediction, ingenious as it is, research has uncovered several sources of error that are critical for you to be aware of before going down the rabbit hole of your mind's fantasies. For example, one of the reasons your expectations do not often match your future reality is that previews tend to emphasize the events of early happenings rather than later occurring moments. Just as people often remember past events by their endings, they appear to fantasize about future events by their early stages.

A critical consequence of focusing on early-arising moments is that previews take little account of your capacity for adaptation. As you have found with your mindfulness practice, emotions tend to dissolve over time, which is important since previews highlight the early diagnostic moments that evoke the most intense feeling. This becomes significant because research has demonstrated that healthy people consistently over-rate how unhappy they would be with ill health. Their previews of illness emphasize the early moments in which they make the difficult transition from being healthy to sick, ignoring the numerous moments that follow through adapting to their new circumstances. People imagine the early stage of *becoming* disabled rather than the later experience of *being* disabled, and emerging into this condition is often much worse than being with it. Over time, most people adapt at least somewhat to disability.

Another reason for your poor predictions of emotional reactions to future events is that people adapt to distressing circumstances more rapidly when they cannot undo them than when they can. When faced with an illness that cannot be cured, individuals can adapt more quickly to this experience. Unfortunately, you don't consider this when you are simulating your potential emotional response to future events.

A further concern in terms of the reliability of your future predictions is that your preview of a future event tends to overlook features related to the event, but that may have a significant impact on your emotional reactions. For example, studies have shown that people overestimate how happy they would be to move to a warm climate like California. The optimistic prediction is based on their previews of positive defining features, such as sunshine and ocean beaches, but fails to include accompanying troublesome but tangible elements, such as traffic gridlock and poor air quality. I know this flawed prediction process to be accurate because when I fantasize about winning a lottery, I imagine the positive aspects of wealth but conveniently neglect to consider pesky problems, such as taxes and previously unknown relatives, or even strangers masquerading as kin, coming out of the woodwork looking for a handout!

In addition, researchers also found that accurate predictions require that the context in which previewing occurs be similar to the actual event. That is, your future prognostications are not just reactions to the previews but are also shaped and influenced by the situation you are in when these previews are envisioned. As a simple example, you feel happier imagining eating chocolate cake when you are hungry rather than when full and satisfied after a big meal. Regarding an illness, predicting the future when given a new diagnosis can look very different and much scarier when you are in the throes of initial shock instead of a later, more rational outlook.

What all this means is that while receiving the diagnosis of a chronic or life-limiting illness is, of course, a challenging and often harrowing experience, predicting how your life will now be going forward is suspect. Therefore, at this time, the attitudinal foundations of beginner's mind, of opening to each moment without knowing what will arise, coupled with acceptance, non-judging, non-striving, patience, and trust, provide a healthier and more compassionate strategy.

ILLNESS AS "ROUGH INITIATION"

As if it were not enough to have the reality driven home that predictions about your new future are suspect, illness makes even more demands of you. The psychotherapist Francis Weller (2015) notes that illness throws you into a "rough initiation." All initiation events throughout the ages have a common theme: it takes you into an unknown and unshaped world. In an initiation, nothing is as it was, nor is it intended to be. It is a time of shedding and endings. It is now undeniably evident that the familiar world is left behind, and you have no choice but to continue your life journey into the unknown. Like it or not (usually not!), you are in a time of radical change.

Weller further notes that a prominent aspect of this upheaval is the identity you have known for your entire life can feel dissolved. Illness carries you into places of great uncertainty—*Will I ever get better? Will I ever feel "normal" again? Who am I?* You can no longer lean on what you know for a feeling of stability. You can feel a sense of depersonalization, adrift in a new uncharted world, and as in all authentic initiations, you fear that you are not up to the unasked-for task.

Weller specifically notes that while a significant focus in your mind is the hope of getting back to where you were before a sickness began, this is not going to happen. The roots of the word "recovery" literally mean "to get back something we lost." Even with successful treatment of an illness, you will not return to your life exactly the way you were before the ailment arrived. You are forced to accept that your illness has uprooted you and your life as known. Physically, psychologically, socially, and spiritually you are compelled to navigate your new world. Like any authentic ritual process, you will come out of the experience profoundly changed.

Illness sheds all excess, winnowing you down to the bare essentials. Weller writes: "When the choice of denial has been stripped away, as it is in illness, we are brought face-to-face with our own mortal lives, our tender vulnerabilities, the old wounds that linger in our hearts, the fragility of flesh, and the immensity of soul. We are ushered into a darker night that sheds an astonishing light on our deeper and more genuine shape."

This descent into a darker night is often accompanied by physical, mental, and emotional obstacles that make it very difficult to live in the moment. Of course, the discipline of medicine will be available to address physical illness and its symptoms biologically. Psychotherapy and counselling can also be helpful to deal with the cascade of emotional concerns that arise. So, what can mindfulness offer to you in the throes of a chronic/life-limiting illness?

MINDFULNESS MEETS ILLNESS

When I posed this question to the group, I was gratified by the multiple responses that quickly arose. In essence, the group's answers echoed what they had been learning and applying to all complex physical, cognitive, and emotional situations over the past six weeks. The newly learned and practised mindfulness strategies also apply to chronic/life-limiting illness because it presents challenges on physical, emotional, and cognitive levels. In essence, mindfulness meets illness through a two-pronged approach of self-regulating attention to the present moment coupled with changing your relationship to whatever the moment presents.

Since chronic/life-limiting illness entails physical, emotional, and cognitive constituents, often all tossed together at once, you know by now how to satisfy mindfulness goals. First, utilizing your anchor of awareness through the four levels of response facilitates your capacity to self-regulate attention at the moment. Mindfulness allows you to respond more thoughtfully instead of simply reacting in a knee-jerk fashion to whatever your thoughts, feelings, or body sensations are. When you respond rather than react, you have the opportunity to make better decisions and are less likely to suffer from negative repercussions.

LET DOWN BY MY BODY

Second, applying the attitudinal foundations helps develop a more receptive, accepting, healthier, and compassionate response to whatever arises, critically needed in the face of chronic/life-limiting illness.

However, many people with a chronic/life-limiting disease may feel that their body is not their friend as it has betrayed them. Karl angrily related his disappointment at coming down with prostate cancer even though he had spent his life proactively nurturing his health. Carlos also voiced dismay that his injured right hip did not fully heal and deteriorated into a degenerative arthritic condition despite his conscientious and active participation in his rehabilitation program. Other group members nodded their agreement when Sanjay rhetorically asked, "Why would you ever want to be friends with your body when it has let you down?"

It is essential to emphasize that the attitudinal foundation of acceptance of what is—befriending your body—doesn't mean that you must like what is happening. Instead, it means you are kind and gentle toward your body and that you can be with it even in difficult times. This is similar to what you can experience with close friends. You can be with good friends even when they are going through painful, challenging, and difficult times and may not be the best of company. Nevertheless, through a sense of acceptance, patience, non-striving, beginner's mind, trust, and non-judging, you can compassionately be with them.

Benefiting from the attitudinal foundations takes time, but knowing and applying them provides a helpful road map for how your relationship can shift and better "embrace" each moment. Within depth psychology, it is said that "what you resist persists." However, when you turn toward and pay attention to discomfort, pain, complicated feelings, or challenging thoughts, the mindfulness practice allows you to become more mentally flexible and better able to "go with the flow." When you are mindful in the present moment, you can experience a sense of curiosity, balance, openness, and spaciousness toward whatever arises. At the end of the day, you become a better friend to yourself, especially in the midst of one of life's challenging experiences.

A SHRINKING WORLD

Dr. Susan Bauer-Wu is the president of the Mind and Life Institute and has worked extensively with patients experiencing severe illnesses. Dr. Bauer-Wu (2011) notes that in addition to the challenging thoughts, feelings, and body sensations that arrive with a chronic or life-limiting illness, it's very common for patients to feel as if their world has become smaller, more restrained and constricted. Because of the illness, individuals may spend more time confined to the house or hospital. Even if you can physically get out and about, your thoughts and feelings can be consumed with your condition and its spinoff effects so that you don't even really notice the immediate world around you. Others may purposefully shut out what is happening to and around them as a defence against the illness.

Chronic/life-limiting illness may seem to lock you into a more constricted world, but it also opens the door to expanding your mindfulness practice, as it offers additional strategies to self-regulate your attention and foster healthier relationships with physical and emotional challenges.

Dr. Bauer-Wu found that anyone feeling trapped inside the body or confined to a limited living space (hospital or your own home) could profit from additional mindfulness practices. She specifically notes that mindfully paying attention to not just your body experience but also to the sights and sounds around you can be very worthwhile and gratifying.

CHANGING YOUR ANCHOR OF AWARENESS

The moving of your anchor's attention—from the breath or hand sensations to sights and sounds in the environment—can promote a more stable mind. Expanding your anchor of awareness also fosters a sense of spaciousness and acceptance. For some people, it can unveil an appreciation of their immediate surroundings, even though the environment had previously felt oppressive.

However, you will notice that even though you are moving your focus of attention from your usual anchor, you still maintain an anchor, albeit now through other senses. Keeping your attention on sights and sounds allows you to continue to experience the experiential network in your mind instead of getting pulled into your analyzing and judging narrative network.

SOUNDS AS ANCHOR OF ATTENTION

A retired TV journalist friend once told me about the challenges he and colleagues confronted whenever they searched for a quiet place to film an interview or "stand-up" report-to-camera in an outdoor location where a story had occurred. "There is no truly quiet place," he said, "when you're listening through a high-quality condenser microphone. Any seeming silence, when monitored by earphones attached to a shotgun mic, typically teems with sounds: wind, bird calls, dog barks, far-off people's voices— even the drone of a distant freeway or invisible passing plane—something always broke the silence, just when you thought you'd found the best silent place."

Similar with many other experiences in life, you can be indifferent to or not even be aware of a multitude of sounds occurring in any one moment. Just as with a high-powered microphone, mindfulness allows you to consciously expand your field of awareness to explore a variety of different sounds. This change in concentration means that you can scan the various sounds around you and then choose to focus on any particular sound to which you are drawn.

Just as you become a curious explorer of the body region that holds intrusive and persistent thoughts, feelings, and physical sensations (Level Two strategy), the goal is to explore the sound you are using as your anchor of awareness. Be curious about the sound's quality—loud or quiet, high or low pitch, tone (often referred to as colour), direction (arriving through both ears or only one), timbre (bright or dull), and so on. Notice the ambient sounds that may mask or interfere with the distinct sound on which you are focusing. Does the sound resonate in your body, and if so, where do you feel it? The mantra is again to be curious about this sound sensation that has become your anchor of awareness.

As with previous explorations of physical sensations, be aware that your mind is skilled at offering judgments, stories, and other assorted shiny objects to hijack your intended focus of attention. I recall several years ago sitting at a bedside vigil with an elderly patient close to death. At three thirty a.m., the hospital ward was peacefully quiet, punctuated by only her ragged breaths and the dull hum of an air pump at the end of her bed, inflating her mattress. However, the pump's hypnotic buzz was interrupted by a repetitive mechanical rattle, occurring only every few minutes but noticeable enough that it captured my attention.

Before I knew it, my mind moved from focusing on the machine's sound to a lengthy analysis of why the pump was malfunctioning. Without evidence, I became convinced that there was no doubt that the pump was made on a Friday afternoon before a holiday weekend, so the workers' attention was more on their vacation plans than on their assembly tasks. Someone forgot to tighten a critical bolt on the fan, resulting in a slightly off-track rotation, hence the intermittent but regular rattle. The quality assurance workers were also excited about their upcoming weekend, hurrying their tests and therefore missing the slight mistake playing out in the hospital room, years after their sloppy workmanship. There you have it—not just another instalment of the world according to my inventive imagination, but the *absolute correct* version of a situation of which I knew nothing. Another example, as if I need it, of the mind having never met a condition to which it cannot attach a story!

Moving your anchor of awareness from your breath or hand sensation to sounds co-occurring around you also fosters one of mindfulness's central goals: to self-regulate attention and promote a stable mind. A stable mind, one that is not caught in judgment or non-acceptance or striving to be something or somewhere different, allows you to respond to your environment instead of simply reacting to it. My TV journalist friend noted that he sometimes took pains to film the source of the intruding sound they couldn't eliminate, such as for instance a loud bird calling, so as to incorporate it into the sequence later in the edit suite. In his own way, my friend "mindfully" accepted the intrusion and in a non-judgmental manner, allowed it to become one of the story's "anchor of attention."

With focused attention, you can realize that certain sounds are associated with feeling grounded, relaxed, or even energized, while other sounds make you feel tense, sad, or upset. Positive sounds could involve the ticking of a clock that makes you feel centred, the sound of gentle rain on the roof that washes away your worries, or even the hum of hospital equipment (when working correctly) that engenders a sense of rhythm within.

The practice of awareness of sound grounds you in your direct experiences in the present moment through a different sensory modality: your hearing capacity. You can consciously move your attention toward sounds that stimulate a sense of comfort, which is another example of how mindfulness can allow you to respond to the present situation rather than just react.

SIGHTS AS ANCHOR OF ATTENTION

As an enthusiastic but amateur photographer, I continue to be amazed with the power offered through different camera lenses. I particularly enjoy the detailed exposure of far-off objects through my zoom lens, while also am amazed at the hidden details of close-up focus through my macro lens. Both lenses open new worlds that have always been available but hidden by my limited visual acuity.

Similar to the camera's enhancement of my visual perceptions, the capacity to expand your day-to-day awareness goes beyond sound as it can also include other sensory modalities, including vision. As noted earlier, a commonly reported experience of living with a chronic/life-limiting illness is that your world becomes much smaller. This can certainly include the sense of sight where your focus becomes much narrower, often missing much of what transpires around you. Mindfulness is an opportunity to expand your awareness of whatever is arising at the moment, including the visual stimuli.

Just as with sound meditation, focus your awareness on the qualities of the object you are viewing. When you attune your attention to your surroundings, the variety of shapes, colours, shades, lights, and shadows brought into your field of awareness from one moment to the next is boundless.

Similar to utilizing sound as your anchor of attention, you can intentionally search your visual field of awareness and choose to enlarge the range of what you are seeing. As you pay attention to your visual world, you will recognize how certain things you see make you feel more relaxed, peaceful, or invigorated. In contrast, other visual cues make you feel angry, irritated, upset, or pessimistic.

By opening your awareness to all the sights available, you choose to use your sight as your anchor of attention. It again is imperative not to get caught in the stories, lodged in the past or projected into the future, regarding the object upon which your vision is focusing. The goal is to simply use sight as your anchor of awareness to expand your attention of the time and space in which you presently, at this moment, reside. Be curious about what you see—explore what your visual attention is drawn to.

AN EXPANDING WORLD PERSPECTIVE

"The voyage of discovery is not in seeking new landscapes, but in having new eyes," concludes the writer Marcel Proust. "New eyes," and "new ears," illustrate Dr. Susan Bauer-Wu's (2011) findings that when you develop the capacity to listen and see mindfully, you will notice how the world around you takes a different perspective. She identifies specific qualities that emerge, which include vividness and spaciousness.

Vividness corresponds to a deepening and enriching of your experience through refining your senses. It allows you to experience that even during a chronic/life-limiting illness, it is possible to create feelings of richness and vibrancy by simply expanding and focusing on listening and seeing awareness.

Spaciousness is the opposite of feeling confined. It relates to a sense of expansiveness brought about by an awareness of the range of sounds or sights available to you at any given moment. Dr. Bauer-Wu concludes that "you can move out of feeling confined, like a hostage to bodily limitations and circumstances, and move toward the infinite possibilities of experiences accessible to you right now."

Dr. Bauer-Wu's contribution to mindfulness practice is significant. There are countless sounds and sights all around in every moment, but your constricted or distracted attention means that you may rarely hear or see what is being offered. However, it is possible to intentionally bring awareness to different sounds and sights and then notice how your body and mind respond.

The practice of mindfully attending to sounds and sights can bring more richness to your experiences and give you a feeling of openness and connectedness with the world around you. Opening to sights and sounds that have always been available but often overlooked is a further invitation to live more mindfully by paying attention, on purpose, in the present moment, non-judgmentally.

Utilizing sights and sounds as your anchor of awareness is another way to claim some degree of agency over your life experiences. While being subjected to an illness can understandably lead to feelings of powerlessness, mindfulness reminds you that your capacity to consciously open to the vividness and spaciousness that is here, at this moment, has not been lost. You can decide how much, or how little, you are consciously bringing into your awareness and experiencing at this moment. Whether facing ongoing health challenges or not, all of us live the reality that you only have this moment . . . and this moment . . . and this moment. Mindfulness is the key to opening and expanding your experience of life at this moment.

MINDFULNESS REVISITED

The sight and sound anchors of awareness are a very significant aspect in the mindfulness journey. I didn't want the group to miss the impact of these beneficial additions, so I offered a short synopsis.

Beginning at Week One, you learned that the definition of mindfulness is *paying attention, in the moment, on purpose, non-judgmentally*. Critically, even though you have expanded your anchor of attention beyond body sensations of touch or breath to now incorporate sights and sounds, you maintain your allegiance to the core meaning. Your attention uses the larger world around you as your anchor, the place to hold your awareness of the present moment. This enlarged focus of awareness brings you closer to mindfulness's overarching goal—to pay attention to all occurring in each moment. Crucially, though, you continue to stay within the mind's experiential neural network by focusing on the qualities of sights or sounds that you encounter and not falling into the mind's narrative network by judging, analyzing, adding stories, fantasizing about the future, etc.

Critically, you are opening to the world that has patiently been waiting for your embrace, as the poet David Whyte beautifully reminds us:

"Everything Is Waiting for You"

Your great mistake is to act the drama
as if you were alone. As if life
were a progressive and cunning crime
with no witness to the tiny hidden
transgressions. To feel abandoned is to deny
the intimacy of your surroundings. Surely,
even you, at times, have felt the great array;
the swelling presence, and the chorus, crowding
out your solo voice. You must note
the way the soap dish enables you,
or the window latch grants you freedom.
Alertness is the hidden discipline of familiarity.
The stairs are your mentor of things
to come, the doors have always been there
to frighten you and invite you,
and the tiny speaker in the phone
is your dream-ladder to divinity.

Put down the weight of your aloneness and ease into
the conversation. The kettle is singing
even as it pours you a drink, the cooking pots
have left their arrogant aloofness and
seen the good in you at last. All the birds
and creatures of the world are unutterable
themselves. Everything is waiting for you!
(Whyte, "Everything is Waiting for You" 141)

PRACTICE OF THE WEEK

This week, I recommend that you continue to practice both **1) formal** and **2) informal mindfulness practices.**

3. Formal Meditation Practice: Sights/Sounds

Guidelines:

- This week it is recommended that you increase your formal meditation practice to **forty-five minutes each day.**

- As an alternative to sitting or walking practices, I recommend trying the Sights/Sounds meditation. Focus on either sounds or sights for extended periods during the practice—to shift back and forth quickly can make it more challenging to stabilize the mind.

- Perhaps do two sessions of twenty to twenty-five minutes each day. Try sticking with either sight or sound meditations for the shortened session.

- Experiment with the Sights/Sounds meditation both indoors as well as outdoors. Notice if you find it easier doing it inside or outside. After the session, explore why one may be more manageable, or not.

- As with all the homework assignments, you can either use the audible guided set of instructions or just read them to yourself before starting the practice. You may want to start with the audible ones and, as the week progresses, experiment doing sessions without them.

- In the spirit of making mindfulness your own practice, please experiment and see what works best for you!

- Remember to record your homework on your **Tracking Your Practice** sheet under the Formal heading.

FORMAL MEDITATION INSTRUCTIONS (SIGHTS/SOUNDS):

Gently close your eyes. . . . Become aware of the feeling of being held at this moment . . . supported . . . grounded . . . noticing your body . . . your posture as you sit on your chair . . . noticing your feet on the floor . . . your hands resting comfortably. . . .

Notice the breath . . . the chest and abdomen expanding and contracting . . . rising and falling. . . . Maybe notice the temperature of the air as it enters the body . . . as it exits the body. . . . Notice your hand sensations as they lie on your lap or thighs. . . . Be aware of the sensation of the clothing under your hands and fingers . . . allowing your breath or hand sensations to become your anchor of attention . . .

. . . .

As your eyes remain closed . . . consciously change the anchor of attention from your breath or hand sensations to the sounds in this room . . . but perhaps you have a challenge with hearing. . . . If so, just listen as best you can. . . .

Allow your attention to audibly scan the room . . . noticing whatever sounds you hear . . . not engaging with any stories or judgments about the sounds . . . just noticing them . . . expanding your awareness to all the sounds in this room . . . and then expanding your attention to the sounds in the larger house or building that you are in. . . . You may notice voices, phones, people walking in the hall or on the stairs, appliances, air conditioning. . . . Perhaps it is very quiet. . . . Silence is what you hear. . . . Just notice whatever sounds come into your awareness. . . .

Bring awareness to how your body feels as you listen to all of these new sounds. . . . Notice any thoughts and feelings as you scan the different sounds inside this room. . . . Don't allow your attention to be pulled into any stories or fantasies about these sounds. . . . Just notice them. . . . Is there any place in your body that these sounds resonate? . . . Physical sensations that may be pleasant? . . . Unpleasant? . . . Neutral? . . .

. . . .

Now focus your attention on just one sound. . . . Allow this one sound to become your anchor of awareness. . . . Just notice whatever sound you hear . . . without any judgment. . . . Whatever the sound may be . . . can you notice the quality of this one sound? . . . Can you notice the pitch—high or low?. . . The loudness? . . . The quietness? . . . The timbre or tone—bright or dull? . . . Is the sound continuous . . . or intermittent? . . . Is there a rhythm to the sound? . . . Do you hear the sound through one ear? . . . If so, which one . . . or both ears? . . . Is the sound pleasant . . . or unpleasant . . . or maybe just neutral? . . .

As you listen to this sound, tune into your body. . . . Notice if the sound resonates in your body . . . and if it does, where do you feel it? . . . Can you notice any thoughts or feelings that may have arisen as you listen to this sound? . . .

Become aware of any stories that may be playing out in your mind that are connected to this sound. . . . Just notice . . . label it as "story" or "judgment" or whatever it may be . . . and then let your awareness return to focusing on the sound . . . of the sound qualities being your anchor of awareness . . . just the bare sensations of the sound holding your anchor of attention. . . .

When you are ready . . . allow your attention to notice another sound in this room. . . . There is no need to rush, so take your time. . . . You are in control of what sound you want to focus your anchor of awareness on. . . .

Notice the quality of the new sound. . . . Be curious about this new sound. . . . It is one that you have chosen out of all available sounds open to you. . . . Listen to this sound as if it were the first time you have ever heard it . . . a mystery sound that has now come into your awareness. . . . Can you notice the pitch—high or low? . . . The loudness? . . . The quietness? . . . The timbre or tone—bright or dull? . . . Is the sound continuous . . . or intermittent? . . . Is there a rhythm to the sound? . . . Do you hear the sound through one ear? . . . If so, which one . . . or both ears? . . . Is the sound pleasant . . . or unpleasant . . . or maybe just neutral? . . .

Do you notice any feelings that arise with the sound? . . . Maybe it's irritating. . . . Perhaps it's calming. . . . Where do you feel it in your body? . . . Just notice . . . and consciously bring your anchor of awareness back to the sound itself . . . the bare sensation of the sound. . . .

Are there any thoughts associated with that sound? . . . Again, be aware of any stories that may arise. . . . If so, notice . . . label it as a "story" or "thought" . . . and gently come back to the sound as your anchor of attention. . . .

. . . .

Let's move our attention to the sounds outside this room. . . . Can you notice different kinds of sounds? . . . Perhaps cars . . . birds . . . raindrops . . . wind . . . a fountain . . . sirens . . . dogs barking . . . emergency sirens . . . construction machinery . . . airplanes . . .

Perhaps there isn't much sound, and it is very quiet. . . . Then just listen to the essence of the quietness . . . of the stillness . . . of the silence. . . .

If you do notice sounds outside of the room, choose one to focus on. . . . Again, notice the quality of the new sound. . . . Be curious about this unique sound. . . . Notice how loud or soft the sound is. . . . Can you notice a rhythm? . . . The timbre or tone—bright or dull? . . . Is the sound continuous . . . or intermittent? . . . The pitch—high or low? . . . Is this sound pleasant . . . or unpleasant . . . or maybe just neutral? . . .

Be aware of how these sounds may affect or not affect your body. . . . . Notice emotions that may surface in response to these sounds. . . . These sounds may have triggered a memory. . . . Just notice how it feels and where you feel it. . . . Be aware if you start to get pulled into a story surrounding the sound. . . .

Keep your focus on the quality of these sounds . . . how the sound changes from one moment to the next. . . . Notice the silence between the sounds. . . . Allow the sound or the silence to be your anchor of attention. . . . Enjoy your new appreciation of sound . . . sound that has always been but often outside of your awareness. . . .

. . . .

As you change your attention from sound to sight . . . please gently open your eyes . . . keeping your gaze soft . . . and without moving your head, just notice what is within your field of vision . . . the light . . . objects . . . colours . . . shapes. . . .

Now let's gently and slowly begin to scan the room . . . notice the colours . . . and the shades of colours. . . . Are objects shiny . . . or dull? . . . Are you drawn to bright colours . . . to earthy colours . . . muted colours? . . . How does your body and mind react as you look at the different colours? . . . Maybe it is a pleasant feeling . . . maybe unpleasant . . . perhaps neutral. . . . Just notice. . . .

Now focus your attention on the different shapes . . . large . . . small . . . boxy . . . square . . . round . . . irregular . . . notice the texture . . . rough . . . smooth . . . soft . . . hard . . .

Now focus your awareness on the light and the shadows. . . . Does that change the colour . . . shape . . . texture of what you are looking at? . . .

. . . .

Explore and settle into the experience of just seeing . . . slowly scanning the room with a beginner's mind . . . as if never seeing these objects before. . . . Just visually explore with curiosity and non-judgment. . . .

Again, if stories are beginning to arise, just notice them as a thought, and then bring your attention back to the objects of your sight. . . . If emotions draw your attention away from the sight . . . just notice . . . label it . . . and return to scanning the objects as your anchor of awareness. . . .

Now focus your attention on just one sight. . . . Allow this one object to become your anchor of awareness. . . . Maybe you see a clock . . . the hands slowly moving . . . maybe a piece of furniture . . . perhaps part of the wall décor . . . or the ceiling décor. . . . Maybe the object is stationary . . . or moving ever so slightly. . . . Just notice . . . .

Has anything changed within your body at this moment of focusing on one object? . . . A new memory, a new feeling . . . no need to judge yourself. . . . If so, just notice that your awareness has been pulled away from the object that has been your anchor of awareness. . . . Gently bring your attention back to the object. . . . Rest your attention on the sight of the object as your anchor of awareness. . . .

. . . .

Now bring your attention to space between objects. . . . How one thing ends and before another one begins there is a space. . . . It may be a very narrow and small space . . . or it may be quite an expansive space. . . . Be curious about this space. . . . Begin to notice how your body and mind feel as you explore this sense of space. . . .

. . . .

Gently close your eyes. . . . Become aware with all of your senses of your whole being, of your sense of self . . . this bag of bones present in this space. . . . At this moment . . . be aware of what you smell . . . of what you hear . . . of the darkness that you see with your eyes closed . . . of your body sensations sitting on your chair . . . of any taste you may be experiencing. . . .

Notice how your body is feeling right now . . . in this moment of time . . . never before experienced in quite this way . . . because this moment has never before existed . . . being aware of the awe and mystery of this body . . . of this mind . . . in this space . . . at this moment. . . .

. . . .

Now allow your awareness to return to your usual anchor of awareness . . . your breath . . . or your hand sensations. . . . This will be your anchor once again. . . . Knowing that you can decide where the anchor of your attention will be . . . feel your anchor—your breath or hand sensations—as like an old friend . . . always available . . . never judging . . . just there for you to rest within . . . to hold you within any turbulence that may arise in your body or mind. . . .

Now slowly and gently open your eyes . . . continuing to attend to your anchor of awareness—your breath or your hand sensations . . . and also to

be aware of your surroundings . . . noticing that you can hold both awareness of your anchor as well as the sights and sounds around you at the
same time . . . and if your attention is drawn to a specific sound or sight . . .
and if you decide to explore that sight or sound . . . consciously move your
anchor of attention to the sight or sound . . . knowing that your attention,
if you choose, can gently move from your breath or hand sensations to
the sound or sight as your new anchor of awareness . . . feeling the flow
between your anchors of attention if you decide to do so . . . of trusting that
you can rest in your anchors. . . .

Know that your anchor will usually be your breath or hand sensations . . .
but you can also, gently and effortlessly, shift your anchor to the exploration
of a sight or sound. . . . Know that you will always have an anchor to hold
your attention. . . . You do not have to fall into a thought . . . or an emotion . . .
or a body sensation. . . . You are fully present in this room at this moment . . .
and at the same time you are using your anchor of attention—whether it be
your breath or hand sensations or a sight or a sound . . . to hold your awareness on this moment . . . not getting hijacked by thoughts, emotions . . .
body sensations . . . not being dragged into the past . . . and not falling
into the future . . . just being fully open and present at this moment . . .
and this moment . . . and this moment . . . allowing yourself to experience
all that is unfolding before you and within you. . . . Feel the awe of being
so present . . . of being held in the mystery of this moment . . . just this
moment . . . of gratitude for the capacity to be with this moment . . . to hold
this moment . . . to be held in this moment. . . .

4. Informal Mindfulness Practices

Guidelines:

- As we have discussed during the last few weeks, outside of the formal
  practice sessions, there are ample opportunities to continue learning
  to be more mindfully present. These informal practices arise out of
  the daily activities that comprise your life and therefore are readily
  available to be of service to your learning process.

- This week, I invite you to continue exploring informal mindfulness practices daily. Be creative—stretch your imagination and try new ones.

- Remember, while it is easy to identify many daily activities to which you can apply your burgeoning mindfulness skills, they all share a commonality of being ones you probably don't pay much attention to. The activity itself is not what is critical. Rather, any activity that allows you to slow down the process to experience it with your senses entirely is what makes it an informal mindfulness practice and, therefore, a good one to choose.

- Remember to record your homework on your **Tracking Your Practice** log under the Informal heading.

- Continue to check in with your new best friend, your anchor of awareness! Setting the intention to pay attention and be curious about your anchor at various times throughout the day will strengthen your relationship with it.

MIDWEEK CUPPA...
REFLECTIONS ON
PATIENCE AND AGING

WEEK SEVEN

This book is premised on a central theme that aging brings to light the realization that your time for living is limited. It is also abundantly clear that the best of intentions, most fanciful dreams, or mournful pleadings will not slow the passage of time. It follows, therefore, that with a conscious acknowledgement of the inevitable passing of limited time available, the inevitable recurring and pressing question is, "Why wait? Why wait to live this life that is yours totally and wholeheartedly? Why squander the moment-to-moment opportunities that are open to you but overshadowed by your undisciplined mind bouncing from one shiny object to the next?"

The impetus to live more fully in each moment is the guiding principle underlying awareness that time during your aging years is known and unknown. You acknowledge that your time alive is limited while also holding the uncomfortable reality that you don't know when it will end. You are addressing these concerns through learning that mindfulness sensitivity is a practical and effective response to the urgent question of "If not now, when?"

But hold on! Just as you accept the critical imperative not to wait, now you are asked to appreciate and hold the attitudinal foundation of patience. Patience, meaning "calm endurance," invokes images of self-control and steadiness with tolerant perseverance to meet hardship, provocation, pain, and delay. I earlier told you that patience is a form of wisdom indicating that you understand and accept that life will evolve in its own time. Patience doesn't seem compatible with the commitment to get going, not to wait, so what gives?

HURRY UP AND WAIT

It may sound like a contradiction to merge the concepts of not waiting with patience, but it turns out that both are critical to befriending yourself through the mindfulness platform. Developing consciousness requires the capacity to hold ambiguous or competing thoughts together at the same time, so "hurry up and wait" is, in fact, precisely what is demanded!

The capacity to embrace seemingly incompatible thoughts and feelings is best characterized as the attitude of equanimity. Equanimity is an even minded mental state that invokes balance and impartiality; to be capable of experiencing all that arises including the capacity to "gaze upon" or observe without judgment or interference.

COMMITTING TO BOTH

Picking up this book and starting your mindfulness practice satisfies the first commitment to change your relationship with time by declaring your intention to pay attention, on purpose, in the present moment, non-judgmentally. You took the challenge to learn a new way to experience each moment more fully. You fulfilled your pledge to "hurry up."

However, it didn't take long to realize that making this commitment was much easier than fulfilling it. Paying attention in each moment is a challenge. It requires multiple strategies to remain within your experiential neural network rather than being pulled into the narrative that professes that every gleaming object, whether it be a thought, feeling or physical sensation, is a must-see.

Learning to live mindfully is no easy feat—your experience through these six weeks of practice makes it abundantly clear that you cannot rush the learning process of paying attention, on purpose, in the present moment, non-judgmentally. Therefore, patience, in accord with beginner's mind, acceptance, non-striving, non-judging, and trust comprises the supportive attitudes facilitating your capacity for equanimity, to both *hurry up* and *wait.*

EXPANDING INDIVIDUAL MOMENTS TO A LIFE

While patience proves to be a critical supportive attitude to make mindful awareness workable, it has a more prominent role to play during your aging years. By this point in the course, each of you knows through your experience that mindfulness, with the assistance of learned Jungian psychological strategies, focuses on fully living each moment of your day. One of the core tenets of mindfulness is the belief that to live each moment fully is not only beneficial for you at the time, but the accumulation of lived individual moments leads to your capacity to then experience a full life. So, you are not only learning to experience life moment by moment, but through this immediate process, you are also creating a life—the accumulation of millions and millions of mindful moments equals one fully lived life!

The macro view of life comprised of micro individual moments is important to comprehend and illuminates a more significant role that patience plays in supporting your personal growth and development journey through your aging years. "Hurry up and wait" turns out to be not only the rallying cry of individual moments but also of the immense task of meeting the life that is yours.

INDIVIDUATION COMES CALLING

Our old friend and companion during our mindfulness quest, Dr. Jung, offered that each of you has a built-in imperative that seeks your development to become all of who you are. As I introduced earlier, he called this personal growth "individuation" to mark the inner desire and drive to realize your potential to become the unique individual you are.

The impetus for individuation can occur at any time but is felt especially during the latter half of life. Questioning whether you are on your path toward individuation often arrives without warning through complex life events. Experiences such as illness, divorce, death of a loved one, ending of career, and so on compel you to question more significant life matters— *Am I living my own life? Am I fulfilling my potential? Am I content and satisfied with my life? Who am I?*

These existential queries are like a knock on the door of your life— truth be told, more often felt like a thunderous jolt to be sure—arriving at your consciousness with enough discomfort not easy to dismiss or ignore. While occurring at any time, aging years portends the likelihood of unasked-for events that can deplete your coping strategies, that often feel like you have hit the wall or hit bottom. Becoming more mindful, that is, to be aware and capable of experiencing each moment, including the challenging ones, increases the chances that you can meet and hold these difficulties through your appropriate attitudinal foundations. Painful as it often is, awareness that something in your life is amiss, not quite right, is the opening to becoming more conscious on your journey toward individuation. Especially when occurring during aging years, it is the slap on the side of your head that makes it abundantly clear that you must not wait.

A dream I had over thirty years ago exemplifies how the initial awareness of needed change in one's life can be compellingly and graphically presented:

I am with a group of followers in a large wood-frame building that is empty of furnishings except for a glass display case. The male leader of the group, unable to continue living his life as he had, sweeps his arm through the case, smashing his trophies and icons of achievement to the ground. Weeping deeply, he buries his head in his hands and falls to his knees. With no awareness or sense of control over where his life will now lead, feelings of despair, as well as resignation, fill him as the building explodes into flames.

My dream ego's action of relinquishing a life of achievement reflected my real-world experience. After establishing a psychological consulting company that proved successful with offices in several cities across Canada, I fell into a depression. My personal and career life achievements felt empty and barren—they essentially had withered to the point where I lost all interest and motivation. My dream's ending of the building exploding into flames symbolically mirrored my psychological distress and compromised functioning. While I often feel like a slow learner with life's lessons, there was no misconstruing the message that I could not continue as I had—an unmistakable mandate to "not wait." Unfortunately, the dream does not illuminate what to do next!

WAKING UP

Similar to mindfulness's challenges of patiently learning to be present in each moment, Jungian psychology offers no immediate or easy relief to the response of not waiting. Instead, it too relies on your awareness and experience of life's moments-to-moments, especially paying attention to those persistent and intrusive struggles that will not transform quickly through mindfulness strategies. Jungian psychology presents a system to change your relationship with long-held impediments through a process of inquiry, reflection, and strategy implementation to not only fully experience each moment but also to fulfill your overarching individuation task. This process, too, demands your patience. Significant life changes will simply not be rushed!

SLOW CHANGE

Contrary to popular belief, personal growth and change is not an instant response to insight. While no doubt some individuals may encounter moments of instantaneous change following illuminating comprehension of an issue, similar in speed to an abrupt religious conversion, my personal and clinical experience indicates that this is the exception rather than the rule. While becoming aware of issues challenging your growth and development is a critical first step, learning what is required and how to bring it to fruition through changing beliefs and behaviours influencing your life's course is a more prolonged process. It demands patience.

LIMINAL STATES

Recognizing and acknowledging that earlier accomplishments, attitudes, and beliefs no longer support your life, as dramatically expressed in my dream, can often leave you feeling baffled and bewildered. Confusion and disorientation are often experienced but can be appropriately understood through the concept of a liminal state, an image initially and fittingly applied to rite of passage initiations. Liminality is a state in-between, with few or none of your past attributes and no compelling visions of the future. It is a moment in and out of time, associated with darkness, wilderness, invisibility, and even death.

Anthropological studies of earlier cultures have identified liminal entities often disguised as monsters who wear only a strip of clothing or even go naked to demonstrate that they have no status, property, or role in society as liminal beings. Your once solid footing in your world has now abruptly shifted, leaving you feeling off-balance, disoriented, confused and unsure of yourself.

The entry into a liminal space comes about through many life experiences, but all arrive with emotions strong enough to grab your attention, not to be ignored. My descent into depression; Gary's (Week Two) anxiety about his upcoming retirement; Kate's (Week Three) listlessness and lack of excitement about her future; Cleo's, Jackson's, Liam's, Emma's and Sarah's (Week Four) unexpected emotional reactions beyond what situations call for; Ted's (Week Five) persistent, albeit unwanted, pesky low mood; and Reid's (Week Six) shame-based identity, all exemplify emotional reactions leading to a state of liminality, an inability to continue living your life as you had, but with no identified plan forward. It is an entry into unknown territory.

Unpleasant and unsettling as they often are, Jungian psychology understands such dramatic experiences of unknowing in a liminal space as essential factors that potentially positively enhance your individuation development. To be contained in these times of unknowing requires you to be still, to have trust and patience for the expectant unfolding of your individuation. Supporting your liminal state of being is your mindfulness practice which has proven that you can be with whatever arises, including the complex and often painful experiences demanded by the process of personal change.

STUCK FOREVER?

During the troubling experience of unknowing in this liminal period, it is essential to remember another critical mainstay of mindfulness: everything is in a constant state of change. Even while it can feel like you will be stuck forever in this place of unknowing, endings always imply beginnings. To be in this liminal state is a time that foreshadows new possibilities or potentials to unfold, often ones of which you are not conscious.

I found that Buddhism has a striking image that captures the liminal unknowing of this experience called "sunyata," defined as "a pregnant void or the hollow of a pregnant womb." The concept of a sense of emptiness that is paradoxically pregnant presents a powerful image of unbounded potentials and possibilities that have not yet been realized or, to continue the metaphor, born.

Just as human pregnancy demands time for the maturation of the developing fetus, personal growth and change also require time—progress cannot be rushed! As you have seen through the examples offered within the Midweek Cuppa sections, tricky complications embedded within personal beliefs/contracts, shadows, projections, vulnerability, and shame prove powerful enough to shade or even impede your ability to experience each moment fully. Each Midweek Cuppa section offered insight and specific strategies to identify problematic and thorny issues, experience them fully, and through curiosity, questioning, and reflection, alter your relationship with them. Upon mindfulness's foundation, Jungian psychology provides additional strategies that have the dual charge of liberating your capacity to experience each moment fully and further your individuation through the process.

However, the Midweek Cuppa examples also illustrate that transformation takes time—change is not as quick and easy as flicking on a light switch. Each individual has to take the time necessary to work through their troublesome snags with patience to satisfy the intention of fully experiencing each moment, which, in turn, aids their individuation course. My journey through depression mirrored a similar need for calm endurance in ways that I had never before experienced.

The depression that I fell into over thirty years ago came as a shock to my then worldview of a happy life. However, over time, it became glaringly evident to me and those close that this "funk" I was in was more than a passing glitch through mid-life. I was fortunate to work with a wise elderly Jungian psychologist who guided me through my liminal state. Gently but persistently, she pushed and prodded me to look deeply into the corners of my life that I had never explored, let alone even considered.

My therapy started with the usual inventory of potential troublesome issues but did not uncover my underlying malady. I had two terrific young daughters in a long-term supportive marriage, a good social network, personal spiritual practices, and I lived on a small commuter island off the coast of Vancouver. As noted previously, I had founded a psychological consulting company a few years earlier that proved successful with offices in several cities across Canada and enjoyed a lifestyle offered by my company's success. In short, I had everything that I believed constituted a happy and satisfying life! Unfortunately, my depressed mood made it abundantly clear that something deep inside had a different opinion.

With the typical red flags underlying a depression put to bed, my psychotherapeutic exploration moved to more profound, previously unconscious issues through dream analysis, active imagination, and symbolic creative expressions of inner complexes. I discovered and connected intimately with previously unknown aspects of myself, especially many shadow ones that I was not particularly eager to acknowledge, in addition to those others that blossomed as gifts. I met an inner "orphan" figure that, over time, transformed from a small child floundering in life to a tall, decisive, and purposeful man utilizing strengths of independence that only aloneness can foster. I also came to know the punitive feelings of shame that I had mightily struggled to hide from everyone, including myself.

A summary of my psychotherapy process can sound like it was over in a week, but I can assure you that it was a lengthy process over many months, which frequently tested my patience. However vehement my protestations during the acute treatment phase, it was painfully clear that I was not in control of any potential resolutions—endurance and patience, although not always of a "calm" nature if truth be told, became the only fallback position.

While over time an expanding and evolving sense of myself lifted many of the oppressive depression symptoms, it was only through a significant excavation of the contracts and belief systems with the universe I had constructed that the foundational cause of my malaise rose to the surface.

In essence, like an episode out of a bad sci-fi movie, I realized that the life I was living was not my own. It sounds crazy, but when this thought arrived, it truly felt like not only were my eyes finally opened, but a mighty weight had lifted. Let me briefly explain.

My father was an immigrant from Scotland who viewed Canada as the land of opportunity for his burgeoning business spirit. To make a long career history short, he eventually became a small airline senior executive. Not bad for someone who dropped out of school to join the British Merchant Navy, but he always held the definition of success to be definitively more; it had to be corporate CEO or president. Unfortunately, he never met his bar of success before retirement.

Unconsciously, for I am sure my dad never asked me, I took the baton and continued the race to become a corporate "winner." Starting and then expanding my small consulting company was not exactly an Amazon-level corporate fairy tale; however, it still did satisfy his concept of success, albeit vicariously through my efforts.

What did I get out of it? With a lengthy Jungian therapy, I came to understand that my co-dependent contribution to his idea of success was an attempt to obtain the love and respect that I had never felt from him.

I honestly had no awareness of this underlying and unconscious game plan, but I knew deep in my bones that it was true when it came to light. Another example of the power of not only the unconscious but also underlying attachment wounds that can become evident through mindfulness and Jungian psychology.

With this core insight, I was able to gradually experience life moment to moment, again enjoying the small gifts offered by daily life. The lifting of depression also allowed me to disentangle myself from the script that I had written but became so toxic. Of course, there was nothing inherently wrong with the life that I had created, for it bestowed many gifts to my family and me—the problem was that it just was not MY life!

My individuation process to become more of who I am required a different path. Over time, which again demanded considerable patience, I extricated myself from the company I founded; returned to graduate school to earn a doctorate in clinical psychology (with an emphasis in Jungian psychology); raised our girls on a rural property in a smaller community; lived my dream of having horses on an acreage (affectionately known as "Thistle Dew Ranch" with a nod of appreciation to the attitudinal foundation of acceptance); and with my wife, Lynn, opened a private psychotherapy and assessment practice, which was well received and proved successful. Still, by learning to listen to my inner voice of individuation, it continued as a small private practice with only a couple of contract employees—sorry, Dad, corporate flights of fancy were permanently grounded!

MANAGING EXPECTATIONS

Holding patience as an attitudinal foundation is critical in managing expectations of both mindfulness practice and your individuation journey. The initial excitement of beginning a mindfulness training course can quickly plummet into frustration and premature declarations of its worthlessness because it is not a quick and easy fix. Even with the explicit notice that developing a mindfulness sensitivity takes time and practice, I have witnessed students drop out early because of a desperate and often manic rush to escape their present life experiences not being met. All the attitudinal foundations create a framework for healthier and more realistic expectations of not only what mindfulness practice, but life in general, offers.

Therefore, patience is also an essential attitude when confronting the inevitable tangles of human life that require more than what mindfulness can provide. Jungian psychology presents a complementary process of awareness, experience, and relationship with the thorny intrusive habits, patterns, and personal characteristics that interfere with not only moment-to-moment experience but also your overarching life journey. Developing a different and healthier relationship to such struggles is again not a quick-and-easy fix, so patience becomes your needed and trusted companion. The time necessary to satisfy awareness, experience, and relationship of each moment, which by extension creates awareness, experience, and relationship of this life that is yours, is not to be rushed. "Hurry up and wait" proves to be the non-debatable prescription demanded by time!

HOLD ME TIGHT: COMPASSION AND SELF-COMPASSION

WEEK EIGHT

REVIEW SIGHTS AND SOUNDS PRACTICE

There was no way to miss the upbeat mood crackling through the group as they gathered for their eighth session. The buoyant mood echoed the group's universal affirmation that the sights and sounds practice of the past week proved to be a winning life exercise! To pay attention, to explore everyday sights and sounds that had been taken for granted previously, was like a whole new world opened before them. Bethany was brought to tears with the lilting coo of a mourning dove; Sam marvelled at a budding magnolia tree with curiosity as if never before seen; Cassie was surprised with the diverse array of colours offered by books on the shelf; Sybil found beauty in the gnarled bark of an old cedar tree; Ken was mesmerized by attending to the sound of an ambulance's siren; Juanita was intrigued by the space in-between her family photographs hanging on the wall; Cindy was shocked by the cacophony of environmental sounds while sipping coffee on an outdoor patio; Richard, with his technical sensitivity, became fascinated by the silence to which he awoke early one morning.

Opening to the world and all that it offers presents an unlimited bounty for your senses. The simple practice of paying attention to not only what is occurring inside of you (using the breath or hand sensation as your anchor) but extending it to the world around exemplifies Dr. Bauer-Wu's promise of increased vividness and spaciousness. Your attending to sights and sounds did not create them, so they were always available, echoing David Whyte's poetic declaration that "Everything is waiting for you."

To Dr. Bauer-Wu's identification of increased vividness and spaciousness, I would add that focusing awareness on sights and sounds also opens you to a sense of awe and wonder. While the concept of awe originated from feelings of fear or terror (expressed through words like awful or awestruck), it also evokes images of reverence, amazement, astonishment, and marvel. Awe often is elicited by the experience of being in the presence of something vast that transcends your understanding of the world; it is something bigger than you, which is probably why it initially evoked fear.

Mindfulness harnesses your experiential neural network rather than getting caught in your chatty default narrative, highlighting the awesome intricate and complex features of everyday sensory experience as it did with Sam's magnolia tree, Cassie's colourful bookshelf, and Bethany's mourning dove. Research on awe finds that it can expand your perception of time, with time seemingly slowing down while engaged in the flow of the moment. Awe engenders connection with others and the larger world, feeling more generous, cooperative, and kind, as well as improving well-being with an accompanying decrease in stress—a pretty good payout for simply focusing attention on what has always been available to your awareness.

The week's exercise highlighted appreciation for life's 10,000 joys, which elicited Betty's query of "Since this is so wonderful, why didn't we start the mindfulness course with this practice?" A fair question, with the short answer being that I didn't want to oversell mindfulness and misrepresent expectations.

I am confident that by now, each of you has realized that the simple definition of mindfulness—to pay attention in the moment, on purpose, non-judgmentally—is not that easy to do. It has taken weeks to introduce and practise a basket of strategies facilitating self-regulation of your attention. It has also taken weeks to support the attitudinal foundations of beginner's mind, acceptance, non-judging, trust, non-striving, and patience needed to meet each moment in a healthy manner. To have begun with an emphasis on the awe-inspiring experiences of sensory awareness could have misrepresented the focus and the true power of what mindfulness can offer. That is, it is pretty easy to rest in the moments that bring you pleasure and satisfaction. It's another thing to stay with those moments of pain, loss, sorrow, and the inevitable thousand and one other sufferings that this human existence can present—the very sort of suffering that tends to happen more often in our senior years.

Therefore, leading with the amazement, marvel, and reverence attached to sensory awareness practices only temptingly extends shiny objects that make mindfulness appear seductively easy. Remember that wondrous sensory awareness of everyday moments has always been available to you—it is not as if the course hid them. However, what is not so readily apparent, and the central core of what mindfulness offers, is that you have the potential for awareness of a multitude of thoughts, feelings, physical sensations, and environmental stimuli of a complex and challenging nature; tolerance and resilience to experience them thoroughly; and you are curating a healthy relationship with whatever arises through establishing a confident and stable attitudinal foundation. That is the challenge and, most critically, the true gift of mindfulness.

Make no mistake that the amazement, marvel, and reverence attached to awareness of sensory events is to be honoured and enjoyed—but you also know that it is not all life presents. If you don't develop a healthier relationship to the more challenging experiences, you are left to pursue only happy and upbeat moments in a manic and desperate fashion. Therefore, a more beneficial response is to meet *all* of what life presents through being able to focus your attention where you want it and develop a kinder and more compassionate relationship with yourself concerning whatever arises. This response reflects what you have now viscerally experienced, which is the long answer as to why the course did not start with the easier sensory awareness experiences.

LETTING GO

Letting go is the final attitudinal foundation of mindfulness to review that is essential in establishing a new and healthier relationship with your human experience. By now, you know that negative thoughts and feelings may repetitively intrude into your consciousness, festering and undermining not only your capacity to experience the moment but also your health, happiness, and well-being. Similarly, inviting memories of satisfying experiences and pleasantly expectant fantasies of the future to swarm your waking awareness is also destructive to your capacity to live in each moment. While many would agree that experiencing each moment is a boldly healthy attitude to hold, the ability to let go of both positive and negative ruminating thoughts and feelings is a challenging task! Like many of the earlier attitudinal foundations, letting go sounds easy, but it is difficult to understand and skillfully implement.

In the mindfulness field, a richer sense of the concept of letting go can be attained through a story about a particularly clever way of catching monkeys. As one variation of the story goes, hunters in Thailand will cut a rectangular slot in a coconut just big enough for a monkey to put its open hand through. They then hollow out a cavity inside the coconut through the slot, place a sweet paste that monkeys desire inside the coconut, and secure the coconut to the base of a tree. The hunters then move away and watch as the monkey approaches, puts his open hand through the slot and takes hold of the sweet paste. The monkey grabs the treat, but the hole is shaped so that while the open hand can go in, the clenched fist gripping the treat is too big and cannot be pulled out. The monkey is trapped! Unfortunately, no one has told the monkey that all it has to do to be free is to let go of the sweet paste and their hand will then slip out, but it seems that most monkeys won't do so anyway. They lose their instinctual freedom because of not letting go.

The mind is similar in terms of the power it has to latch on to specific thoughts and feelings you have a tough time letting go. When you pay attention to your inner life through the mindfulness lens, you quickly recognize particular thoughts and feelings the mind wants to hold on to because they are enjoyable. These are the memories or fantasies you enjoy replaying and therefore try to hold as long as possible.

On the other hand, there are many thoughts, feelings, and experiences, either from your past or projected on potential future happenings, that you try to eliminate or block because of their unacceptable, painful, or worrisome nature. Daily life becomes a struggle between the push and pulls of the wanted and unwanted, which is exhausting and acts as a barrier to experiencing what is happening in the present moment. Your mind's frenetic jumble of what it likes and what it doesn't is often referred to as "monkey mind."

In the mindfulness practice, you learn to deliberately loosen your grip on such cognitive, emotional, or physical events so as to not get caught like the monkey in the coconut trap. Instead, you acknowledge and accept your experience to be what it is and become a curious eyewitness to each moment, letting go of the attachment you have to either the positive or the negative. Letting go is a way of letting things be, of accepting things as they are. When Sir Paul McCartney sings his song "Let It Be," I imagine him recognizing and honouring the ever-changing nature of experience.

Letting go is not the same as giving up. Instead, it is a conscious acceptance that you are not in control of all aspects of your inner or outer worlds. Letting go supports all attitudinal foundations, including acceptance, beginner's mind, non-judging, non-striving, trust, and patience.

When you observe your monkey mind holding or pushing away, remember your task is to let go of those reactions. To review, you started the mindfulness practice with the simple identification of thoughts, emotions, or body sensations that pulled your attention from your breath or hand sensations, you labelled them, and then returned to your anchor of attention. You then learned additional strategies to work with more powerful intrusions to your attention, with the common theme of simply letting them go. Don't latch onto them, don't judge them, don't fight them, don't debate them, don't analyze them, and don't feed them with stories. You simply let them be, and in doing so, you can let them go, like clouds dissipating in the hot summer air or waves washing over the sand or some sweet allure inside a clever trap that you decided you'd be better off avoiding.

Dr. Jon Kabat-Zinn's (1990) initial introduction of the letting go concept likened it to falling asleep, so it is not such a foreign experience to anyone of us. You do it every night when you go to sleep. To get to sleep, you lie down and let go of your mind and body. What happens if you don't let go—if your mind will not slow down, if your emotions just will not subside? No doubt you found that you just don't get to sleep if you don't let go. Like the monkey who will not let go of the desired object, you too will lose your natural freedom to fall asleep if you don't let go of the mind and body.

As Dr. Kabat-Zinn reminds us, you are already an expert in letting go if you can go to sleep. The challenge now becomes consciously applying this skill in waking situations as well. And that is where the mindfulness method that you have been learning and practising will serve you well. But as you have also found, to change your relationship to your old unmindful way of being is not easy!

MINDFULNESS 101 REVIEWED

Your mindfulness practice to this point has been an attempt to more clearly experience what is happening in the present moment without judgment. It means being open to the raw thoughts, feelings, and sensations that each experience on an ongoing basis—to be with them without judgment or feeding them with the ongoing narrative in our minds.

When starting mindfulness, it can seem that purposely focusing your attention and awareness on what is happening at the moment can cause more suffering. However, this is not true because the suffering has always been there—it is just that each of you, as a good student of our culture, has been good (in varying degrees) at finding ways to ignore, deny, avoid, or numb yourself to it. Increased awareness of the present moment simply brings with it an increased sensitivity and intimacy with your inner and outer worlds. Somewhat surprisingly, you can hear your thoughts more clearly; you can feel emotions more powerfully; you physically encounter the body in new ways that you perhaps have never felt before.

As we have talked about throughout this course, suffering is not optional—it simply is part of the human existence and its 10,000 joys and 10,000 sorrows. So, your choice in life is to either try to avoid suffering (which I think every one of you by this time of your life knows doesn't work that well) or find a different way to be with the inevitable pain, loss, and sorrow we will all experience. The poet Allen Ginsberg rightly noted that finding a different way directly involves your attitude: "The suffering itself is not so bad; it's the resentment against suffering that is the real pain."

COMPASSION

Within mindfulness meditation, you have endeavoured to establish an acceptance of whatever arises within you, a non-judging of it, a non-striving to try and change it, as well as just to let it be and to let it go. All these attitudes address Ginsberg's observation of resentment through establishing a different relationship to whatever life challenges and difficulties arise. With a mindful attitude, turning *toward* whatever is emerging in the present moment rather than turning *away* is to better *respond* to the moment rather than *react* to it. However, mindfulness is cognizant that this is not an easy task, so a companion strategy to change your relationship to suffering is offered through compassion.

Compassion comes from the Latin roots *com* (with) and *pati* (suffer) or to "suffer with." From its etymological beginnings, when we offer genuine compassion to another, we join a person in his or her suffering. We abandon our fear or resistance to the other person's pain, which means that compassion cannot be undertaken in an emotionally distant manner. Instead, the experience of compassion is the complete abandonment of the inclination to resist emotional discomfort. It is total acceptance—of the person, the pain, and your reactions to the pain.

The British meditation teacher Christina Feldman (2005) concludes: "Compassion is the most precious of all gifts. . . . It is the force of empathy in your own heart that allows you to reach out and touch the broken heart of another." Compassion extends yourself through kindness, empathy, and care to the suffering of another. Self-compassion is simply giving the same positive qualities to yourself that you would provide to others.

SELF-COMPASSION

Twelve years ago, my wife, Lynn (a psychotherapist), and I developed and facilitated workshops titled "Meeting Suffering Mindfully." It was a way to use mindfulness and other teachings and methods from depth psychology and spiritual traditions in being better able to move toward and befriend the inevitable pain, loss, and sorrow that each of us will experience. Interestingly, the two sections of the workshop that were the most impactful with participants involved the concepts of self-compassion and self-forgiveness. During the many workshops that we presented, these two areas evoked the most emotional reactions. Long after the seminar ended, we received feedback from individuals who found those sections challenging but helpful, particularly significant to continue exploring for their well-being.

From the workshops, we found that one of the greatest challenges of self-compassion is that it demands a form of acceptance. Mindfulness meditation teaches that acceptance usually refers to what has happened *to* us, to accept a feeling or a thought or a body sensation that has arisen. However, self-compassion sees it differently in that acceptance becomes *of* the person to whom it's happening. That is, it is *acceptance of yourself* while you are in pain or sorrow. You start caring for yourself *because* you are suffering. Christina Feldman (2005) directly connects mindfulness and compassion: "The purpose of mindful attention is to bring to all moments of suffering and contraction the compassion that liberates your heart from pain."

There is an essential distinction between care and cure. Cure is what you try to do when you have some way to fix a problem. However, as we have discussed, pain, loss, and sadness are inevitable pieces—not the whole but pieces—of this human existence that defy easy management. Care is what you do when all efforts of curing have failed. Therefore, it is essential to emphasize that you care for yourself when you work with self-compassion because you are suffering. The sooner you stop struggling to create a mythical pain-free existence in emotional life, the better.

From my personal life and professional experience (both within individual/couples psychotherapy and in group workshop settings), it is clear that holding a sense of self-compassion to ourselves is not easy, nor is it something that our culture has embraced. However, against our harsh self-criticalness, including shame discussed in Week Six, it is interesting to note that the Buddha reportedly said, "You can search the whole world over and not find anyone more deserving of your love and compassion than yourself."

OPENING SELF-COMPASSION

A prominent researcher and writer about self-compassion is Dr. Kristin Neff, a psychologist at the University of Texas in Austin. Her work has identified critical elements of self-compassion and other factors that would be considered the opposite of self-compassion.

Dr. Neff (2011) notes that one of the significant components of self-compassion is *self-kindness.* A self-compassionate person responds to difficulties and setbacks in a warm, understanding, and accepting manner—that is, with kindness to yourself. The opposite of self-kindness is *self-judgment*—to react to whatever arises with an inner judgment of harshness and criticism. This self-condemnation is exemplified by the Week Six review regarding the punitive and destructive inner judge of shame.

The second component of self-compassion is a realization of each of our membership in a *common humanity.* The awareness of shared humanity brings relief from feeling alone and isolated. It leads you to understand that others, in fact, share your experience. As you will recall from the Introduction chapter, one of my favourite characters is a fellow by the name of Wavy Gravy. His wry, tolerant sense of humour succinctly portrays our common humanity when he concludes: "We are all bozos on the bus, so you might as well sit back and enjoy the ride."

This understanding of each of us being part of a common humanity is vital because when you experience misfortune or difficulties in life, you may often feel that you are the only person in the world who is suffering. You can also feel shame about the misfortune as if you alone are responsible for it. You don't want the world to see what you believe about yourself (negative self-judgments), so as a reaction to shame, you try to hide. Mother Teresa observed that "the biggest disease today is not leprosy or tuberculosis but rather the feeling of not belonging." These adverse reactions can lead to the opposite of common humanity, which is a sense of *isolation*.

The third major component of self-compassion is *mindfulness*. As you have been practising, mindfulness is open awareness that supports your ability to accept painful thoughts, feelings, and physical sensations in a more accepting and steady manner. Mindfulness awareness helps you recognize whatever is occurring and meet it with new skills and attitudes. It vividly demonstrates that when you are in pain, when you are criticizing yourself, when you are isolating yourself, and the thousand other events you may have, simply paying attention to them in an accepting and non-judgmental fashion can change not only your experience, but critically, your relationship to them.

Your mindfulness practice has demonstrated that sometimes by just holding thoughts, emotions, and body sensations in your awareness, they change in their presentation, location, and intensity or even dissolve completely! The opposite of mindfulness is *over-identification*—this happens when you lose yourself in emotional reactivity. Obsessing and fixating on everything wrong is to lose contact with your capacity for mindfulness and, therefore, descend into an over-identification with the negative—or, as Wavy Gravy would conclude, miss out enjoying the "ride" that is your life.

UNINTENDED CONSEQUENCES TO LACK OF SELF-COMPASSION

I still recall a psychotherapy client from many years ago who exemplified the personal anguish brought about through a lack of self-compassion. Amisha's relationship with her sister had never been exceptionally close, but while attending her sister's sixty-second birthday celebration, Amisha found that her built-up resentment abruptly overflowed in a raging tirade. Amisha recognized that there had been many incidents over the years when her sister undermined her sense of self, but Amisha had never addressed them. Still, this explosive reaction to her sister shocked not only other partygoers but especially Amisha herself.

Leaving the party as quickly as she could, Amisha felt riddled with guilt and shame for her behaviour. Even after later phoning her sister to apologize, she continued to beat up on herself for this transgression. Days later, she continued to not only condemn herself as a "bad sister," but also denigrated her worth as a person. She had never seen anyone else act in such a manner, so she concluded that there must be something fundamentally wrong with her character. While she attempted to carry on with her daily life, her thoughts and feelings continued to convict her as a singularly unworthy person.

Amisha's experience is, unfortunately, not a unique one. Dr. Neff's (2011) research found that when bad things happen to us, we often tend to have three unfortunate reactions: self-criticism, self-isolation, and self-absorption. Amisha's explosive expression of her shadow's denial of her pent-up anger toward her sister mirrored all three reactions. Her lack of self-compassion amplified the underlying interpersonal issues with her sister creating not only a messy scene but, more importantly, savaging Amisha's sense of self.

Dr. Neff's three self-compassion components could direct Amisha precisely in the opposite direction: self-kindness, recognizing the common humanity in her experience, and a balanced mindfulness approach to negative emotions. The gift of self-compassion arrives with caring and gentle responses that direct a very different outcome!

SELF-COMPASSION SCALE

One of the common healing elements in mindfulness and self-compassion is a gradual shift toward friendship with emotional or physical pain. As you have been working on, mindfulness is a way to *turn toward* the pain you experience and simply pay attention to it in an accepting and non-judgmental manner. Self-compassion practice is an additional method for whittling away our stubborn tendencies to resist pain and grasp for pleasure. Mindfulness joins hands with self-compassion, bringing in feelings of sympathy, forgiveness, tenderness, and love.

Mindfulness shows you that to open your heart to self-compassion, you first need to open your eyes. You need to be aware of what is happening to you at the moment, which is the benefit of mindfulness practice. Mindfulness says *feel the pain* while self-compassion adds further benefit by saying *cherish yourself during the pain*. These are two ways of embracing your life more wholeheartedly, even in the presence of pain, loss, and sorrow.

Amisha's experience demonstrated her lack of self-compassion, but what about you? How self-compassionate are you? Continuing in the spirit of mindfulness, an assessment of your self-compassion is an important first step in learning how you react or respond to challenging situations. Dr. Neff's Self-Compassion Scale is accessed online at www.self-compassion.org/test-how-self-compassionate-you-are. It is an easy-to-complete questionnaire that measures the degree to which you show self-kindness or harsh self-judgment, have a sense of common humanity or feel isolated by your perceived imperfections, and are mindful or overidentify with your suffering. Take a moment and see how you fare on this critical self-care continuum.

LEARNING SELF-COMPASSION

Having just begun the course eight weeks earlier, the members of the mindfulness group displayed mutual feelings of trust and respect as they reflected with surprise and some disappointment on their results from the self-compassion questionnaire. Rachel was shocked at her low score on the common humanity scale, for she had believed herself as more accepting. However, when she quickly reviewed the past few years of her life, she realized that she has felt more separate from others as her health concerns increased. Sam realized that his low score on the self-kindness scale really was an accurate reflection of the harsh self-judgments he lays upon himself when he does not meet his self-imposed high standards. Devon quietly offered that through the mindfulness course, he realized that he easily gets carried away with his feelings when something upsets him. With a quick smile though, he assessed, "But I know I'm getting better at staying present—just takes me time!"

While considerable differences were registered in the three self-compassion components, many had a low composite score. But instead of berating themselves for this unwanted mirroring image (which would only reinforce their low self-compassion), they were able to hold their feelings in an accepting and curious manner. Without an urgency to flee from their feelings, they could share personal stories and realize their common humanity in a self-compassionate fashion. Beth's summary of the discussion as "welcome to the world of the imperfect" was met with smiles and quiet nods of acceptance.

Self-compassion does not spring to life independently, but it is a skillful attitude that can be learned. Self-compassion practice, also known as loving-kindness, builds on the foundation of mindfulness. Self-compassion and mindfulness transform the way you relate to what is happening in your life, and therefore, they are known as relational practices. However, as we have discussed, there are times when mindfulness meditation is extremely difficult, such as when experiencing chronic pain or grief.

Self-compassion offers another way to be with pain—physical and emotional—through moving your focus from being *with* the difficulties to cultivating a connection with your *intention and desire* for well-being. Whereas mindfulness meditation primarily uses *attention,* self-compassion meditation employs the power of *intention.*

Self-compassion works more with motivation and connection than with attention by directing goodwill toward yourself. Self-compassion soothes the mind like a loving friend who is willing to listen to your difficulties without advising until you can sort your problems out for yourself.

Self-compassion focuses explicitly on you and your experiences. When you are suffering intensely, it is beneficial and reassuring to feel held or embraced by another person. While that other person can be a real, physical human being, it no less effectively can also simply be a compassionate part of yourself—to metaphorically wrap your arms around yourself in a warm and caring manner.

PLAY NICE WITH YOURSELF

Sharon Salzberg (2005), an early proponent and champion of self-compassion or loving-kindness meditation, emphasizes that the practice is not expecting to fix all your worries or concerns magically but rather to hold the intention that you experience more kindness and connection with yourself. It is a "wish" that you are extending just as you send a birthday card to a friend, wishing them well in the year to come. The tone of the practice is not one of petitioning or pleading but rather that of gift-giving—kindness and generosity of spirit. The common feedback from people engaged in self-compassion practices is that it feels good when you do it and that the more you do it, the more you want to do it. Over time, a positive cycle develops, strengthening and deepening the initial motivation to practice.

Loving-kindness practice doesn't *directly* change how you feel, but it helps to gently hold yourself, allowing emotions to change by themselves. You utilize the power of intention when you practice self-compassion meditation as it works with your deepest motivation—goodwill. Self-compassion meditation teaches you how to be a better friend to yourself.

In keeping with the respect you have for how easy it is for your attention to be pulled into stories, analysis, judgments, and anything else available as a distraction, self-compassion practice continues to employ the benefits offered through holding an anchor of awareness. However, self-compassion practice or loving-kindness meditation uses words instead of the breath/hand sensations as your anchor of attention.

LOVING-KINDNESS PRACTICE

Traditionally, four loving-kindness phrases are employed as your anchor of awareness. These wishes or intentions comprise a kind, gentle, and compassionate attitude toward a broad range of life experiences. Specifically, if you are in danger, you wish for safety; if you are emotionally upset, you want contentment and happiness; if you are physically sick, you wish for health; and if you are struggling to meet continuing needs, you hope for the capacity to complete each day with greater ease.

The phrases used are neither exhaustive nor etched in stone—the idea is to find words that evoke sensitive, caring feelings inside of you. The terms can change over time in response to specific challenges and difficulties that you are experiencing. However, it is best to keep the phrases simple and easy to repeat. Be creative! Find the words that best mirror your compassion needs at the moment.

To start your exploration, let's use the phrases that typically begin a self-compassion meditation. These would include:

May I be safe.

May I be happy.

May I be healthy.

May I live with ease.

The phrases are repeated silently and gently over and over during the meditation. You may find that you only need to repeat one word of a phrase, such as "safe," "happy," "healthy," "ease." The idea is to take your time and repeat the phrases gently to yourself while keeping an image of yourself in your mind's eye. Savour the meaning of the words. Use the words as an anchor of not only your attention but your intention.

LOVING-KINDNESS TO YOURSELF

In the spirit of being a good friend to yourself, loving-kindness meditation usually begins with offering your good wishes to yourself. However, many find that this starting point is anything but easy!

My psychotherapy client Sylvia came to the loving-kindness practice after the death of her husband. Her grief was wedded to her anger as his violent death was so senseless and unnecessary with him simply being an innocent bystander in a store robbery. Sylvia held little hope that a loving-kindness practice would be of any benefit, but her friend had sensibly argued that she had nothing to lose by trying it.

However, Sylvia's first loving-kindness meditation was a disaster when she could not offer the loving-kindness phrases to herself since she felt that she did not deserve them. Even though she could not have prevented her husband's death, her ongoing feelings of survivor's guilt intruded in her attempts to use the phrases as her anchor of attention. She simply did not see herself as deserving such kind wishes.

Sylvia's experience is not uncommon, as many find it strange or difficult to give yourself care and love. Even if not manifesting as a shame-based identity, the feelings of unworthiness are powerfully convincing in our Western culture, such that this makes it difficult to offer yourself good wishes meaningfully. The record of Sylvia's unfolding experience over the weeks that followed stands as a compelling example of one person's dogged approach in learning to love herself.

After relating her struggles, Sylvia took my suggestion and found a picture of herself as a young child. Sylvia used the photo to summon a more affectionate and caring attitude to herself by seeing the image of herself as an innocent young person holding the excitement of a life yet to come. Her young self's endearing image inspired a more positive, open, and caring frame of mind that she could use in the next loving-kindness meditation session.

Over the subsequent sessions, Sylvia discovered that she could empathetically extend good wishes to herself. While initially awkward, the phrases became more accessible in a manner that felt real to her.

When Sylvia could offer herself loving-kindness wishes meaningfully, she found that her mind did continue to wander at times from her focus on the loving-kindness phrases. This attention slippage is expected, so she knew that she could gently return to her anchor of attention by repeating the expressions when they occurred.

When Sylvia found that phrases would sometimes become meaningless, she revisualized herself as the young girl and began reciting the wishes. Sylvia also found that if both the image of herself as a young girl and the words became vague or blurry, she simply placed her hand on her heart and recalled her intention to fill herself with loving-kindness.

EXTENDING LOVING-KINDNESS TO OTHERS

As noted earlier, one component of self-compassion is that it allows you to feel a connection with all of humanity. That is, it moves you from a sense of isolation into a realization of belonging to the common humanity that we all share in this mortal existence. Therefore, the next step in loving-kindness meditation is to extend the good wishes that you hold to another person, allowing the connection to others to become particularly evident.

BENEFACTOR

After offering the loving-kindness statements to herself, Sylvia then learned to provide them with traditionally what has been called a benefactor. A benefactor is someone who has your well-being at heart, who has helped you or inspired you, such as a mentor, a child, a spiritual guide, a pet, or even an aspect of nature. Sylvia always felt taken care of by her older brother Frank, so she brought his image vividly to mind and allowed herself to feel what it is like to be in his presence. She allowed herself to enjoy the feeling of being in his embracing and supportive company. Sylvia then offered the same wishes to Frank, repeating them slowly and gently while feeling the importance of her words. She again used the aspirations that Frank be safe, happy, healthy, and live with ease as her anchor of attention and the focus of her intention.

FRIEND

Continuing to expand her goodwill, Sylvia then extended the loving-kindness to a friend—a supportive person to whom she feels trust and gratitude and mainly had positive feelings. Like offering loving-kindness to her benefactor, Sylvia brought her friend Claire's image clearly to mind and let herself feel what it is like to be in her presence. She again allowed herself to enjoy Claire's supportive company and then gently and softly repeated her friend's aspirations to be safe, happy, healthy, and live with ease. When Sylvia's mind would wander, she gently brought it back to the words as her anchor of attention as well as the focus of intention.

NEUTRAL PERSON

It is also possible to extend the loving-kindness meditation to a neutral person. This targeted individual would be any living being you don't know and therefore neither like nor dislike. Despite its dull name, this can be a very interesting category. It is an opportunity to develop loving-kindness toward any of the billions of people in the world that you may encounter in your lifetime. Since the neutral person is someone you don't know yet and therefore someone for whom you have neutral feelings, your main challenge will be to maintain the energy of loving-kindness.

Sylvia visualized the teenage girl in front of her at the grocery checkout line the day before. Even while not knowing this person (or any of the other billions of individuals on earth that she could have chosen), Sylvia held the teenager's image in her mind's eye and offered her loving-kindness wishes. Your sense of the importance of the words by gently and slowly repeating them can remind you that the neutral person is a vulnerable being just like you, subject to the 10,000 joys and 10,000 sorrows of life.

DIFFICULT PERSON

You may want to extend loving-kindness to a final category called a diffi-cult person—someone who has caused you hurt or toward whom you have negative feelings. It is understandably more challenging to hold a difficult person in mind—you need to drop to a deeper level within yourself to evoke and sustain loving-kindness toward those who have wronged you. Because this is so challenging, it has been said that difficult people are your best friends on the path of loving-kindness.

When confronted with the category of difficult person, Sylvia immedi-ately thought of the criminal who had killed her husband. However, not surprisingly, this degree of difficult person was too emotionally charged, and I suggested that Sylvia choose a mildly problematic person. Sylvia's instructions were to select someone she felt comfortable enough visual-izing in meditation. When beginning loving-kindness with a challenging person, Sylvia was instructed to remember the difficult person is also struggling to find their way through life, but in so doing they have caused her hurt or sorrow.

Sylvia chose a previous co-worker, Betsy, as her difficult person. Recognizing that it can be difficult to generate positive feelings for such a person, Sylvia utilized the often-recommended introductory statement: "Just as I wish to be safe, may you too find inner safety." This preface allowed her to consciously establish a shared expectation with someone with whom she had previously conflicted. While some want to continue the loving-kindness statements on their own ("May you be safe," "May you be happy," etc.), Sylvia decided to continue to link them with the wish for herself: "Just as I wish to be happy, may you too find inner happiness; just as I wish to be healthy, may you too find good health; just as I wish to live with ease, may you too live with ease."

DIFFICULT PEOPLE BE GONE!

One of the challenges people have found when working with a difficult person is that you may feel that you *do not want* the difficult person to be safe or happy or healthy or at ease. But it is important to note that when we offer a problematic person loving-kindness, we are not accepting bad behaviour or hoping the person will escape the consequences for their action. Instead, we wish for the person to become a healthier human being.

However, some people find that they do not even want to think about their difficult person. Many people instinctively wish that their difficult person would just disappear or die. However, it can be helpful to remember an old Tibetan saying: "Don't waste your time and energy wishing your enemies will die; they will do that anyway."

The difficult person target of the loving-kindness meditation can undoubtedly be very challenging. Feelings of aversion, anger, sadness, revenge, and so on may arise. You may find that the loving-kindness phrases sound hollow alongside these emotions. Should this occur, simply give a label to the feelings you are having (sadness, anger, etc.) and practice compassion for yourself—("May I be safe," "May I be happy," etc.). When you feel more centred, you can again try loving-kindness with your difficult person.

If you continue to have strong feelings of aversion with the difficult person meditation, go back to your friend, benefactor, or neutral person. Don't feel that you *must* bring a difficult person into your meditation—that would only be another form of self-judgment that goes against the meditation's intention. Take it slowly—be gentle with yourself—and over time, see if it is possible to extend your good wishes to such a difficult person.

At the end of the meditation session, you can collectively offer good wishes and intentions to everyone:

May I and all beings be safe.

May I and all beings be happy.

May I and all beings be healthy.

May I and all beings live with ease.

HEALING ELEMENTS

Loving-kindness practice is always on the wishing side of the aspirational equation rather than the outcome side. Positive outcomes may likely come with time, but we primarily learn to cultivate a kind attitude, no matter what happens to us or others. Holding the wish and remaining unattached to the outcome is the definition of unconditional love and being consistent with the mindfulness goal of being fully present in the current moment non-judgmentally.

Self-compassion practice is primarily the cultivation of goodwill rather than good feelings. Feelings come and go, but the ground of your being is the universal wish to be safe, happy, healthy, and free of suffering. That is where you put your trust. Affirmations are an effort to encourage yourself by saying things you may not believe, like "I'm getting stronger every day!" Self-compassion practice isn't trying to fool yourself that your situation is better than it is. Therefore, the phrases you use must credibly reflect your intention—goodwill toward yourself and others.

DOES SELF-COMPASSION WORK?

Before beginning the loving-kindness practice, I asked the group if they had any questions or concerns. Richard, whose technical worldview continued to scrutinize the efficacy of what appeared to be simple training, succinctly asked, "Does it work?" The short answer is yes—there have been many studies demonstrating that the seemingly innocuous and straightforward loving-kindness phrases contribute to increases in self-compassion and general well-being.

For example, in a study at the University of Wisconsin, Dr. Ritchie Davidson (Neff 2011) trained a group of subjects to practice compassion meditation (similar to loving-kindness) for thirty minutes a day for two weeks. A comparison group of subjects learned to cognitively reappraise difficult situations in their lives by looking at them with different viewpoints. After two weeks, only the compassion meditation group showed significant improvement on the Self-Compassion Scale developed by Kristin Neff (the same one you completed online).

Then the participants were brought into Dr. Davidson's lab and exposed to images of human suffering (such as a child with a dramatic eye tumour) while their brains were scanned in an MRI. The compassion meditation group had more increased activity in the brain's insula area (which shows empathy) as opposed to the other group. The more active the insula was while the participants looked at the distressing photographs, the higher their scores on self-report scales of well-being and self-compassion.

Dr. Davidson then gave the subjects the chance to donate their $165 honorarium to a cause of their choosing. Amazingly, activation in the insula measured by the MRI predicted how much money the subjects donated—the more insula activity, the more money subjects contributed! This study demonstrates that only two weeks of loving-kindness meditation can change brain activity, make people feel more compassionate toward themselves and others, and even elicit generosity.

After all her years of research, Dr. Kristin Neff concludes that self-compassion is an excellent emotional strength and resilience source. She notes that this is difficult for some people to understand because they think self-compassion means being weak—self-compassion is for "sissies." But the research shows that people who have more self-compassion are more resilient to get through difficult times.

For example, a study by Dr. Hiraoka (2015) assessed American soldiers returning from Iraq and Afghanistan. She measured their self-compassion levels (using the same Self-Compassion Scale that you did earlier) and, over time, whether they developed post-traumatic stress disorder (PTSD). After accounting for combat exposure and the soldiers' baseline PTSD symptoms, the Self-Compassion Scale predicted PTSD symptom severity at the 12-month follow-up. This suggests that self-compassion may influence the degree of chronicity of PTSD symptoms among combat war veterans. This also suggests that increasing self-compassion through training sessions may be beneficial to some war veterans who are struggling with PTSD symptoms. Robust self-compassion has the potential to inoculate you against many of the trials and challenges of life. Not bad for such a simple meditation practice.

Dr. Neff concludes that the crucial question becomes, "Are you an inner ally or an inner enemy?" Unfortunately, as discussed throughout this book, many individuals have an inner critic or judge that undermines them, which harms them. However, when you have an inner voice that supports you through whatever you are experiencing—not one that undermines you—you have an incredible source of strength and resilience that is yours. You become a friend to yourself!

Further studies have shown that simply learning about compassion does not necessarily increase empathetic and benevolent behaviour. In an earlier session, I mentioned that just learning about mindfulness in and of itself did not result in changes in participants' neural (brain) wiring—it took practice to bring about such changes. In the arc, from empathizing with someone's suffering to reaching out to help, participation in loving-kindness/compassion meditation has been found to increase the likelihood that an individual will become involved in a supportive manner. The longer people practice loving-kindness/compassion meditation, the stronger their new brain circuitry becomes through neuroplasticity and in turn, their tendency to become actively involved in a compassionate manner.

A Chinese proverb says, "If you keep a green tree bough in your heart, the singing bird will come." Self-compassion reminds you there are tangible benefits to always keep a green bough in your heart.

PRACTICE OF THE WEEK

Guidelines:

- It is recommended that with loving-kindness meditation you limit it to two shorter sittings, which may be better than one extended sitting. Therefore, try the loving-kindness practice for **fifteen to twenty minutes once, if not twice per day**. The brain develops a habit of doing whatever it is doing, so the more you can generate the intention to be loving and compassionate, the greater likelihood that this will lay down new neural connections. Dr. Shauna Shapiro (2020) reminds you that "What you practice grows stronger."

- Experiment with the phrases. Find ones that meet your present needs and intentions.

- You can work with the phrases any time, night, and day. Even during the day, as you are going about your business, you may offer such wishes to yourself or anyone you encounter.

- Some people find it very pleasing to do the loving-kindness meditation for even a few minutes before sleep.

- Experiment with the timing of the practice—perhaps start your sitting mindfulness meditation with ten to fifteen minutes of loving-kindness, and then do your formal sitting practice. Or end your formal sitting meditation with loving-kindness.

- As with all the homework assignments, you can either use the book website's audible guided set of instructions or just read them to yourself before starting the practice. You may want to start with the audible ones and, as the week progresses, experiment doing sessions without them.

- In the spirit of making mindfulness your own practice, please experiment and see what works best for you!

- Remember to record your homework on your **Tracking Your Practice** log.

LOVING-KINDNESS MEDITATION INSTRUCTIONS:

To begin the loving-kindness meditation, assume a comfortable posture that facilitates your focus . . . and bring your attention to your breathing. . . . To support your groundedness at this moment, choose the part of the body that allows you to feel the breath coming in and going out . . . through the nostrils, focusing on the chest area, or on the belly. . . .

Allow your focus to be anchored on the breath and the part of the body you are using to hold your awareness . . . allowing the breath to be natural . . . noting its inflow and outflow, without trying to force or control it in any way . . . allowing yourself to settle into the breath's rhythm . . . allowing the mind to rest in this place . . . feeling the movement of the breath. . . .

After a few breaths to centre and ground yourself, turn your attention and awareness to the loving-kindness phrases that you have chosen. . . . Typically, four loving-kindness phrases comprise a kindly and gentle attitude toward a broad range of life experiences. . . . Find ones that mirror your intention at this moment. . . . The phrases that are traditionally used are neither exhaustive nor etched in stone. . . . The idea is to select words that evoke tender, warm feelings inside . . . words that reflect your intention to befriend yourself and others. . . . It is best to keep the phrases simple and easy to repeat. . . .

Before beginning to recite the phrases silently, bring up an image of yourself in your mind's eye . . . either a picture of you today . . . or of you as a young, innocent child . . . or when you were experiencing challenges and needed loving-kindness and self-compassion . . . whatever image that allows you to hold yourself in a positive and kindly manner. . . .

Loving-kindness begins with yourself. . . . The phrases that are typically used to start a self-compassion meditation would include:

May I be safe. . . .
May I be happy. . . .
May I be healthy. . . .
May I live with ease. . . .

Repeat the phrases, slowly, silently, and gently over and over during the meditation. . . . You may find that you only need to repeat one word of a phrase, such as safe . . . happy . . . healthy . . . ease. . . . The idea is to take your time. . . . Repeat the phrases gently to yourself . . . while keeping an image of yourself in your mind's eye. . . . Savour the meaning of the words. . . . Use the words as your anchor of attention and intention. . . . When you notice that the mind has wandered (which it will inevitably do), come back to your anchor by repeating the phrases again. . . .

If the words become meaningless, revisualize yourself and begin repeating the words. . . . If both the image of yourself and the wishes become vague or blurry, put your hand on your heart and recall your intention to fill yourself with loving-kindness . . . with self-compassion. . . . Perhaps change the image of yourself to a more positive one. . . . An endearing image of yourself can inspire a more positive, open, and loving frame of mind. . . .

A critical aspect of self-compassion is that it allows you to feel a connection with all of humanity. . . . It moves you from a sense of isolation into a realization that we all experience this human existence. . . . We each experience the good, the bad, and the ugly of life. . . . No one gets off scot-free. . . . Therefore, the next step in loving-kindness meditation will be to extend the good wishes that you hold to another person. . . .

After offering the loving-kindness statements to yourself for a few minutes, you can now offer it to someone else who has been called a benefactor. . . . A benefactor is someone who has your well-being at heart, who has helped you or inspired you . . . such as a mentor . . . a child . . . a spiritual guide . . . a pet . . . or even an aspect of nature. . . . Bring the benefactor's image clearly to mind. . . . Allow yourself to feel what it is like to be in that person's presence. . . . Allow yourself to enjoy the excellent company . . . and when it feels right, offer the exact wishes to your benefactor. . . . Repeat them slowly and gently while feeling the importance of your words. . . . Again, use the phrases as your anchor of attention. . . .

Benefactor: May you be safe.

                May you be happy.

                May you be healthy.

                May you live with ease.

After a few minutes of offerings to your benefactor . . . when it feels right to you . . . extend the loving-kindness to another . . . to a friend . . . a supportive person toward whom you feel trust and gratitude and have primarily positive feelings. . . . Again, bring the friend's image clearly to mind. . . . Let yourself feel what it is like to be in that person's presence. . . . Allow yourself to enjoy the good company . . . then gently and softly repeat the offerings with the intention that your friend be safe, happy, healthy, and live with ease. . . . If your mind wanders, gently bring it back to the words as your anchor of attention. . . .

Friend: May you be safe.

          May you be happy.

          May you be healthy.

          May you live with ease.

After a few minutes of offerings to your friend . . . when it feels right to you . . . extend the loving-kindness meditation to a neutral person. . . . This would be any living being whom you don't know and therefore neither like nor dislike. . . . Visualize a neutral person as anyone in the universe . . . and offer them the loving-kindness wishes. . . . Use the words as your anchor of attention and intention. . . .

Neutral Person: May you be safe.

                   May you be happy.

                   May you be healthy.

                   May you live with ease.

After a few minutes of offerings to a neutral person . . . when it again feels right to you . . . extend loving-kindness to what has been called a difficult person . . . someone who has caused you pain or toward whom you have negative feelings. . . . It is obviously challenging to hold a more difficult person in mind. . . . Therefore, choose a person who is mildly difficult . . . not a person who has hurt you badly . . . or who is causing massive hardship on the world stage. . . . Let it be someone you feel comfortable enough visualizing in meditation. . . . Remind yourself that the difficult person is struggling to find their way through life. . . . In their own, often misguided way, they too are trying to become healthier . . . but, in so doing, are causing you pain. . . .

Bring the difficult person into your mind's eye. . . . You can begin this meditation by saying to yourself:

Difficult person: Just as I wish to be safe and free from suffering, may you too find inner safety.

Just as I wish to be happy, may you, too, find inner happiness.
Just as I wish to be healthy, may you too find good health.
Just as I wish to live with ease, may you too live with ease.

Alternatively, you may decide to just use the short phrases on their own . . . "May you be safe. . . . May you be happy. . . . May you be healthy. . . . May you live with ease. . . . "

When engaged with the difficult person, feelings of aversion . . . anger . . . sadness . . . and so on, may arise. . . . You may find that the loving-kindness phrases sound hollow alongside these emotions. . . . Should this occur, simply give a label to the emotions you are feeling . . . sadness . . . anger . . . or whatever has arisen . . . and practise compassion for yourself . . . "May I be safe. . . . May I be happy. . . . May I be healthy. . . . May I live with ease. . . ."

If with the compassion directed to yourself you find that you can return to the loving-kindness meditation with the difficult person, then do so. . . . However, if it feels too painful or challenging, continue the practice with yourself . . . or with your benefactor . . . or with your friend . . . or your neutral person. . . . You can always return to the difficult person at another time. . . . When you feel better, you can again try the loving-kindness with your difficult person. . . .

You can continue your loving-kindness meditation for a set time . . . or offer good wishes and intention to each person two or three times . . .

whatever feels right to you. . . . At the end of the meditation session, you can then invoke good wishes and intentions to all beings. . . .

May I and all beings be safe. . . .
May I and all beings be happy. . . .
May I and all beings be healthy. . . .
May I and all beings live with ease. . . .

MIDWEEK CUPPA... REFLECTIONS ON AGING AND LETTING GO

WEEK EIGHT

By the time you are in your fifties or later, you've chalked up many experiences through your aging life! While many of these past experiences were undoubtedly positive and are now enjoyable memories, you have also had the opportunity to accumulate many other incidents you regret, resent, or feel guilty about. You know which difficult ones I'm talking about—those harsh and unpleasant encounters with others, hurtful offences inflicted by others on you, spiteful actions you took toward others, resentful thoughts that you harboured, crushing words that you spoke in anger, and so forth. In short, experiences that are difficult to let go of!

The oldest couple I saw in my psychotherapy practice were in their eighties. Alfred and Irene were married almost sixty years ago, with the presenting issue that brought them to therapy being his inability to let go of resentments held toward his wife. Irene readily admitted that she spoke in a derogatory manner to Alfred during the first few years of their marriage. However, Irene had apologized for her thoughtless and angry outbursts multiple times over the ensuing years. While Alfred could cognitively acknowledge that the personal slights that she threw at him were not that significant and did not represent a pattern of her ongoing behaviour toward him, he still felt their sting and couldn't let go. Even with the passage of the intervening years and all the other experiences that he had with Irene, Alfred continued to be held hostage to those words spoken in moments of anger over half a century ago. They were both quick to clarify that this did not result in them experiencing daily conflict. Instead, Alfred's resentment created a barrier, insulating him from fully emotionally investing with Irene.

Not diminishing Alfred's experience and the pain he felt, while sitting in the room with them, I felt a wave of sadness blanket over me—sadness for the loss of deep intimacy that they missed developing with the impenetrable wall of resentment that stood between them. Such is the power of resentment—and the inability to let go!

REGRETS, RESENTMENTS, AND FORGIVENESS

The Christian professor of theology Lewis Smedes (1984) observed: "To forgive is to set a prisoner free and discover that the prisoner was you." Alfred's experience of holding resentments is not unusual but somewhat reflective of the human experience. While Alfred's grievance is specific to his life situation, you, too, have likely been on the receiving end of words and actions that have hurt. As well, whether wittingly or not, you have probably said or done something to cause pain and sorrow to another person. Therefore, the issue is not *if* you have regrets or resentments but rather what you will *do* about them. How do you deal with them ethically and sensitively to yourself and others in a way that allows you to let go—to let go of the destructive power that they can exert over you? How much lighter and more easeful would your life be?

In addition to compassion toward yourself and others, letting go through forgiveness is a direct action that offers you the power to break down the barriers of regrets and resentments. Without the capacity of forgiveness, your life would flood with the accumulation of all the pains and sorrows that living in a societal community inevitably brings.

The Oxford Dictionary defines *forgive* as "cease to feel angry or resentful toward; pardon an offender or offence." This definition conveys the literal aspects of the word but lacks the power that forgiveness holds. A better, and what I've found to be more emotionally meaningful, understanding of forgiveness is that "forgiveness means giving up all hope for a better past." I have been unable to locate the original author of this quote but it certainly feels much more sensitive, robust, and accurate!

Please take a moment to digest the essence of this understanding of forgiveness and how it relates to your life. Do you hold onto the past, hoping that it will be different in a positive way? Do you wish that not only the big-ticket events of your life would be better but also the many more minor transgressions? Maybe not wholesale better but perhaps hoping for even just a nudge better?

Forgiveness at its core is, therefore, really about your well-being. Forgiveness is a way to let go of the pain you, just like Alfred, have carried. Forgiveness releases regret about what you have said or done to others as well as resentments of those actions imposed upon you. What would your life be like without the collection of regrets and bitterness that you carry? How much lighter and more easeful would your life be?

REGRET WITH OTHERS

Through the process of mindfulness meditation, you have the opportunity to move closer to feelings of regret that you may be carrying because of your hurtful words or actions to another. To recognize the feeling without defensively ignoring, avoiding, or justifying it away allows for an honest reflection on how your words or actions may have harmed another. I am talking about the more significant events that you may have caused or participated in and those lesser but still powerful transgressions that have caused pain or sorrow to others. You know the ones I mean—a sharp rebuke, a dismissive action, a thoughtless gesture, satisfying a selfish desire at the expense of another, a turning away when witnessing the suffering of another, and so on—all potentially creating hurt and pain to another person whether you meant it or not.

Asking for forgiveness from the other that you harmed takes courage. To sincerely ask for forgiveness means recognizing the negative effect of your words or actions through empathic attunement to the other's hurt that you caused. To be open to this recognition also means holding your own pain because of your actions or words—the pain cuts across both you and the other. Mindfulness helps to prepare you to fully be with whatever emotions arise, while loving-kindness practice provides a compassionate holding environment for your experience. This is not an easy process even with such practices, but true forgiveness cannot occur without a conscious meeting of the other's and your suffering.

It is also essential for you to take full responsibility for your words or actions—do not justify or analyze or share the blame. The other may have played a role in the situation, but your words or actions created your feelings of regret in the end. The other's involvement is their responsibility to deal with.

Also, taking full responsibility for your words or actions needs to be coupled with your declaration that you will not do this again. Without such an assertion, asking for forgiveness stands as just a hollow and meaningless exercise.

The courage needed to ask for forgiveness arises from feeling powerful and painful emotions both within yourself as well as the other and because you have no control over the outcome. The acceptance or not of your request of forgiveness is entirely out of your hands as it recognizes the other person's sovereignty—they may or may not be willing or able to accept your offering at this time or anytime in the future. Mindfulness practice helps prepare you for this reality through the attitudinal foundations of acceptance, non-judging, beginner's mind, trust, non-striving, letting go and patience.

RESENTMENT WITH OTHERS

Just as Alfred experienced over many decades, holding resentments about what others have said or done to you is a compelling and potentially destructive outcome over and above the original transgression. However, forgiving someone for offences they committed against you also takes great courage. It is important to remember that forgiving the other who has hurt or harmed you does not mean that you are condoning their actions or trying to forget what took place. Instead, forgiveness is releasing you from the often painful and limiting cage that your resentments have built and fortified.

A well-known Tibetan Buddhist story tells of two monks who meet each other years after being released from prison, tortured by their jailers. "Have you forgiven them?" asks the first monk. "No, I will never forgive them! Never!" scoffed the second. "Well, I guess they still have you in prison," the first monk sadly replied.

Forgiving another is often a very long process that will not be rushed. Forgiveness can feel like it has a life of its own with a hidden timetable, and therefore, it is vital to honour the process. You may also experience an increase in emotional upheaval when initially exploring forgiveness. This emotional response is certainly not unusual, but know that it doesn't mean that forgiveness is impossible.

Forgiveness is not to be taken lightly or entered impetuously. Forgiveness has been mistakenly described as a weakness of character or surrender to the perpetrator, but true heartfelt forgiveness is anything but! In addition to not condoning the other's words or actions, a critical component of forgiveness is the declaration that you give to yourself to do everything in *your* power not to fall prey or to allow such breaches to occur again. Therefore, compassion for yourself at such times is offering a powerful gift with healing intentions.

Mindfulness and compassion practices can hold and nurture the capacity to be with resentments to develop and establish a new relationship with the harm you sustained. Just as you learned to work with powerful pain and grief experiences, mindfulness supports you in recognizing and holding the painful emotions associated with wrongs you have experienced. When the feelings are particularly powerful, to touch up against them—hold them as your anchor of awareness through a half-breath or one breath or two breaths (Level Four response)—begins to establish a new relationship with them—a new relationship to ensure that they're not keeping you in prison!

Loving-kindness practices, primarily directed to yourself, can also be very beneficial. While you may want the perpetrator of the wrong you experienced to be the difficult person you utilize in your compassion practice, be reasonable and gentle with yourself regarding whether this is manageable. Don't rush the forgiveness practice—it will unfold as it will. It is again important to note that through the mindfulness practice you have been developing, the attitudinal foundations of acceptance, non-judging, beginner's mind, trust, non-striving, letting go and patience will do you well.

But it is essential to be clear that there are devastating experiences that individuals have had, primarily regarding abuse and trauma, which require professional assistance in terms of changing one's relationships with them. The field of trauma-focused psychotherapy has developed by recognizing that some traumas can reshape the body and the brain and require specialized interventions. Compassion for yourself can motivate you to explore forgiveness, but wisdom will help you know how best to bring it about. If in doubt, it is prudent to consult with a mental health professional.

REGRET AND RESENTMENT WITH YOURSELF

While regret and resentment with others are usually the focus of forgiveness, it is also essential to recognize the harm you may have caused *yourself* through your thoughts, beliefs, and actions. Speaking or acting in ways that can harm others can also be painful to you not only because of your regret but also due to a change in the relationship itself. Unfortunately, harmful words or actions have the potential to rupture family or long-term friendships irreparably.

In addition, you may have experienced harm through the negative judgments you have laid upon yourself, such as proclaiming yourself incompetent, stupid, ugly, fat, unlovable, or the thousand other declarative verdicts that undermine your sense of self. Harming yourself may also have come about through the decisions you made based not on a reasonable assessment of the facts but instead on your fear. The education you passed up, the jobs you didn't try for, the promotions you turned down, the pleasurable experiences you denied, the children you didn't have, the people you didn't open your heart to love, can all arise because of fear of failure or other negative consequences.

To thoughtfully review your life's choices and acknowledge the limitations you have imposed upon yourself is a step toward forgiveness—forgiveness compassionately directed toward yourself! The review needs to catalogue your choices and identify the causes and conditions that led to your beliefs and actions. To recognize that your decisions arose not from some characterological flaw but rather your limited or mistaken understanding of who you were at the time, as well as your capacity to meet and hold the often-conflicting feelings that such decisions entail, opens the possibility of forgiveness.

It is also imperative to recognize that every decision involves a sacrifice—whenever you choose one thing, you are by default not getting something else. It is simply impossible to get everything, so know that this means that your limitations in life are not restricted to you—limitations are part of the human experience. By recognizing the common humanity of self-compassion, the goal no longer becomes getting "everything" in life but rather to consciously understand *what* you would be sacrificing through your decision and rationally and emotionally evaluate what you are *willing* to sacrifice. This becomes yet another opportunity to mindfully respond and not just react.

Mindfulness and compassion practices allow you to forgive yourself for whatever beliefs, decisions, and actions you have taken. Remember, however, that genuine forgiveness also demands a declaration that you will not act in a similar destructive manner in the future, which therefore requires a different way of being toward yourself. Becoming more conscious of what is important to you and then having the courage to pursue such goals is facilitated through self-forgiveness. Mindfulness and compassion practices provide you with the opportunity to establish a new foundation, no matter your age, to live this life that is yours entirely.

THE REST OF THE STORY

Regarding the story about Alfred's resentments toward Irene with which I began this section, I am unfortunately unable to tell you how it ended. They only attended one session, and while they made a follow-up appointment, they later cancelled and never rescheduled. I was never given a reason why—it is possible they may not have felt confident in me to accompany them through this issue, or it could have been that one or both of them may not have felt ready to do the work of psychotherapy. During the first session, I explained that working with me would entail exploring their emotional relationship as a couple and, critically, within themselves, which may have been too threatening. I don't know, but, over the years, I have wondered what happened to them and hoped with a sense of compassion that they did find someone else to help them with their long-suffering struggles.

I also have wondered whether seeking professional assistance many years earlier would have made a difference in resolving Alfred and Irene's difficulties. I don't know if it would have, but knowing that forgiveness is often a long process with its hidden timetable, it is a good reminder not to put off addressing the regrets and resentments that each of us has experienced. Ernest Hemingway told us: "Today is only one day in all the days that will ever be. But what will happen in all the other days that ever come can depend on what you do today." With the recognition of time limitations, our aging years provide the impetus to compassionately question: If not now, when?

ENDINGS IMPLY BEGINNINGS— STAYING AWAKE

WEEK NINE

REVIEW LOVING-KINDNESS PRACTICE

The aliveness and enthusiasm infusing the final group session mirrored nature's annual proclamation that a vibrant new season had arrived. From the dark days of late February, nature had once again transformed from a barren and bleak hibernation to the late April riot of colourful blossoms and foliage. Similarly, the group had undergone their own growth over these eight weeks, learning and practising mindfulness, Jungian principles, and self-compassion to transform from uncertain aging students into confident adventurers meeting time in a respectful, healthier, and more conscious manner.

The previous week's loving-kindness and self-compassion meditation had proved to be another winner with the group. Helen's affirmative summary that the daily practices were an endearing way to open the heart and create a loving spirit with yourself and others met with unanimous nods of approval. Beth's experience of finding the "difficult person" incredibly challenging echoed through most of the group. While Rachel, George, and Josie affirmed this challenge, each found that falling back to direct loving-kindness to themselves and others created more resolve and resilience to then include their difficult person. Cassie tried this strategy on a few occasions but to no avail—as she wryly noted, "There is no place set at my table—yet—for my problematic infuriating cousin!"

Carlos changed the targets of his loving-kindness wishes from the standard categories to family members. Unexpectedly, but perhaps not surprisingly, Carlos concluded that by directing wishes to each member of his extended family, he still ended up identifying benefactors, friends, neutral, and even difficult persons!

Jessica extended her good wishes to her father, who passed away two years ago. I appreciated Jessica's extension to beneficiaries who have passed, as, depending upon your spiritual beliefs, they can be worthy recipients of continuing good thoughts and wishes. Each evening when I take our old dog, Sophie, out for her last walk of the day, I look to the stars and offer wishes to my stillborn grandson: "Bowen, may your spirit be enriched and strengthened by the love you receive. May your spirit be at ease and at peace."

Loving-kindness is a spirit that can be awakened, nurtured, and encouraged to grow in our hearts. Over the years, I've found it to be a lovely nourishing practice to foster. When experiencing challenging and complex life events, I have benefited from practising loving-kindness meditation exclusively for months at a time, so I was pleased that the group also discovered its supportive and enriching qualities.

The room fell silent as Richard, whose technical background exemplified the group's initial skepticism about the merits of meditation, quietly expressed his growing admiration of mindfulness and loving-kindness practices. He offered that his way of dealing with suffering throughout his long life had always been reactive, living with underlying anxiety as he waited for the next "something bad" to happen. And when it did (as it inevitably did), his fallback game plan was to ignore the pain or sorrow for as long as he could, find some logical, rational reason why it occurred, and then just "gut it out." However, over these eight weeks, with loving-kindness as the crowning touch, he has discovered a different way of meeting life's challenges based on inner support and confidence that he didn't know existed. In a slow, gentle, but discernable manner, he has viscerally experienced the strength and resilience that comes with meeting the difficulties of life consciously and with a softening of his heart.

With his eyes tearing up, Richard disclosed it had taken seventy-four years to learn that he does not have to live in anxiety of the next "catastrophe" to befall him. Instead, he has tapped into an inner aliveness and confidence that with his newfound skills he can courageously meet whatever arises with an open heart and a bemused appreciation of himself as just another "bozo on the bus." Richard concluded, "While I've heard the phrase about being a 'better friend' to yourself many times during this course, I thought it was just an empty saying—nice words but didn't mean much. But now I know that this is true—I can honestly feel that I AM my own best friend!"

TIME HAS COME TODAY

We began this shared journey eight weeks ago to explore valuable ways of becoming a better friend to yourself through consciously reflecting and practising how you meet time. But why time—what is so special about time? Because aging is the embodiment of time passing, and with advancing age comes the reality that your time resource is diminishing. How you maintain awareness of this certainty, how you experience each moment, and what your relationship is to each moment becomes an imperative not to be ignored.

You have been introduced to a new lens through which to experience time by diligently investing in your emergent mindfulness practice and Jungian psychological strategies. I'm sure that you also noticed that time did not stand still or even take a break while you engaged in learning these ways of being present in each moment. Your life continued during these weeks as it always has, presenting you with gratifying and satisfying moments, with complex and sometimes painful challenges, as well as interspersed between with everything else.

The group's experience was no different. Josie enjoyed the birth of a new grandson. Sybil had an emotional reunion with her long-estranged daughter. Betty's cancer went into remission. Malik began his long-planned retirement. Cindy suffered heart concerns not yet diagnosed. Henry tentatively entered a new romantic relationship. Devon's idiopathic pulmonary fibrosis condition progressed, making it more difficult to use his breath as his anchor of awareness, so he switched to using his hand sensations. Sanjay emotionally struggled mightily on the first anniversary of his wife's passing. Juanita decided to move to the country to kick-start the next chapter of her life.

These brief examples are yet another persuasive lesson that time stops for nothing, including the beneficial intention to develop a healthier relationship with it! There is simply no negotiating or bartering to placate time—with or without your active participation, time and all that comes in its wake will continue to advance, moment to moment, hour to hour, day to day, month to month, year to year . . .

Over the previous weeks, every member of the group had met both the highs and lows of a lived life, learning to be with jubilant and sombre events ranging from silly playfulness to weighty emotional and physical discomfort stemming from chronic pain or grief or chronic/life-limiting illness. No one in the group recounted that this journey had been a walk in the park, but still, each had demonstrated to themselves that they could meet their goals of being with time more healthily and satisfyingly. Just as Richard found, they were experiencing a new foundation of companionship, becoming a better friend to themselves as they live through the 10,000 joys and 10,000 sorrows of a life lived!

THREE INVITATIONS REVISITED

You will recall that you started this journey to meet time as you age more healthily and enjoyably through accepting three invitations. The first invitation was to be *aware* that there is no avoiding, escaping, denying, or numbing the truth of ever-limited time available as you age, evoked and remembered through the rhetorical question, "If not now, when?" Mindfulness proved to be an influential teacher of this reality. Moment-to-moment awareness drove home the truth that every moment is different, constantly changing, requiring active monitoring to not miss what transpires. Especially during your aging years, with diminishing time available, this awareness is a crucial ability to harness.

Moment-to-moment awareness laid the foundation for the second invitation by inviting you to *experience* time completely. Experiencing time is to metaphorically and literally "wake up" to the unfolding terrain of each moment that defines your life. Mindfulness offered you a framework to direct and hold your attention where you want it when you want it. It presented a structured process to harness your attention in service of being aware of whatever occurs in terms of positive and negative and neutral thoughts, emotions, physical sensations, and events. Establishing an anchor for your awareness and learning that you have strategies through four incremental levels of response to whatever may disrupt your objective is the gift of attention self-regulation. This skill acquisition created a solid structural foundation, building a new house to hold your emerging self-friendship.

The third invitation encouraged you to establish a new *relationship* with time, one cloaked with integrity, respect, and aliveness fuelled by courage. Your awareness and experience of neutral, positive, and especially negative thoughts, feelings, physical sensations, and events made it abundantly clear that the quality of your relationship with each moment depends not so much on what occurs but critically on your attitudes and beliefs to whatever arises. The French Nobel laureate Andre Gide exemplifies this relationship when he concludes: "To be utterly happy, the only thing necessary is to refrain from comparing this moment with other moments."

Holding the seven attitudinal foundations as the lens through which you experience each moment provided a framework to further this relationship goal. Attitudes of beginner's mind, non-judging, acceptance, trust, non-striving, patience, and letting go come together in a synergetic and interactive way to establish a context of understanding and knowing with confidence that you can meet, accept, and be present with everything that life offers, including those of an unwanted and painful nature.

Now, eight weeks later, you appreciate the positive and are able to better meet the challenging and complex moments. Your attitudinal acceptance of pain and loss and sorrow can evolve, echoing Tennessee Williams's observation: "Don't look forward to the day you stop suffering, because when it comes, you'll know you're dead." Your self-friendship mindset expands exponentially, primarily through your accepting and non-judgmental relationship with time. Critically, the attitudinal foundations support the basis of self-friendship, creating a way of being that feels like a home to welcome and embrace your self-regulation of attention to each moment.

THE SYNERGY OF JUNGIAN INSIGHTS

You also found that while mindfulness is a powerful way of being in the world, it is not a panacea to encountering all challenges. While mindfulness provides a playbook to facilitate meeting each moment, stickier intrusive issues will arise that veil or hinder or impair your ability to be present. Those beliefs, attitudes, personality characteristics, and learned reactions, often of a long-standing and unconscious nature, intrude in your quest to pay attention, on purpose, in the moment, non-judgmentally. Fortunately, Jungian psychology presents complementary strategies to meet and unpack these issues in furthering mindfulness's goal and support your individual growth and development journey through your aging years.

The "Midweek Cuppa . . . Reflections on Aging" sections in Weeks Two through Eight provided a parallel but integrated process to address many of these troublesome issues, including the unknown future, personal shadows, projections, rigidity, criticalness, vulnerability, shame, expectations, regrets, and resentments. Bringing these concerns to the light of consciousness positively impacts your relationship to each moment and furthers your psychological maturity and overall individuation process. While these matters are not amenable to easy or pithy answers, insights and strategies for transforming the small limiting version of yourself to becoming the more extensive and authentic embodiment of you were offered, expanding your mindset through opening another door to become a better friend with yourself!

WHERE DO WE GO NOW?

Over the past eight weeks, learning to pay attention, on purpose, in the moment, non-judgmentally has been presented in a structured step-by-step manner to facilitate your skill development. While you may not have recognized it as you participated in each week's practices, I assure you that you have been following an arc constructing a solid foundation to explore, learn, and practise your budding mindfulness skills. You have now arrived at a point where the more comprehensive experience of mindfulness becomes accessible to you!

You may have heard this before (only kidding, because I know I can sound like a broken record!), but its prominence needs to be again emphasized: the importance of attention self-regulation has been a critical underlying theme of your mindfulness, self-compassion, and Jungian practice training. Attention is a vital skill to hone because it is essentially the brain's boss—wherever attention goes, most other cognitive and emotional processes follow.

To address the importance of attention, you started the course by practising *focused awareness*, which involved establishing a defined reference point to place and hold your attention. This was likely a new experience, so it demanded a concerted effort to maintain awareness where you wanted it and when you wanted it.

In Week One's Body Scan meditation, you focused on individual areas of the body to start developing the ability to hold and shift your attention at will consciously. You then extended this skill in Week Two by creating a defined anchor of awareness (your breath or hand sensations), which became your attention's safe haven when it inevitably was hijacked by intrusive thoughts, emotions, and physical sensations. Your focus of attention was narrow and specific to your anchor. Remember my young untrained horse, Fionn—the one who was without a doubt and with no discussion between us, definitely calling the shots during my initial ride? Well, during that first somewhat frightening ride, holding a tight rein (in addition to the goal of hanging on for dear life) would be similar to focused awareness as an attempt to establish a line of communication, directly and emphatically signalling where and on what I am asking Fionn to focus her attention.

You later extended your attention to sights, sounds, and other sensory experiences so that you could expand your focus from a narrow perspective (just your breath or hand or feet sensations) to a broader field focusing on a variety of objects in your environment. You continued to use an anchor of awareness (new sights and sounds or other sensory experiences) with you deciding what your anchor would be. This is referred to as *flexible awareness* practice, where you make a conscious decision to shift between and among objects as your anchor of awareness. The effort required is variable, with there being a lessening of the amount demanded with fixed awareness. Your field of attention is both expansive and narrow, but you continue to focus on specific objects. Flexible awareness allows you to exercise your freedom to choose where your attention is focused.

With more time in the saddle on Fionn, this stage would be like loosening the reins as more effective communication is established. I am still conscious of the need to focus her attention but without holding such a tight grip—trusting that Fionn and I are learning to become partners in directing where attention (both hers and mine) is placed and, by extension, where we are going.

Moving through fixed and flexible awareness prepares you to meet the whole mindfulness experience now. An incredibly significant benefit and one of the long-term goals of mindfulness practice is to experience *open awareness* or *choiceless awareness*. This means sitting in the middle of experience and remaining attentive and open to whatever arises, staying within the experiential neural focus and not being pulled into the default narrative one. Your mind tends to rest in a place of effortless awareness rather than a defined anchor, which happens on its own—you simply don't have to try so hard consciously. Staying utterly present in the moment, you don't seek any unique experience, nor do you reject whatever arises. You remain present, open, and receptive to whatever unfolds in your awareness. Thoughts, feelings, body sensations, sounds, sights, and smells arise and pass away, opening the endless series of direct experiences through this moment, and this moment, and this moment.

Open awareness is very much like what many of us experienced as a child on a warm summer afternoon lying on the grass and simply watching the clouds go by, which allowed for an open and present sensory awareness. After Week Seven, Cassie experienced it as she sat by a flowing stream, fully attentive to the sights, sounds, and smells of the moment, witnessing the ever-changing world in and around her, marvelling at the wonders available in every moment. Betty sat in open awareness during a chemotherapy session, simply being in the moment with her attention wide open and accessible, moving from sights to sounds to smells offered in the hospital environment.

With Fionn, open awareness further loosened the reins needed to hold her attention in sync with mine. It is trusting she can focus her attention where it needs to be while meeting our shared goals. It is the thrill of galloping through open fields, directly experiencing the oneness of two animal bodies and spirits in tune with the world—this time, unlike my first in the saddle, not just along for the ride but as an active participant!

OPENING TO AWE AND WONDER

Much of the course has been learning new skills and attitudes to meet the challenges and struggles of life. This goal has been essential since most of us have, from an early age, mistakenly believed that the only reaction to pain and loss and suffering is to ignore, avoid, or numb ourselves to it. Correcting these misperceptions has necessitated the extended emphasis of increasing your understanding and felt experience of how to meet suffering openly and directly.

However, that is not all that you have experienced over these eight weeks—you have also perceived beautiful moments of joy, playfulness, satisfaction, and wholeness that are also always available to you. You have also likely touched upon moments of open awareness, wholly immersed in the sensory perceptions offered to you.

While moments of open awareness or choiceless awareness can be fleeting, they are also a potent reminder that to be fully immersed in just this moment opens the opportunity to touch the absolute beauty of human existence. You met this marvel during Week Seven, when you discovered the experience of awe through sight and sound meditations. Awe arises when your attention is drawn on its own to something in the environment, often a gift through nature, music, or art that holds you effortlessly in the experiential neural focus. Your senses are readily awakened by awareness of what is occurring around you and to you. Awe is opening to the felt sense of aliveness in its grander sense to experience your place in this vast world viscerally.

To be held in awe also allows you to see that the phenomenal world, and therefore you, are miraculously ever-changing. You and the world in and around you simply don't stay the same, which fosters a reverence for the unfolding mysteries of life.

GRATITUDE

To experience each moment mindfully is to be aware of the magnificent complexity of the world in which you inhabit and participate. Paying attention to each moment's awe and wonder and aliveness is to be emotionally moved by and consciously appreciate what you are experiencing. The poet David Whyte (2014) reminds us: "Gratitude is the understanding that many millions of things come together and live together and mesh together and breathe together in order for us to take even one more breath of air, that the underlying gift of life and incarnation as a living, participating human being is a privilege; that we are miraculously, part of something, rather than nothing."

Gratitude is the embodied appreciative relationship you share with an awareness of each moment. As the thirteenth-century Christian mystic Meister Eckhart concluded, "If the only prayer you ever said was 'thank you,' that would suffice."

Gratitude is often thought of as a process of taking inventory of your life, to count and reflect upon the "good" stuff that you encounter or possess. This is undoubtedly an aspect of gratitude. Studies demonstrate that keeping a gratitude journal to document activities, objects, and people you appreciate or are thankful for is an effective method to feel better physically and mentally, enjoy fewer symptoms, feel happier, less isolated, and more optimistic.

However, gratitude is much more than an accounting exercise to convince yourself of life's value. Gratitude is a robust attitude to cultivate, important enough to be recommended as the eighth attitudinal foundation of mindfulness.

Gratitude is an attitudinal gift to be cherished, but it requires you first to be aware of your inner and outer world experiences. Without such awareness, you simply miss the opportunity to marvel at the wonders that are continually available and present to you. Exploring these marvels, even very simple ones through your senses—like Bethany, brought to tears with the lilting cooing of a mourning dove and Sam marvelling at a budding magnolia tree—brings them into focus, experiencing the splendid nuances of sight, sound, touch, smell, and taste. Comprehending moments as the gift that they are, never before experienced in just this manner, at just this time, through your unique senses, opens a personal relationship of wonder and appreciation for, as the poet Rumi (1995) tells us, "This being human is a guest house." Each moment, we as a "guest house" host the grand array of thoughts, feelings, and sensory experiences that are constantly occurring within, around, and to you. Mindfulness and self-compassion simply allow this ever present and constantly unfolding reality to become conscious.

LIVE YOUR LIFE GRATEFULLY

Brother David Steindl-Rast, a Benedictine monk, has devoted his life to exploring and promoting the healing qualities of gratitude. His YouTube video of "A Good Day" (A Network for Grateful Living 2007) has been viewed over 1.5 million times. It beautifully captures images of simple daily activities that make life a gift, engendering a sense of appreciation and thankfulness if only you pay attention to them. He expands gratefulness to not only those times when you take stock of your life but espouses that a bigger and better goal is to every moment fully live your life gratefully. He illustrates developing this way of being similar to how children are taught to cross a busy street. To safely cross, as well as live life gratefully, requires you to "stop, look, and go."

"Stop" is to slow life down to be more acutely aware of what is occurring. To become quiet allows you to consciously be aware of the small qualities and aspects that comprise this miraculous existence that is laid out before you. "Look" is to open your senses to experience the glorious wonder of all that is life. There is no end to being appreciative of what is available before you, around you, and within you. Take it all in and hold it with a sense of wonder and awe of the miracle called life. "Go" is to respond now, to do something with whatever life offers to you. With a sense of appreciation and thankfulness, recognize that this moment has provided you with an opportunity to engage and participate more fully in the marvel of life. Sounds familiar? It sounds like mindfulness to me!

However, just like mindfulness, Brother Steindl-Rast also is realistic in acknowledging that life events and experiences can be painful and difficult. At this time, most people find gratefulness challenging to engender. Therefore, the key to a grateful life is not only focusing on the "positive stuff," objects and events you cherish and enjoy but also on gratefulness for the *opportunity* that this miraculous world presents each moment you are alive. The gift to respond by meeting whatever arises, including the painful challenges, through your human assets and capabilities is what you can be grateful for.

Victor Frankl (2006), an Auschwitz survivor who went on to develop a school of mental health treatment called Logotherapy, bases his work on the potent power of response that we all possess: "Between stimulus and response there is a space. In that space is our power to choose our response. In our response, lies our growth and our freedom." The fact that you can respond to everything that occurs, even including the horrors Frankl found in a concentration camp, is to truly appreciate and be thankful for your life, to live your life gratefully.

Intuitively you know that gratefulness and happiness go together, but not in the order that many believe. It is not happiness that makes you grateful, but gratefulness that makes you happy.

CONNECTEDNESS AND INTERCONNECTEDNESS

Developing an encouraging, less judgmental, and more confident connectedness with yourself—in essence, being grateful for yourself—is a skill you have been developing through mindfulness and loving-kindness meditation skills, augmented with Jungian psychological practices. Consciously connecting with gratitude has become more accessible through the deepening self-friendship you have been developing and experiencing through the weeks. By extension, expanding and maintaining a positive and supportive relationship with yourself have been central to enhancing awareness, experience, and relationship with time. Feeling more grounded and at peace with yourself, notwithstanding the quirks and foibles that your being human will undoubtedly continue to exhibit, strengthens the appreciative and thankful connection you have with yourself in each moment that comprises your life!

In addition to developing increased personal connectedness leading to self-friendship, many individuals who have been able to sit in the awareness of awe and wonder report a sense of powerful connectedness with their immediate surroundings, and by extension, with all of existence. Mindfulness teaches you that sights, sounds, sensations, smells, tastes, emotions, thoughts, and body sensations arise and, over time, fall away, only to be replaced with something else. Awe, wonder, presence of mind, and gratitude of the ever-changing world opens you to a sense of interconnectedness, of being part of the infinite mystery of life.

A DIFFERENT PERSPECTIVE ON REALITY

The theologian Howard Thurman (1999) concludes that to know the truth of interconnectedness, we need to look at the world with what he calls "quiet eyes." Thurman connects "quiet" with a kind of inner profound composure and trust, reflecting an outer posture of calm, confident presence. I believe mindfulness is an embodiment of "quiet eyes" as it facilitates balance and clarity at the interface between inner and outer worlds. Sharon Salzberg (2005) clarifies this gift of mindful quiet eyes when she concludes: "We take in what is appearing before reactions and conclusions get fixed. When we relax into this mode of perception, a different perspective on reality becomes available to us."

Through the mode of perception offered by the lens of mindfulness, self-compassion, and Jungian psychology, you have been exploring and creating a different perspective of your life. Your awareness, experience, and relationship to each moment have opened a deeper self-friendship, awe, wonder, gratitude, presence of mind, and interconnectedness with all of existence.

This development has provided you with a different perspective of time during your aging years, which I suggest is healthier, more alive, and more satisfying. I envision accessing this continuing perspective as more like entering an interactive spiral pattern rather than straight-line developmental stages to be met and surpassed. Specifically, this new perspective of your aging life can be accessed at any time and place since one door opens to another and then another. Awareness leads to awe just as awe leads to awareness. Experience leads to all of the attitudinal foundations just as the attitudinal foundations lead to the experience of each moment. Relationship leads to gratitude just as gratitude leads to relationship. Interconnection leads to wonder just as wonder leads to interconnectedness, and round and round it goes.

A different and novel mode of perception leading to a healthier perspective toward time and your aging years has been the goal of this course. As we come to the end of the course, I believe that this goal has been met. However, what is critical to your life is not my assessment but rather your evaluation of its benefit.

YOU BE THE JUDGE

As promised in the Introduction, you have been in charge of the time and effort invested in developing a mindful disposition toward advancing time and, by extension, your aging years. While there were suggestions made each week about specific practices and committed time to build and strengthen the scaffolding of your mindfulness skills, it has been presented in the spirit of fully recognizing your sovereignty. If you are like most students in the group, there were days when you met completely the suggested practice sessions and other days where you either showed up for a shorter period or missed them altogether. No matter what your record of practice, you are now ready to carry out your promised second appraisal task, to judge for yourself if mindfulness proved to be of benefit to you.

Before arriving at your global value assessment, it can also be helpful to review the layers of skills and practices that encompassed your eight-week course to understand more precisely what, if anything, proved to be of worth. When I asked the group if any particular aspect proved especially helpful during the course, hands shot up, and responses tumbled out swiftly:

- Jasmine likes the body scan and continues to use it when having difficulty falling asleep at night.

- Karl finds the sitting and walking meditations calming, especially when his mind starts racing with worry and fear about his prostate cancer condition.

- While Bethany also enjoys sitting and walking practices, she relies heavily on the four levels of response to persistent intrusions because, as she dryly noted: "Those little intrusive SOBs just won't stay away—like a magnet pulled to metal, they keep grabbing for my attention when I'm meditating!"

- Josie loves the attitudinal foundations because they encompass all the qualities that she wants from a friendship—especially the self-friendship that she tearfully reported was developing "quite nicely!"

- Cleaning counters continues to be a "quietly satisfying" daily practice for Betty. Somewhat to her surprise, she also enjoys discovering many other everyday activities that, when slowed to notice what they entailed step-by-step, are amazingly rewarding!

- George shyly confided that during the course, he "fell in love." To tease the group's anticipation, he waited a full few seconds before declaring that the identity of his new love was his breath!

- Darnell quietly informed the group that uncovering his shame-based identity continues to be a colossal eye-opener for him. Utilizing the Jungian practice exercise coupled with his ongoing counselling, Darnell declared that he feels more confident meeting life, including his continued grief over his mother's passing.

- Cindy identifies looking and listening practices to be especially important as she is going through ongoing medical investigations for her heart concerns: "I can quickly spiral out of control when fear of what my heart condition might be grabs me, so to pull myself back into living this moment by focusing on sights and sounds has been critically important!"

- "Who would have known that our lives are bigger than what we believed?" exclaimed Malik. He related that his previous caution and fear of being negatively judged has given way to his newfound experiences of vulnerably "being real" with his partner and with his friends, which has opened his eyes to an expanded, and hugely rewarding sense of himself.

- Juanita claims that her increased awareness of the wonderous and nuanced aromas and flavours of wine has blossomed to the point where she can now "taste the smells!" But since life is more than just appreciating wine, she also welcomes exploring the multitude of other activities that open her to informal meditation practice.

- "I love being on the lookout for what the day will bring," declared William. "While I know that not everything is sunshine and rainbows, I wake up eager to discover what may happen today."

- Bernie simply declared that the loving-kindness practice had been the best thing to happen to him since bread was twenty-five cents a loaf—and he chuckled that he is old enough actually to remember when bread was that cheap!

- "While I don't look forward to the negative things that happen each day, I am more aware of how I have previously let those events dictate how I feel during the rest of the day," offered Rachel. "Now, I can see them for what they are—still not pleasant—but I don't have to let them hold me hostage for the next week or even the next twenty-four hours. Let them be and let them go is my new best friend!"

WHAT ABOUT YOU?

Take time to reflect on your experience during these eight weeks of developing mindfulness and loving-kindness sensitivity to whatever arises in your existence. What was helpful? What was not particularly beneficial? What were you drawn to, and what didn't "click" with you? Do you notice increased awareness of individual moments during your day? Do you find your sensory faculties more acute, both in terms of positive as well as challenging events? Are you able to hold the attitudinal foundations in mind as a template to develop a healthier and more expansive mindset of who you are? Specifically, do you find yourself more open to meeting each moment as the new unknown one that it is? Are you more accepting, non-judging, non-striving, patient, and trusting with yourself and others? Are you able to let be and therefore let go of thoughts, feelings, physical sensations, and events more easily? Are you able to respond and not reflexively react to demands placed upon you? Are you a better friend to yourself? Are you more grateful for your life? Are you perfect (only kidding!)?

AND THE WINNER IS . . .

The mindfulness group also met the challenge of being their own judge by reflecting on their overall experience. The conclusions were, as to be expected in any group, wide-ranging. While the above comments make it clear that specific aspects of the training resonated deeply on an individual basis, the overall assessments indicated that the last eight weeks had been positive, with no one concluding that it had been a wasted investment of time and energy.

When asked how many in the group intended to continue a formal daily mindfulness practice (explicitly focusing on body scan, sitting, and walking meditations), nineteen of the twenty-five participants raised their hands. Of those who decided not to continue the formal practice, all indicated that their newfound appreciation of paying attention, on purpose, in the present moment, non-judgmentally would be honoured through informal daily practices—essentially, through a commitment to "stay awake" and be present. Through continuing formal and informal practice, each remained dedicated to further discovering and enhancing their way of being with the delights and challenges human life offers. Each felt committed to continue developing more vital awareness, experience, and relationship with aging.

WHAT NOW?

What about you? Has your awareness, experience, and relationship to time been positively affected by your mindfulness practice? Do you believe that continuing a mindfulness practice will be beneficial? The decision to continue with a formal and informal mindfulness meditation practice is, of course, a personal one likely based upon your experience to date, coupled with how it would fit with your life commitments. But in making your decision, know that research is continuing to further our knowledge that active participation in meditation practice is critically important to optimize long-term physical and psychological benefits.

STATES TO TRAITS

One of the more recent focuses in mindfulness research is better under-standing the movement from more temporary "states" that individuals can experience with short periods of mindfulness training compared to what has been called "traits" (more long-term qualities or attributes), which are observable in individuals who have extensive practice in meditation (Goleman, 2017). This was particularly evident when discussing the impact of mindfulness on pain during Week Five, where experienced meditators and a control group experienced the same physical sensations of pain. While each group received the same degree of pain, the meditators' brains did not react to such stimuli in the way that nonmeditators' brains did. The findings of alteration in an individual's anticipation—reactivity—recovery process after exposure to painful stimuli were demonstrated convincingly in individuals with extensive meditation experience. (As you may recall, the long-term meditators showed little sign of anticipatory anxiety, a short but intense reaction involving the physical experience of pain itself, and then a rapid recovery.) The brain activity for such individuals was dramatically different compared to the control group with no meditation experience.

It is the development of states into traits that makes ongoing medita-tion practice so critically valuable. As I have mentioned numerous times throughout the course, the formal meditation practices we have been doing for homework are only "batting practice" for life itself. That is, the goal of mindfulness is not to become a "better" meditator during those formal twenty or thirty or forty-five minutes of practice per day, but rather to be able to transfer what you experience during those times to everyday life. The challenge is to engage in enough practice to lead to decreased reac-tivity, increased calmness, inner balance, and a clear focus on whatever you experience during the day. While the amount of time and expertise necessary to change states into traits through mindfulness practice is not yet definitively known, the research clarifies that it is critical to *continue practising* for such momentary changes in states to become more long-term altered traits.

NEUROPLASTICITY

So why is mindfulness practice so important? What we know so far indicates that formal and informal meditation practices provide an opportunity for the brain to purposefully lay down new neural pathways that, over time, will manifest in your life when engaged in day-to-day activities. One aspect of mindfulness that has been especially intriguing concerns the brain's neuroplasticity to shape the brain's neural structure by repeated experiences. As noted earlier, it has been found that brain neurons that "fire together wire together," which means that ongoing practice will strengthen the benefits that even short training courses in mindfulness can produce.

One of the most critical findings from brain scan research is that mindfulness practice results in an increase in activity in the experiential focus network within the brain and a decrease in the activity of the default narrative focus network. The shift to more of an experiential neural focus allows you to be more present at the moment without feeding it stories about the past or future, which allows for more capacity to respond to whatever is arising (both inside yourself and out in the environment) rather than react. It demonstrates that mindfulness can influence how the brain processes experience—how you experience your life unfolding and what you tell yourself about it. Overall, mindfulness allows you to be more aware and, therefore, experience wholly the ongoing moments of life . . . this life . . . your life!

TIME . . . TIME . . . TIME . . .

However, by now, you have no doubt realized that the main barrier to continuing a formal practice is time. As you found, committing to a formal practice means setting aside time to participate in body scan, sitting, or walking meditations—these are practices that require a dedicated time allotment to complete. Isn't it interesting that you started the course because of time—seeking to meet it more healthily and satisfyingly—and here it is, once again, a critical component influencing your commitment!

Time will not gently fade into the sunset—another powerful lesson on how time is a crucial factor affecting all of your life.

There is simply no denying that maintaining a formal meditation practice means that time is the most significant potentially challenging factor to consider. But as you have discovered, time in and of itself is not the end of the story. How you experience and relate to the present moment determines the quality of time—remember that, like the ancient Greeks, while you do not have control over time as Chronos, you possess the ability to create Kairos moments! While the extent of time remaining in your life is usually out of your control, you do have more agency over the quality of the moments presented to you. Your aging years, beginning through attention to this present moment, offer a Kairos window—an acknowledgement that this is the *right time* to live this life that is yours with more intention, aliveness, and curiosity.

STAYING AWAKE

"Don't go back to sleep/You must ask for what you really want/ Don't go back to sleep," the poet Rumi (1995) cautions us.

In keeping with the theme that time is not an insurmountable barrier and can be skillfully worked with, if you decide that mindfulness has benefits and want to continue with the practice, how do you do so? How do you stay awake and keep it alive?

As you all know, life can become hectic, making it difficult to commit to mindfulness and extend the necessary time and effort required to maintain a meditation practice. A book written by one of the three individuals who were instrumental in bringing mindfulness to the West, Dr. Jack Kornfield (2000), is titled *After the Ecstasy, the Laundry.* It aptly recognizes the difficulty of maintaining a practice, even one that we believe is important and beneficial, amid often busy day-to-day commitments. As you all undoubtedly have experienced, it is easy to postpone or avoid the time and energy required to maintain helpful mindfulness practice.

In the spirit of supported inquiry, let's walk through strategies rein-forcing first formal meditation practices and then informal ones to meet Rumi's challenge of staying awake and not going "back to sleep."

LIVING WITH INTENTION

From my perspective, I believe that one of the essential components of staying awake is to *live with intention*. Intention is a critical factor in our behaviour and has been beautifully described by Dr. Jack Kornfield (2008) as the process of "setting the compass of the heart." Increasing the likelihood of maintaining and enhancing being a better friend to yourself means that a commitment is required to invest yourself in the mindful-ness practice continuously. When consciously made and remembered on an ongoing basis, I have found that such intentions can be helpful to get past those times when you would just as quickly put off meditating until tomorrow or the next day or the next day.

Before my retirement, I had a framed prayer flag in my psychotherapy consulting room with the single word "REMEMBER" in large blue capital letters scrolled against a cream-coloured background hung above my door. Clients could see this while in session and passed it when entering and exiting the office. Inevitably, at some point in time, clients would ask what was to be remembered, to which I replied, "Whatever is important to you, but I would suggest that it start with your intention—whatever that may be!" Meeting clients years after ending our therapeutic relationship often elicited fond and appreciative memories of the reminder; it is clear that to remember is a captivating intention in and of itself to hold! I still have the framed prayer flag in my home to continually remind me of this imperative.

I also believe that when setting an intention, it is vital to know that this is not a way to simply "grit your teeth" to get through a difficult or challenging activity. Instead, it is more helpful to approach and hold the meditation practice intentionally as a "friend" whose existence is there to help you—not make life more difficult for you. To even take a moment at the beginning of a practice session to connect sincerely with your inten-tion—your heart's aspiration—can be beneficial.

MAKE THE PRACTICE YOUR OWN

To increase the likelihood of committing to a formal meditation practice, it is recommended that you have an honest reflection of your life as it is presently. Specifically, to review all the challenges and responsibilities that you have and, by so doing, come up with a *realistic* estimate of how much time you are *willing and able* to commit to daily formal meditation practice. While the usual instructions are to practise for forty-five minutes a day, this is just not reasonable for many people. Therefore, if this time is set as the expectation, it is likely that some would not be able to meet it and will experience defeat with discouragement—essentially setting you up for failure.

Recent research from Dr. Amishi Jha (2021) has found that as little as twelve minutes of formal mindfulness practice undertaken five days per week can reap enormous benefits, including improvements in working memory, less mind-wandering, greater sense of well-being, and better relationships. However, it is also known, and reinforced by Dr. Jha, that mindfulness does have a dose-response effect, which means the more you practice, the more you benefit.

To set you up for success, choose a time that you can make an unswerving commitment to meditate at least six days per week. It may be forty-five minutes per day, but it could also be thirty, twenty, fifteen, ten, or even five minutes each day. While more time is likely better, the exact number of minutes to practice is not critical; instead, the goal is to ensure that you can *commit* to a defined practice each day. To put it politely, getting your backside on the cushion increases the likelihood of feeling successful and continuing to practice. Over time, you may find that you can increase the length of each day's formal meditation practice but play it by ear—see how it goes. The intention and accompanying commitment to engage in meditation practice are crucial to maintaining it over time.

MEETING RESISTANCE

In addition to actually setting the intention of maintaining mindfulness practice, you must *do it.* You keep the practice alive by engaging in the non-doing of mindfulness—no matter how much inner resistance you may feel. Over time and with further practice, trust that it can become easier to make it a necessary part of your day. Creating a time for daily mindfulness can become as natural and vital as eating is to feed your body. Meditation becomes accepted and even looked forward to as an essential part of your life and one you do to maintain your inner health and well-being.

However, one of the obstacles that you will likely find arising, even with the best intention of having a mindfulness practice, is having days of simply not wanting to do it. Even though you know in your mind and heart that there are benefits to it and that you have experienced such benefits, there still can arise that thought and feeling of "I just don't want to do it." It is times like this that knowing you have effective strategies available is a critically supportive factor.

To even begin a meditation session knowing that your mind is saying, "I don't want to do this, I don't want to do this," allows you to learn to be with thoughts and feelings that you know may not be in your best interest. It is also an excellent time to recall the prescient bumper sticker that I introduced in Week One that candidly revealed: "Don't believe everything that you think."

Just as we have done with all other thoughts and feelings, it is simply a matter of noticing them, labelling them, and returning to the anchor of awareness. If they continue to intrude and pull your focus away from your anchor, then turn your attention to a Level Two response, using the body sensations associated with such thoughts/feelings of resistance as your anchor of awareness. It is then a matter of becoming very curious about those specific sensations and continuing your practice just as you have done. You also have Level Three and Four responses to fall back on should your resistance prove especially stubborn. These strategies allow you to acknowledge the resistance that you are experiencing but also to work with it in a manner that will strengthen your mindfulness practice.

Resistance is no big deal—it is just another opportunity to be with whatever arises. The meeting of resistance declares that having a mindfulness practice is not only for "good days," but instead on "all days," no matter the thoughts, feelings, or body sensations that arise.

SELF-COMPASSION

Another way to work with the resistance of engaging in formal mindfulness practice is to decide to use the session as one of self-compassion and loving-kindness. Focusing on the good wishes you extend to yourself, even when there is resistance, can establish a different relationship with those thoughts and feelings. However, it is essential to remember that participating in the formal practice even during resistance doesn't mean being harsh with yourself. Gentleness and self-compassion are not optional luxuries but critical in establishing and maintaining a solid and beneficial meditation practice.

STRUCTURAL CONCEPTS TO ASSIST YOUR PRACTICE

There are a few structural concepts to keep in mind that are helpful to establish a daily formal practice. For example, it is beneficial to *set aside a particular time* to meditate. To simply hope that you will get a chance to do it throughout the day increases the likelihood that life will intrude and there won't be any time available. Using the Tracking Your Practice log through the course, you will have explored different times of the day and found the time that works best for you. Most critical about finding the best time is to have one that you can realistically commit to regularly.

Deciding in advance the *duration* of your formal practice (body scan, sitting, walking, loving-kindness) will also help support your practice. As discussed earlier, you are in charge of deciding what length of time you can realistically commit to do each day. This will increase the likelihood of meeting success and, in turn, increase your commitment to mindfulness.

Finding a space to do your daily formal meditation practice is also a way not only to declare your intention but to develop a place that, over time, can feel like it "holds" you.

It is helpful to start your daily practice with a conscious declaration of *arriving* at the moment. This does not need to take long but can involve several deep breaths to let go into the moment and feel supported in your chair with your feet on the floor, which creates a sense of being grounded or held in the moment. It is also possible to use a brief body scan to review the body, which also helps bring you into the moment.

OFF THE CUSHION EXPERIENCES

The title of one of Jon Kabat-Zinn's (1994) books that aptly declares our reality of *Wherever You Go, There You Are,* turns out to be a powerful reminder of living life through mindfulness. Formal practice is of course critical to extend and strengthen your mindfulness sensibility to what counts, which is the moment-to-moment experience of your life. But formal practice is not all that is required or available! To hold a mindfulness sensitivity with informal practices, colloquially known as being "off the cushion," provides continuing opportunities to fully experience each moment, which can reinforce and consolidate your new way of being. Quite simply, holding a mindfulness sensitivity while out in the world is another opportunity to practice, allowing you to reap the benefits of your time and energy investment.

Informal practices arise out of the daily activities that comprise your life and are readily available to be of service to your learning process. As you have practised since Week Four, the activity itself is not what is critical. Instead, any activity that allows you to slow down the process to experience it with your senses entirely is what makes it an informal mindfulness practice and, therefore, a good one to choose. Examples from daily activities abound: brushing your teeth, doing the laundry, eating a snack, tasting wine, cleaning the yard, taking out the garbage, and so forth.

The instructions are the same for each activity: be aware of the steps involved; decide what the initial component of the first step will be; slowly begin working through each stage, focusing on your senses of sight, touch, hearing, smell, and (if appropriate) taste. Be curious as to how you are experiencing each step through your senses. Take your time with this activity you could do in your sleep but want to approach with a beginner's mind as if undertaking it for the first time.

Just as Alice in Wonderland found, you can become "curiouser and curiouser" about each moment, no matter how often you may have participated in it. However, if you don't want to take advice from a fictional character, remember what Albert Einstein concluded: "I have no special talents. I am only passionately curious." Alice and Albert can't both be wrong, so enjoy the process of engaged inquisitiveness!

The informal meditation practices heighten your ability to meet the whole of life with moment-to-moment awareness. As you encounter each moment with awareness to respond and not just react, to be more fully present in the moment and not live in the past or the future, even ordinary tasks, such as washing the dishes, can become more enjoyable. When it comes right down to it, the challenge of mindfulness is straightforward— to realize "This is it! This moment. . . . Right now is my life."

CONTINUALLY REDISCOVERING YOUR ANCHOR OF AWARENESS

In addition to informal, structured activities that provide tremendous opportunities for mindfulness training, I would also recommend that you set an intention to be aware of your anchor of attention (whether that is your breath or hand sensations) from time to time throughout the day. This does not have to entail lengthy periods but rather just momentary noticing of your anchor at that moment. Feel the sensation of the breath rising and falling and be curious as to what the breath is like in that unique moment. Or feel the sensation of your hand/fingers on your body through using pressure or movement.

It is also possible to use daily activities as triggers to remind yourself to notice your anchor. For example, every time you get a coffee or tea, stop at a red light, enter a store, finish a chore, and so on can be a trigger to remind you to pay attention to your breath or hand sensation. The intent is not to take your full awareness off the situation you are in but rather to be curious about your breath or hand sensation in that particular moment. With practice, you will build a greater trust in your ability to be aware of your breath or hand sensations as your anchor of awareness and still be conscious and aware of activities in which you are involved.

THE HOUSE AND HOME OF MINDFULNESS

Strengthening your capacity to pay attention, on purpose, non-judgmentally through formal and informal practices not only provides a healthy and supportive foundation to meet each moment but also normalizes your experience of the human condition. Yes, there is suffering. Yes, there is delight. Yes, there is everything in-between.

What calls you is the courage and wisdom needed to hold all of life in an alive, respectful, open, healthy, and satisfying manner. Every "bozo" like you and I need an inner house and a home for living this life that is ours!

As I noted throughout the course, developing a mindfulness way of being is like building a house. The attention regulation strategies you have learned concerning always having an anchor of your attention and what you can do with intrusive, persistent, and powerful thoughts, feelings, or body sensations that arise, provide the house's structure, the technical how-to-do-it step-by-step instructions. However, these strategies only address the first part of the definition of mindfulness: paying attention, on purpose, in the present moment.

The second aspect of the mindfulness definition is your orientation or relationship or attitude to whatever is occurring. This is critical because what you will encounter at any given moment may not be especially pleasing or fun or wanted. Mindfulness does not reject experience—it allows experience to be a teacher as to how you can meet each moment. Specifically, mindfulness asks you to meet *every moment* in a non-judgmental manner. The attitudes you bring to each moment will determine if your structure is just a house or if the unfolding relationship to whatever arises creates more of a home that feels comforting and inviting, even in the face of the struggles you encounter.

Mindfulness gifts both skill acquisition to regulate your attention and attitudes to create a holding environment needed to navigate through whatever life presents. The attitudinal foundations are a critical component of what makes mindfulness so powerfully effective as a home. It presents an opportunity to establish a way of life that gives you the confidence to face whatever may arise—through mindfulness practice, developing not only a belief but a *knowing* through experience that you can meet whatever life presents. This doesn't mean that life is painless, but you can hold a more confident attitude that provides more ease to navigate each day.

Keeping the attitudes of acceptance, non-judging, non-striving, beginner's mind, patience, letting go, trust, and the latest addition of gratitude, in conscious awareness is a critical component of the mindfulness training itself. They provide a way of directing and channelling your relationship to whatever arises in service of meeting each moment with tolerance and resilience, to be with each moment in a healthy and satisfying embrace. As evidenced through the attitudes, your intentions set the stage for the relationship with life that is possible during your aging years.

FOLLOW YOUR HEART'S ASPIRATIONS

Fulfilling the aspirations with which you began this course depends to a significant degree on maintaining your intentions, to "setting the compass of the heart," as Dr. Jack Kornfield (2008) continues to remind us, through ongoing practice. It is not an easy task, but the key to Rumi's (1995) cautionary advice of staying awake is remembering the skills you have learned, insights you have attained, and the importance of the intentions you hold, all of which have enabled and strengthened your agency over the past eight weeks. Endings always imply beginnings but remember that while this course is coming to a close, the mindfulness and Jungian psychology strategies you've been learning and self-friendship experiences you've been having are only the start of what the mindful approach to aging has to offer.

I envision the continuing mindful approach to aging as embodying the spirit of quiet confidence. It is not showy and brash, puffing out your chest declaring your newfound competence with time and therefore aging. Instead, I imagine quiet confidence to be a close cousin to the concept of "quiet eyes," Howard Thurman's vision of a kind of inner profound composure and trust, reflecting an outer posture of calm, confident presence. Engaging in the daily practices of formal and informal meditation is your affirmative and solemn declaration to meet each unfolding moment with a curious awareness, open experience, and ever-expanding relationship.

Hanging on my wall at home is a wood-carved Coast Salish First Nations mask titled "The Man Who Bumped into the Spirit." It depicts a human face with the left side looking very much alive, its eye open and mouth slightly upturned in a contented, calm, and satisfied expression. In contrast, the right side is incapacitated with a paralyzed and painfully contorted look that includes a closed eye, flared nostril, and droopy mouth. While the art piece is ambiguous as to which side has "bumped into the spirit," there is no doubt that the man's life is altered in a comparatively dramatic manner through its encounter with a powerful energy. I see the contrasting images of the contented versus contorted expressions within this one individual as highlighting your choice in how you are going to meet your aging years. While this is your life and you are free to choose, I have always interpreted the left-sided aliveness as that which has touched the spirit of mindfulness and Jungian individuation, exemplifying the quiet confidence of composure, calm, trust, and confidence that I associate with these intentions.

While you know by now that I am not one to hype and oversell what I present, I truly believe that just as the mask's contented side portends, *embracing aging mindfully* is a transformative process capable of enriching your aging moments. My hope and guiding intention with writing this book has been to provide you with the opportunity to test my belief, because at the end of the day and now as well as the end of this book, your conclusion is the only one that counts.

Through mindfulness and Jungian psychology, you are offered a path to embrace and embody this mysterious gift of your one precious life in each moment bestowed upon you more fully. At its core, it really is very simple. As an unknown Tibetan poet noted, in each moment, all we have and what proves to be all we need is:

One hand on the beauty of the world,
One hand on the suffering of all beings
And two feet grounded in the present moment.

PRACTICE FOR THE REST OF YOUR LIFE

Guidelines—very simply:

- May you live your life wholeheartedly held in mindfulness and compassion.

- May you find and embody the "bozo" life that is yours and yours alone.

- May you enjoy your one precious life!

REFERENCES AND RESOURCES

A Network for Grateful Living. *"A Good Day With Brother David Steindl-Rast,"* YouTube video, 5:32. July 10, 2007.

Bateman, Kim. *Crossing the Owl's Bridge: A Guide for Grieving People Who Still Love.* Asheville: Chiron Publications, 2016.

Bauer-Wu, Susan. *Leaves Falling Gently: Living Fully with Serious and Life-Limiting Illness through Mindfulness, Compassion and Connection.* Oakland: New Harbinger, 2011.

Bly, Robert. *A Little Book on the Human Shadow.* San Francisco: HarperOne, 1988.

Brach, Tara. *True Refuge: Finding Peace and Freedom in Your Own Awakened Heart.* Reprint. New York: Bantam Books, 2016.

Brewer, Judson. *The Craving Mind: From Cigarettes to Smartphones to Love—Why We Get Hooked and How We Can Break Bad Habits.* New Haven: Yale University Press, 2017.

Bridgewater, Peter. *Mindfulness & the Journey of Bereavement.* Brighton: Leaping Hare Press, 2019.

Brown, Brené. *Daring Greatly: How the Courage to be Vulnerable Transforms the Way We Live, Love, Parent and Lead.* Reprint. New York: Avery, 2015.

Cacciatore, Joanne. *Bearing the Unbearable: Love, Loss, and the Heartbreaking Path of Grief.* Somerville: Wisdom Publications, 2017.

Carlson, Linda and Michael Speca. *Mindfulness-Based Cancer Recovery: A Step-by-Step MBSR Approach to Help You Cope with Treatment and Reclaim Your Life.* Oakland: New Harbinger, 2010.

Chabris, Christopher and Daniel Simons. *The Invisible Gorilla: How Our Intuitions Deceive Us.* New York: Harmony, 2011.

Chödrön, Pema. *Living Beautifully with Uncertainty and Change.* Boston: Shambhala, 2013.

Devine, Megan. *It's OK That You're Not OK: Meeting Grief and Loss in a Culture that Doesn't Understand.* Boulder: Sounds True, 2017.

Duff, Kat. *The Alchemy of Illness.* New York: Bell Tower, 1993.

Elison, Koshin and Matt Weingast, eds. *Awake at the Bedside: Contemplative Teachings on Palliative and End-of-Life Care.* Somerville: Wisdom Publications, 2016.

Farb, Norman, Zindel Segal, Helen Mayberg, Jim Bean, Deborah McKeon, Zaiab Fatima and Adam Anderson. "Attending to the Present: Mindfulness Meditation Reveals Distinct Neural Modes of Self-Reference," *Social, Cognitive and Affective Neuroscience* (August 2007): 313-322. https://doi:10.1093/scan/nsm030.

Farb, Norman, Adam Anderson and Zindel Segal. "The Mindful Brain and Emotion Regulation in Mood Disorders," *Canadian Psychiatry* 57, no. 2 (2012): 70-77.

Feldman, Christina. *Compassion: Listening to the Cries of the World.* Berkeley: Rodmell Press, 2005.

Frankl, Viktor E. *Man's Search for Meaning.* Boston: Beacon Books, 2006. First published 1946 by Verlag für Jugend und Volk.

Gardner-Nix, Jackie. *The Mindfulness Solution to Pain: Step-by-Step Techniques for Chronic Pain Management.* Oakland: New Harbinger, 2009.

Gilbert, Daniel. *Stumbling on Happiness.* New York: Alfred A. Knopf, 2006.

Goleman, Daniel and Richard Davidson. *Altered Traits: Science Reveals How Meditation Changes Your Mind, Brain, and Body.* New York: Avery, 2017.

Greenspan, Miriam. *Healing Through the Dark Emotions.* Boston: Shambhala, 2003.

Hanson, Rick. *Buddha's Brain: The Practical Neuroscience of Happiness, Love and Wisdom.* Oakland: New Harbinger, 2009.

Hiraoka, Regina, Eric Meyer, Nathan Kimbrel, Bryann DeBeer, Suzy Gulliver and Sandra Morissette. "Self-Compassion as a Prospective Predictor of PTSD Symptom Severity Among Trauma-Exposed U.S. Iraq and Afghanistan War Veterans," *Journal of Traumatic Stress* 28, no.2 (April 2015): 127-133. https://doi:10.1002/jts.21995.

Hollis, James. *Living an Examined Life: Wisdom for the Second Half of the Journey.* Boulder: Sounds True, 2018.

Hollis, James. *Finding Meaning in the Second Half of Life.* New York: Gotham Books, 2005.

Jha, Amishi. *Peak Mind: Find Your Focus, Own Your Attention, Invest 12 Minutes a Day.* San Francisco: HarperOne, 2021.

Jung, C.G. "Psychotherapy and a Philosophy of Life." In *The Collected Works of C.G. Jung (Vol. 16)* trans. R.F.C. Hull, 84-91. Princeton, NJ: Princeton University Press, 1954. First published 1946.

Jung, C.G. "The Transcendent Function." In *The Collected Works of C.G. Jung (Vol. 8)* trans. R.F.C. Hull, 67-91. Princeton, NJ: Princeton University Press, 1969. First published 1957.

Jung, C.G. *Memories, Dreams, and Reflections.* New York: Vintage Books, 1973. First published 1961 by Pantheon Books.

Kabat-Zinn, Jon. *Full Catastrophe Living: Using the Wisdom of Your Body and Mind to Face Stress, Pain, and Illness.* New York: Delta Books, 1990.

Kabat-Zinn, Jon. *Wherever You Go There You Are: Mindfulness Meditation in Everyday Life.* New York: Hyperion, 1994.

Killingsworth, Mathew and Daniel Gilbert, "A Wandering Mind is an Unhappy Mind," *Science* 330, (November 10, 2010): 932.

Kornfield, Jack. *After the Ecstasy, the Laundry: How the Heart Grows Wise on the Spiritual Path.* New York: Bantam Books, 2000.

Kornfield, Jack. *The Wise Heart: A Guide to the Universal Teachings of Buddhist Psychology.* New York: Bantam Books, 2008.

Kornfield, Jack. *A Lamp in the Darkness: Illuminating the Path Through Difficult Times.* Boulder: Sounds True, 2014.

Kornfield, Jack. *No Time Like the Present: Finding Freedom, Love, and Joy Right Where You Are.* New York: Atria Books, 2017.

Kushner, Harold. *When Bad Things Happen to Good People.* New York: Anchor Books, 2004. First published 1981 by Schochen Books.

Lesser, Elizabeth. *Broken Open: How Difficult Times Can Help Us Grow.* New York: Villard, 2005.

Levine, Stephen. *Meetings at the Edge: Dialogues with the Grieving and the Dying, the Healing and the Healed.* New York: Anchor Books, 1989.

Levertov, Denise. "Talking to Grief," in *Poems 1972–1982.* New York: New Directions, 1978, 111.

Neff, Kristin and Christopher Germer. *The Mindful Self-Compassion Workbook: A Proven Way to Accept Yourself, Build Inner Strength, and Thrive.* New York: Guilford Press, 2018.

Neff, Kristin. *Self-Compassion: The Proven Power of Being Kind to Yourself.* New York: HarperCollins, 2011.

Oliver, Mary. "When Death Comes," in *New and Selected Poems: Volume One.* Boston: Beacon Press, 1992.

Ostaseski, Frank. *The Five Invitations: Discovering What Death Can Teach Us About Living Fully.* New York: Flat Iron Books, 2017.

Rumi, Jalal al-Din. "The Breeze at Dawn." In *The Essential Rumi,* translated by Coleman Barks, San Francisco: HarperCollins, 1995.

Rumi, Jalal al-Din. "The Guest House." In *The Essential Rumi,* translated by Coleman Barks, San Francisco: HarperCollins, 1995.

Salzberg, Sharon. *The Force of Kindness: Change Your Life with Love and Compassion.* Boulder: Sounds True, 2005.

Sapolsky, Robert. *Why Zebras Don't Get Ulcers: The Acclaimed Guide to Stress, Stress-Related Diseases, and Coping.* 3rd ed. New York: Holt Publications, 2004.

Schopenhauer, Arthur. *The World as Will and Representation, Vol. 1.* New York: Dover, 1969.

Shakespeare, William. *As You Like It.* Edited by Barbara Mowat and Paul Werstine. Folger Shakespeare Library. New York: Simon & Schuster, 1997.

Shapiro, Shauna. *Good Morning, I Love You: Mindfulness, and Self-Compassion Practices to Rewire Your Brain for Calm, Clarity and Joy.* Boulder: Sounds True, 2020.

Shuman, Robert. *The Psychology of Chronic Illness: The Healing Work of Patients, Therapists, And Families.* New York: Basic Books, 1996.

Siegel, Ronald. *The Mindfulness Solution: Everyday Practices for Everyday Problems.* New York: Guilford, 2010.

Smedes, Lewis. *Forgive and Forget: Healing the Hurts We Don't Deserve.* New York: HarperCollins, 1984.

Steindl-Rast, David and Sharon Lebell. *The Music of Silence: A Sacred Journey Through the Hours of the Day.* New York: Harper Collins, 1995.

Thurman, Howard. "The Sound of the Genuine." Baccalaureate Address Spelman College, May 4, 1980. In *The Spelman Messenger* 96, no.4 (Summer 1980): 14-15.

Thurman, Howard. *Meditations of the Heart.* Boston: Beacon Press, 1999.

Wallace, Gordon. "Dying to be Born: Transformative Surrender within Analytical Psychology from a Clinician's Perspective." In *Self and No-Self: Continuing the Dialogue Between Buddhism and Psychotherapy*, edited by Dale Mathers, Melvin Miller and Osamu Ando, 143-152. London: Routledge, 2009.

Weller, Francis. *The Wild Edge of Sorrow: Rituals of Renewal and the Sacred Work of Grief.* Berkeley: North Atlantic Books, 2015.

Whyte, David. "Everything is Waiting for You," in *Everything is Waiting for You.* Langley: Many Rivers Press, 2003, 6.

Whyte, David. *Consolations: The Solace, Nourishment and Underlying Meaning of Everyday Words.* Langley: Many Rivers Press, 2014.

Whyte, David. "Sweet Darkness," in *The House of Belonging.* Langley: Many Rivers Press, 2016, 23.

Winston, Diana. *The Little Book of Being: Practices and Guidance for Uncovering Your Natural Awareness.* Boulder: Sounds True, 2019.

Wolfelt, Alan. *The Paradoxes of Mourning: Healing Your Grief with Three Forgotten Truths.* Fort Collins: Companion Press, 2015.

INTERNET RESOURCES

Center for Healthy Minds: www.centerhealthyminds.org
- Excellent resource for innovations, practices and research to improve well-being

Center for Mindfulness Self-Compassion: www.centerformsc.org
- Guided meditations, exercises, courses

Network for Grateful Living: www.gratefulness.org
- Terrific resources for all things grateful

Mindfulness Magazine Website: www.mindful.org
- Good magazine as well as informative website, including their online newsletter

Sounds True Website: www.soundstrue.com
- Podcasts, Online Courses, Books

Everyday Mindfulness Website: www.everyday-mindfulness.org
- Mindfulness Resources

Insight Timer—Meditation App: www.insighttimer.com
- Fee for some material but many courses and a timer for your meditation practice are free

Search online for many of the authors listed above, such as Jon Kabat-Zinn, Rick Hanson, Kristin Neff, Jack Kornfield, Tara Brach, Sharon Salzberg, David Steindl-Rast, Brené Brown, etc.
- Good resources for podcasts, guided meditations, writings, TED Talks, etc.

ABOUT THE AUTHOR

Dr. Gordon Wallace earned a Ph.D. in clinical psychology with a specialization in depth (Jungian) psychology. Over his lengthy career as a psychologist, he provided assessment and psychotherapy treatment to primarily mid-life and older clients. In addition to his clinical practice, he has maintained a mindfulness meditation practice for over thirty years and developed and taught workshops on Jungian psychology and mindfulness meditation to mental health professionals and the general public.

Since he retired from clinical practice in 2017, Dr. Wallace has continued as a volunteer to develop and teach mindfulness meditation courses addressing complex issues presented by hospice bereavement and palliative care patients. In addition, he volunteers for bedside vigils with hospice patients nearing the end of life. This book is, in many ways, a summation of his personal and professional life explorations, offering the foundations of a life lived consciously with more ease, satisfaction, meaning and resilience.

Dr. Wallace lives in the lower mainland of British Columbia with his wife, Lynn, their aging golden retriever, Sophie, and close to extended family and grandchildren.

CPSIA information can be obtained
at www.ICGtesting.com
Printed in the USA
BVHW041246080522
636346BV00002B/4